Smart Technologies for Transforming Next-Generation Agriculture: Deep Learning, IoT, and Blockchain

Edited by

Shefali Arora Chouhan

Department of Computer Science and Engineering
Dr. BR Ambedkar National Institute of Technology
Jalandhar, Punjab-144008, India

Nagendra Pratap Singh

Department of Computer Science and Engineering
Dr. BR Ambedkar National Institute of Technology
Jalandhar, Punjab-144008, India

Banalaxmi Brahma

Department of Computer Science and Engineering
Dr. BR Ambedkar National Institute of Technology
Jalandhar, Punjab-144008, India

&

Shashank Gupta

Department of Computer Science and Engineering
Dr. BR Ambedkar National Institute of Technology
Jalandhar, Punjab-144008, India

Smart Technologies for Transforming Next-Generation Agriculture: Deep Learning, IoT, and Blockchain

Editors: Shefali Arora Chouhan, Nagendra Pratap Singh, Banalaxmi Brahma & Shashank Gupta

ISBN (Online): 979-8-89881-192-1

ISBN (Print): 979-8-89881-193-8

ISBN (Paperback): 979-8-89881-194-5

need for a court order if at any point you breach any terms of this License Agreement. In no event will any delay or failure by Bentham Science Publishers in enforcing your compliance with this License Agreement constitute a waiver of any of its rights.

3. You acknowledge that you have read this License Agreement, and agree to be bound by its terms and conditions. To the extent that any other terms and conditions presented on any website of Bentham Science Publishers conflict with, or are inconsistent with, the terms and conditions set out in this License Agreement, you acknowledge that the terms and conditions set out in this License Agreement shall prevail.

Bentham Science Publishers Pte. Ltd.
No. 9 Raffles Place
Office No. 26-01
Singapore 048619
Singapore
Email: subscriptions@benthamscience.net

CONTENTS

FOREWORD

In an age of rapid technological progress, agriculture—the bedrock of human civilization—is undergoing a profound transformation. The fusion of deep learning, the Internet of Things (IoT), and blockchain technology is revolutionizing the sector, offering innovative solutions to challenges in security, sustainability, and resource management. Smart Technologies for Transforming Next-Generation Agriculture: Deep Learning, IoT, and Blockchain serves as a guiding light for researchers, practitioners, and policymakers striving for a more intelligent, data-driven, and resilient agricultural future.

The agricultural sector faces pressing challenges, including climate change, resource scarcity, and a rising global population. Addressing these issues requires a seamless blend of traditional farming expertise and cutting-edge technological advancements. Deep learning empowers predictive analytics for crop yield optimization, pest management, and weather forecasting. IoT devices facilitate real-time monitoring and automation, while blockchain ensures transparency, traceability, and trust throughout agricultural supply chains.

This book moves beyond theoretical exploration, offering practical applications, real-world case studies, and forward-thinking insights that are shaping the future of agriculture. It demonstrates how these technologies empower farmers, enhance productivity, and foster sustainable practices—bridging the gap between innovation and implementation.

As we step into a new era of agricultural transformation, this work serves as a comprehensive guide to leveraging smart technologies for the benefit of humanity. It stands as a testament to the limitless possibilities that lie ahead and a call for collaboration among technologists, farmers, and policymakers to build a sustainable future.

I applaud the authors and editors for their vision and dedication to advancing agricultural technology. This book will undoubtedly inspire its readers to think creatively and act decisively, paving the way for a smarter and more sustainable farming landscape.

M.P.S Bhatia
Netaji Subhas University of Technology
Delhi, India

PREFACE

Agriculture is the backbone of human civilization, providing sustenance and economic stability to billions around the globe. However, as the world grapples with challenges like climate change, population growth, and diminishing resources, the need for innovative solutions to revolutionize agricultural practices has never been more urgent. The convergence of advanced technologies, including Deep Learning, the Internet of Things (IoT), and Blockchain, has opened new horizons for next-generation agriculture, transforming traditional methods into intelligent, sustainable, and efficient systems.

This book, "Smart Technologies for Transforming Next-Generation Agriculture: Deep Learning, IoT, and Blockchain, explores the transformative potential of these cutting-edge technologies in addressing the multifaceted challenges faced by the agricultural sector. It delves into the integration of artificial intelligence for predictive analytics, IoT devices for real-time monitoring, and blockchain for transparency and traceability in supply chains.

Each chapter provides insights into the latest advancements, practical implementations, and the socio-economic impact of these smart technologies. The contributions from leading researchers and practitioners highlight case studies, applications, and emerging trends that showcase the potential of smart agriculture in enhancing productivity, sustainability, and profitability.

This book is intended for a diverse audience, including researchers, academicians, industry professionals, policymakers, and students. It serves as a comprehensive resource for understanding the synergy between technology and agriculture, paving the way for a future where innovation meets sustainability.

We are thankful to all our authors for contributing their insights in the form of chapters, which will inspire readers to embrace and contribute to the transformative journey of agriculture through smart technologies, ensuring food security and environmental preservation for generations to come. We are also grateful to our professional editors, Tushti and Sakshi, for their editing and proofreading of the book.

Shefali Arora Chouhan
Department of Computer Science and Engineering
Dr. BR Ambedkar National Institute of Technology
Jalandhar, Punjab-144008, India

Nagendra Pratap Singh
Department of Computer Science and Engineering
Dr. BR Ambedkar National Institute of Technology
Jalandhar, Punjab-144008, India

Banalaxmi Brahma
Department of Computer Science and Engineering
Dr. BR Ambedkar National Institute of Technology
Jalandhar, Punjab-144008, India

&

Shashank Gupta
Department of Computer Science and Engineering
Dr. BR Ambedkar National Institute of Technology
Jalandhar, Punjab-144008, India

List of Contributors

Anuj Gupta	School of Engineering and Technology, Sharda University, Greater Noida, India
Ajaypal Singh	Department of Computer Science and Engineering, Punjab Engineering College (Deemed to be) University, Chandigarh-160012, India
Akanksha	Materials Analysis & Research Laboratory, Department of Physics, NSUT, Dwarka Sec-3, New Delhi-110078, India
Bharti Sandhu	Dr. B.R. Ambedkar National Institute of Technology, Jalandhar, Punjab, India
Ekamdeep Singh	Department of Computer Science and Engineering, Punjab Engineering College (Deemed to be University), Chandigarh-160012, India
Indu Sounkhla	Department of Computer Science and Engineering, Dr. B.R. Ambedkar National Institute of Technology, Jalandhar, Punjab, India
Jaspal Kaur Saini	Department of Information Technology, Dr. B.R. Ambedkar NIT, Jalandhar, India
Kanu Goel	Department of Computer Science and Engineering, Punjab Engineering College (Deemed to be) University, Chandigarh-160012, India
Lakshay Aggarwal	Department of Computer Science and Engineering, D.A.V. Institute of Engineering and Technology, Jalandhar, India
Meenu Chahar	Department of Physics, Chaudhary Ranbir Singh University, Jind, Haryana-126102, India
Neeraj Dhariwal	Materials Analysis & Research Laboratory, Department of Physics, NSUT, Dwarka Sec-3, New Delhi-110078, India
Narendra Kumar	Department of Computer Science and Engineering, Dr. B.R. Ambedkar National Institute of Technology, Jalandhar, Punjab, India
Nishi Gupta	Department of Engineering and Technology, Gurugram University, Haryana, India
Pawan Kumar Mall	GL Bajaj Institute of Technology and Management, Greater Noida, India
Preety Yadav	Materials Analysis & Research Laboratory, Department of Physics, NSUT, Dwarka Sec-3, New Delhi-110078, India
Prashant Kumar	Dr. B.R. Ambedkar National Institute of Technology, Jalandhar, Punjab, India
Ruchi Mittal	Iconic Data, Tokyo, Japan
Renu Dhir	Department of Computer Science and Engineering, Dr. B.R. Ambedkar National Institute of Technology, Jalandhar, Punjab, India
Satyam Kumar Sainy	GL Bajaj Institute of Technology and Management, Greater Noida, India
Swapnita Srivastava	GL Bajaj Institute of Technology and Management, Greater Noida, India
Sukhdeep Singh	Department of Computer Science and Engineering, Punjab Engineering College (Deemed to be) University, Chandigarh-160012, India
Sanjay Madan	Applied Artificial Intelligence & Analytics Division, C-DAC, Mohali, India
Shefali Arora	Department of Computer Science and Engineering, Dr. B.R. Ambedkar National Institute of Technology, Jalandhar, Punjab, India

Shashank Gupta   Department of Computer Science and Engineering, Dr. B.R. Ambedkar National Institute of Technology, Jalandhar, Punjab, India

Shikha Gupta   Department of Information Technology, MAIT, Rohini, New Delhi, India

Tamanna Sood   Department of Computer Science and Engineering, Punjab Engineering College (Deemed to be) University, Chandigarh-160012, India

Vipin Kumar   Lovely Professional University, Phagwara, Punjab, India

Vipul Narayan   Galgotias University, Greater Noida, India

Vinod Kumar   Materials Analysis & Research Laboratory, Department of Physics, NSUT, Dwarka Sec-3, New Delhi-110078, India

CHAPTER 1

Harvesting Innovation in Agriculture through IoT and Blockchain Technology

Vipin Kumar[1,*]

[1] *Lovely Professional University, Phagwara, Punjab, India*

Abstract: Innovative technologies like IoT and blockchain transform businesses and other agricultural work. Emerging technologies like artificial intelligence and big data have unlocked new possibilities for operational efficiency and achieved the highest level of productivity through informed decision-making. Using the Internet of Things technologies, sensors transmit real-time data regarding the environment's state, crops' growth, and animals' well-being. Consequently, the information they gain facilitates them in making better decisions, where resources can be utilized to their maximum and output raised without compromising waste. Blockchain technology provides a solution for building agricultural supply chains with integrity and transparency. In this chapter, we explore how integrating blockchain technology with IoT in agriculture can unlock unexplored proficiency, sustainability, and robustness. It utilizes case studies and examines innovative irrigation systems, crop monitoring, and animal management applications. This chapter will explore the various methods of data collection from Internet of Things sensors to analyze and gain insight for more accurate decision-making processes. By examining the data accumulated over several years, business management can develop goals that aim to improve production measures, such as efficiency and effectiveness. The analysis of various aspects of the agricultural industry and the application of blockchain technology demonstrates how it can improve processes by streamlining operations and making the industry more transparent. It examines the identification and effectiveness of data-driven decisions in crop management. The yield data analysis from production is the basis for continuing the growth of the agricultural industry.

Keywords: Agriculture innovation, Blockchain technology, Capital monitoring, Crops management, Internet of things, Smart farming.

INTRODUCTION

Innovative technologies like IoT and blockchain, which are relatively new, have been used to modernize the agriculture industry. As a result, a new era of agricultural transformation has emerged. This way of farming utilizes innovative

---

* **Corresponding author Vipin Kumar:** Lovely Professional University, Phagwara, Punjab, India;
E-mail: vipin.17730@lpu.co.in

breakthroughs, such as advanced accuracy, transparency, and efficiency, from the fields through processing plants to the end consumer. Therefore, farming techniques have been revolutionized for generations. The Internet of Things (IoT) enables sensors in fields, machinery, and livestock to provide us with real-time data on humidity, crop health, and livestock health. Through this provision of a coherent system, the farmer's decisions are informed, hence optimizing the available resources. Blockchain technology ensures that the integrity and traceability of agricultural goods from obtaining them from the farms to the consumer's table is preserved, thus cultivating trust and responsibility in the food supply chains. The agricultural revolution shall create more abilities that meet users' and the planet's needs by applying the combined forces of the Internet of Things (IoT) and Blockchain (BC) technologies. Through this, the future holds a highly informed, unambiguous, and fair agricultural sector. Scratching the paper-based agricultural bookkeeping approach, an old method of recording farm activities, is merely a child's game with this approach. The fact that this is the most dynamic stage of agricultural industry development almost deprives me of control. First, the Internet of Things (IoT) and the blockchain will play a crucial role in the current technological revolution. Undoubtedly, the past decade of technology has been a testament to its success, as it has turned all constraints to dust and touched every segment of society. Now, these two innovations will lay the foundation for a bright future in technology. Regardless of whether it's in engineering, health industries, computer science, or anything at all, their distinctive impressions pervade every sphere in which they are active [1].

Overview of IoT and Blockchain technology

The introduction of new technology, integrating IoT and blockchain, in the agricultural sector has resulted in the creation of various approaches to farming processes. Sensors, drones, and intelligent machines make age-old agriculture technologies contemporary by acquiring data instantaneously about soil moisture, temperature, crop health, and livestock. This data allowed them to drive more precise decisions and resources and significantly reduce the amount of waste and the negative environmental impact [2].

The Internet of Things (IoT) has always been the fastest-discussed and searched trend in the present era. The IoT foundation serves as the "connection" between various IT sector devices within the IoT vision. Furthermore, dimension one points us to intelligent communication and smart metering. Accepting this notion's vision would create room for the development of a significant agricultural subsidiary, which would imply change and additional possibilities for innovation and expansion. With contributions from IoT and resilient sensors that can accumulate large amounts of data, enabling the optimization of production processes, the prosperity of agriculture is advancing rapidly toward a greener and cleaner solution. Automated systems can create vast amounts of high-dimensional information to gain a complete understanding of our system. For instance, Uncrewed Aerial Vehicles (UAVs) can capture images that provide real-time information on crop growth. We can pinpoint particular components of the area that may require more attention. These devices can record enormous amounts of data, which, if comprehended, can result in various desirable outcomes. The data extracted from the Internet of Things typically consists of a substantial volume of information, necessitating the utilization of specific methods to be of any use [3].

As technologies continue to advance and people utilize them more, they have enormous potential to transform agriculture and positively impact farmers' lives worldwide. Smart devices and connectivity inculcation can allegedly be achieved in two ways concerning the Internet of Things in agriculture. For example, you can download weather information from the internet and have intelligent IoT devices implement it locally, update it, and automatically adjust the watering schedule. In this regard, robot technologies intended to observe crops and deliver information on the consumption of chemicals, such as pesticides or fertilizers, through the IoT network will operate autonomously. Eliminating the possibility of human error and providing data input with 100% accuracy is a fantastic result of the standard machine learning ability to teach algorithms how to process image data. One phrase can summaries all these: Boosting the product while consuming less water [4].

Blockchain technology is a genius solution for transparency, traceability, and security in the agricultural supply chain, as it helps maintain a record of every possible movement and transfer of farm products. These records are immutable, as illustrated in Fig. (**1**). This is demonstrated by the fact that customers can find the source of their food and track its quality. It is a distributed database shared among a network and uses encryption to ensure security. Blockchains are becoming increasingly popular. Its design does not allow any changes to be made to the data it stores, making it highly secure and auditable. The cryptocurrency known as Bitcoin, which was initially invented, has the potential to be utilised in a broad range of various businesses.

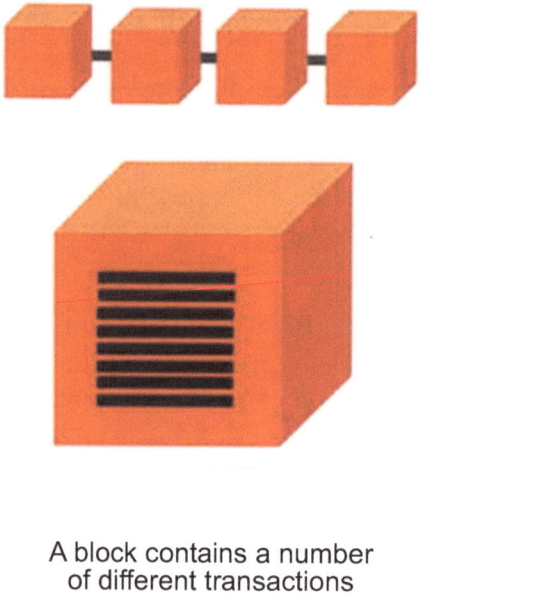

A block contains a number
of different transactions

Each block has its own
hash, transaction details,
nonce and previous hash

Fig. (1). Blockchain and block data.

The role of blockchain technology in existing agricultural systems makes it vital for us to choose it to produce the best results in the problem-solving work that farmers face daily, particularly in terms of financial issues [5].

The Role of Technology in Agricultural Innovation

The Internet of Things (IoT) and Blockchain technology are an impetus to taking agricultural innovation to the next level. Enabling IoT devices in agricultural production has launched possibilities for tracing all critical indicators, including soil moisture, crop health, and weather conditions, in real-time. This information allows farmers to make more reasonable decisions and optimize resource and power consumption, creating more yields with less waste. Also, blockchain technology sustains the availability of information, security, and traceability in the agricultural shipping system by ensuring transaction records and product movements cannot be changed [2]. This levels the playing field and conveys reliable information to stakeholders, permitting customers to trace the source and evaluate the quality of farm produce. Leveraging IoT and blockchain functionalities becomes another powerful driver for innovation in agriculture. This phenomenon fosters sustainable practices, enhances efficiency, and increases resilience against environmental and market pressures. Currently, the Internet of

Things concept has provided various approaches to enhance agricultural production, and we now aim to monitor the progress that has been made. Now comes the blockchain technology. We want precise accountability of where this data was successful, since I am sure that no one wants to go through trial and error when conducting a scientific study. An Internet of Things device will provide the data. Blockchain technology provides a distributed ledger, which can be utilized to monitor and analyze production.

OBJECTIVES

The main objectives of the chapter are:

- Explore the potential of IoT sensors in agriculture to enhance decision-making processes.
- Examine the utilization of long-term accumulated production data to devise strategies that enhance production efficiency and effectiveness.
- Investigate the practical applications of IoT and blockchain technologies in agricultural innovation and transformation endeavors.
- Analyze case studies to illustrate the implementation of blockchain technology within agricultural supply chains, highlighting its role in streamlining operations and promoting transparency.
- Utilize timely insights derived from data analysis to optimize agricultural, water, and fertilization techniques, with a focus on increasing agricultural yields.
- Highlight the importance of systematic production data analysis as a foundational element for continual improvement within the agricultural sector.

APPLICATIONS OF IOT AND BLOCKCHAIN IN AGRICULTURE

The Internet of Things (IoT) has been observed as the most significant game-changer in the agricultural sector, as revealing the revolutionary potential that will clear away all agricultural techniques of the past. Concerning farming, the term "Internet of Things" (IoT), for the sake of definition, is a kind of network of ranked machines, sensors, as well as devices that are scattered throughout the farmers' workplaces, and they are used for gathering and transmitting data on various matter such as the livestock health, crop growth, soil moisture, as well as the temperature. They comprise systems such as robotics, drones, and sensors for soil that are used to collect real-time and reliable data, enabling farmers to make informed decisions about their areas of operation. However, this data is like a magic formula that may help farmers develop improved crops, reduce pests and diseases, use less water and fertilizers, and better manage resources. Through the use of IoT in agriculture, farmers can effectively and efficiently control and monitor their businesses from remote areas, provided that IoT is implemented effectively [6]. Fig. (**2**) illustrates the comprehensive impact of IoT on agriculture. An individual should be aware that this disruption affects agricultural practices and makes the ecological footprint more sustainable, thereby helping to address the challenges of feeding a constantly growing global population in a continually changing environment.

Fig. (2). Applications of IoT.

Blockchain technology offers several applications in agriculture that can enhance transparency, traceability, and efficiency throughout the food supply chain. Some of the critical applications include:

Smart Irrigation System

The installation of the sensing unit in the Smart Irrigation System is based on the use of the Internet of Things (IoT) in agriculture. These sensors collect real-time information on soil moisture, weather, and crop health and release this information to the central hub for further analysis. The system to be implemented enables autonomous control of the actuators for opening and closing solenoids or drip irrigation systems. Algorithms that consider factors such as soil type, crop type, and previous history are typically used to achieve this. With mobile devices, farmers can manage the system right out in the field, making adjustments or reviewing reports and data, thereby ensuring optimal water management. As a result, more crops are produced, and money and the environment are saved as water wastage and runoff are decreased [7].

Crop Monitoring and Management

Additionally, the IoT technology enables excellent and profound crop control and development. By the end of the process, the network will be fully operational, with AR and sensors providing real-time information about the plants, including their health parameters such as humidity, weather, and moisture. The epoch-interconnected Internet of Agri-Things (IoAT) in birds represents the new generation of agriculture, as exemplified by the introduction of beef in reality. The data, including crop assessments and future risks such as insect invasions, pest problems, and nutrient insufficiency around the system, are collected. The cloud or the central system is the destination for the analysis and management conducted using the same processes. The segmentation of the algorithms ensures that they gather data in this manner, allowing the ads customers receive to be generated based on that data. We cannot help but observe that the farmers must use different pest control methods, products, and dosages at various times and approaches. Adoption of best resource use practices ensures exceedingly high yields in that field. The Grotte de la Vache Pila was situated in a border area between Saharan communities and savannahs. Thus, the modern agricultural model emerged after real-time observations of the arts raised concerns about agricultural failure. As with automated irrigation systems, drones equipped with navigational aids, and other advanced sensors, more sophisticated technology is integrated to reduce farming operation costs and promote optimal yields. When incorporating new technologies into crop and livestock production, agricultural scientists demonstrate ingenuity in automating cognitive functions such as data collection, analysis, and reporting, which informs essential decisions supported by the gathered data. A significant step that will consequently increase production is in operation. The business will be profitable, and adhering to environmental provisions will be the best course of action [8].

Livestock Monitoring and Tracking

The Internet of Things (IoT), which incorporates various sensors, GPS, and animal behavior tracking devices, enables comprehensive animal health monitoring and farm management at different life stages. Let me point to a few devices that can track animals using GPS, accelerometers, temperature sensors, and heart rate monitors attached to them, or the devices can be contained within wearable gear. Sensors can continuously track various inputs and wirelessly transmit the captured data to a central point or cloud storage for further analysis. Farmers are allowed to track which animal is doing what, how to observe indicators of unwellness or distress, and what grazing preferences the latter has, as well as map the movement of livestock within the given area by advanced analytics and machine learning algorithms. These data are conducive to creating rational strategies for adopting proactive measures, such as treatment time rescheduling and the provision of just-in-time treatment. For example, various problems may occur, and the manager may cope successfully. Implementing the IoT in the monitoring and tracking of livestock increases production efficiency and welfare. It minimizes operational losses while adhering to prevailing regulatory rules and standards [9].

Supply Chain Traceability

Blockchain enables end-to-end traceability of agricultural products from farm to fork by recording every transaction and movement on the distributed ledger. It makes the product supply chain transparent, allowing consumers to track the product's journey and ensure quality, authenticity, and safety. This blockchain can be used to share the origin of products and quality verification certificates, as well as to monitor compliance with food safety regulations.

Provenance Verification

The Integration of blockchain technology can provide tamper-proof record storage, allowing it to be used to store the origin and history of agricultural products and enable customers to verify the authenticity of a product's original state. By recording tamper-proof information, such as production, processing, distribution, and sales, on the blockchain, various stakeholders can establish trust among themselves and credibility with final consumers. They can differentiate their product in the market and prevent fraud and harmful quality products.

Smart Contracts for Agreements and Payments

An agreement between farmers, consumers, and distributors is essential. It enforces the rules, regulations, and terms of trade. The temperament of anything in these documents may create a big problem. Smart contracts can make the agreement channel; blockchain technology makes it tamperproof. It facilitates real-time payments based on predefined supply, demand, and quality conditions. Farmers can receive immediate payments for their products and delivery to buyers; it eliminates any delay and dispute because it is unchangeable [10].

Data Management and Sharing

Data storage and sharing with partners are essential to agriculture. In the case of blockchain, the data is stored on nodes instead of the central server; this removes the possibility of a single-point frailer. Agricultural data, including soil health, production, and weather conditions, enable analysis and informed decisions to enhance production. Data sharing is also effortless and secure using blockchain, which is tamperproof. Blockchain data sharing enables faster and safer data exchange, facilitating knowledge sharing among stakeholders. Researchers can then analyze and gain valuable insights into the data.

BENEFITS OF IOT IN AGRICULTURE

Utilizing IoT and blockchain technology in agriculture offers numerous benefits, as illustrated in Fig. (**3**). It can ease farmers' work, reduce expenses, better utilize resources, and improve productivity. This technology can provide a sustainable option for meeting the high demand for high-quality agricultural products.

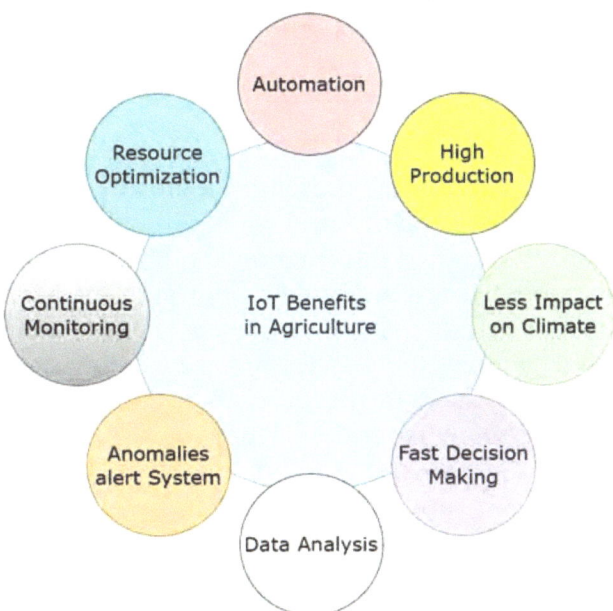

Fig. (3). Benefits of IoT in agriculture.

Improved Efficiency and Productivity

The ability of the Internet of Things to read and analyze data in real-time on the elements of crop farming, such as irrigation, soil moisture, and animal health, is a significant reason for the rapid rise in the effectiveness and production of the agriculture industry [11]. The Internet of Things connected with the fields has 'sensors' and 'devices' installed throughout the farm areas. It is possible to use this methodology to monitor soil moisture, temperature, crop health, and other vital indicators with varying levels of precision that weren't previously available. With this method, based on data collection, farmers will make informed decisions related to irrigation, fertilization, pest control, and other activities. Through this, the farmers will optimize resource usage and increase the number of crops harvested. Israel not only faces a rainfall shortage, but many crops also require more water than our environment can provide; therefore, the digitalization of farms could be introduced to alleviate this problem. Additionally, the Internet of Things enables the automation of mundane operations, such as scheduling irrigation and monitoring equipment. Through AI, these farmers can reduce their manual labour and thus have more time for business development. They have the option to monitor and manage farm situations from anywhere by implementing remote monitoring and management techniques. This will be a good idea for responding to interventions promptly and initiating preventive measures in risky circumstances. Arguably, fundamental IoT changes traditional farming methods; however, insights are acquired that can be implemented, operations become more efficient, and eventually settle on agronomic sustainability, both in production and profitability.

Reduction in Resource Consumption

The agricultural Internet of Things presented tomorrow is the primary variable that will help improve crop quality and yield. Intelligent farming technology enables farmers to access detailed information about natural elements, such as soil moisture content, temperature, humidity, and nutrient levels, that has never been available on their farms before, using built-in sensors and intelligent devices. The 24/7 release of such data paves the way for precise farming methods that precisely create irrigation schedules, accurately regulate nutrient applications, and precisely implement crop management practices. Moreover, Internet of Things-enabled technologies, such as drones and satellite imaging, are widely used on plantations to monitor their farms. Intelligent sensors in agriculture can diagnose early warning signs of insect infestations, diseases, and nutrient deficiencies, thereby enabling immediate response measures to mitigate and reduce output losses. The next element is that advanced machine learning methods analyze a massive amount of information processed by predictive analytics algorithms to determine planting seasons, crop rotation, and harvesting time rather than the exact one [12]. This setup facilitates reaching the highest output possible by keeping the resources used to a minimum. By applying Internet of Things technology to post-harvest procedures such as storage and transportation, farmers can sustain the quality of crops, ensure high-quality products, and maintain product freshness, thereby inevitably reducing monetary loss and delivering superior products to markets. Eventually, the agricultural sector will be transformed entirely into a data-driven precision farming industry that constantly focuses on providing the best quality and higher-yield leafy greens to the planet's fast-growing population. IoT revolutionises the face of the agricultural sector as the sales of arable land soar, and the global population of the Earth keeps rising.

Enhanced Crop Quality and Yield

The use of Internet of Things technology in agriculture represents a paradigm shift in improving crop quality and productivity. All the information that farmers used to have to go out to the fields to find can now be quickly looked at, as long as they use different sensors and other connected farm equipment that the fields have. Instant data enables the execution of technologies such as irrigation schedules, fertilizer application adjustments, and similar processes that impact crop management. Moreover, the Internet-of-things empowered technologies, such as drones, and remote sensing enable supervisory practices through crops. Such devices can detect subtle signs of insect infestations, ailments, and deficiencies in supplementary nutrients, allowing for timely intervention measures and significantly minimizing output losses. Additionally, the predictive analytics control algorithms are heavily loaded with vast amounts of data to develop timely planting durations, crop rotations, and harvest recommendations. This building presents an opportunity for maximizing production and reducing resource waste. In general, there are cost-effective approaches to implementing IoT technologies in post-harvest operations, which include transportation and storage, that aim to sustain the quality and freshness of harvested crops, thereby minimizing monetary losses and ensuring the shipment of high-quality goods to marke [13]. Ultimately, through the seamless integration of Internet of Things technologies, agriculture evolves into a data-driven, precision-focused industry capable of consistently delivering higher crop yields and superior-quality produce to meet the demands of a growing global population, while fostering sustainability and environmental stewardship.

BLOCKCHAIN TECHNOLOGY FOR AGRICULTURE

There is a vast array of applications for blockchain technology in agriculture, ranging from crop monitoring and recording to supply chain management.

Decentralized distributed ledger and smart contracts are the two main uses of blockchain in the agriculture industry:

Blockchain and Distributed Ledger Technology

Blockchain and Distributed Ledger Technology (DLT) are innovative systems for securely and transparently recording and verifying transactionsithout intermediaries [14]. At its core, blockchain technology is a decentralized database that stores data in interconnected nodes. It stores records called blocks, which are linked together and secure the data using the cryptography method of distributor ledger technology. This helps to store the data in a decentralized manner. The main concepts of blockchain and decentralized ledger technology are as follows:

- *Decentralization:* Instead of storing data on a central server, it is distributed across various connected nodes, with no single central authority controlling the data. Blockchain ensures that every participant stores a copy of the data. The decentralized architecture ensures that multiple copies of data are stored on various nodes, making them immutable and tamper-proof.
- *Consensus Mechanisms:* Blockchain Technology is based on a consensus mechanism to validate the data and transactions. Different concession mechanisms are proof of work, proof of stake, and proof of storage. These are used to achieve agreement among in-network participants and also maintain security and integrity
- *Immutability:* Once a transaction is recorded, it cannot be altered in any shape and form. This ensures the integrity and transparency of the ledger, making it best suited for applications where data integrity and security are critical, such as financial transactions or agreements between partners.
- *Cryptography:* Blockchain transactions are mainly based on cryptography and hashing. Each block has a hash of the previous blocks for refrain tempering. Digital signatures verify the authentication and secure transfer of data. Encryption techniques are used to store and transfer data, ensuring consistency among transactions.
- *Transparency and Traceability:* Blockchain-powered transparency lets you view any transaction entering the ledger. The transparent nature of blockchain enables stakeholders to trace the legitimacy of assets or transactions back to their source, making it particularly suitable for logistics tracking, provenance, and auditing applications.

In general, blockchain and distributed ledger technology provide a secure, transparent, and decentralized platform for transaction recording and verification, with applications that can be found in cryptocurrency and banking, supply chain management, healthcare, and more. With technological progress, existing industries can be reshaped by introducing innovations that enhance efficiency, channel resources, and increase trust and security in digital transactions.

Smart Contracts and Supply Chain Management

Smart contracts are powerful tools for creating contracts and applying business rules in supply chain and resource management between various parties. It is very transparent, secure, and easy to use. This aspect eliminates human error, as the contract terms are predicted and implemented when a specific condition is met, without involving intermediarie [15]. Regarding supply chain mechanisms, smart contracts offer numerous advantages. A smart contract is a digital document of agreement written in code. It ensures the following:

* *Automating Transactions:* Smart contracts automate the process in the supply chain. Transactions are automatically executed when a specific condition is met. Supply chain processes, such as procurement, ordering, invoicing, and data updates, are executed automatically by smart contract code and stored permanently in blockchain nodes. They can automatically trigger the order to the supplier and payment settlement. It eliminates delays and reduces the risk of disputes.
* *Enhancing Transparency:* Smart contracts ensure integrity and transparency in transactions executed in a decentralized ledger. All the blockchain participants participate in the transaction. It fosters trust among stakeholders, allowing them to track the movement of goods and verify the authenticity and quality of the product.
* *Improving Efficiency:* Automating tasks without human intervention improves efficiency. Automated supply chains and smart contracts generate shipping documents and invoices, resulting in cost savings and faster delivery. Tracking of goods and alarm systems provide the end user with essential and critical information, enabling them to make better decisions.
* *Reducing Fraud and Errors:* Smart contracts can prevent document forging and modification. They can also prevent the double-spending of digital assets, verify the authenticity of product shipments using IoT sensors and RFID tags, and ensure that payments are made only when goods are delivered as agreed upon.
* *Facilitating Trustless Collaboration:* The classical type of contract often involves trust serving as a moderator for the businesses involved in the supply chain operations. However, human nature will contribute a lot to the advent of such a system, where it may be possible for some people to specialize in topical business issues, and balance amongst all stakeholders will be observed as the officials will have to coexist with society. Nevertheless, honest mediators are imperative factors for functioning. Yet they are not necessarily required, as

contracts will ensure that trade agreements are made and transactions are conducted without intermediaries or trust. Its functionality is not limited to the supply chain alone, but it also facilitates the convenient handling of disruptions.

Indeed, smart contracts, among other methods of supply chain regeneration, can automate existing disparities in business relations, provide greater transparency, and enhance business ethics. Such a floor to the smart contract can be said to be the result or achievements of the breakthroughs in technology, where the evolution is most likely to be seen in the business model where there will be an increase in capital efficiency and the monitoring of the full accountability of the production, commerce and consumption of the goods [16]. Thus, the same high-efficiency level is predicted to be saved by using a streamlined model of global supply chains shortly.

INTEGRATION OF IOT AND BLOCKCHAIN IN AGRICULTURE

Utilizing IoT devices and blockchain technology will enhance traceability, transparency, and efficiency in the agricultural sector. It will hence offer a revolutionary example for complete industry reshaping. Such change can be achieved in both technology areas and by their implementation. The machines feature different types of sensors, drones, and intelligent agricultural tools, which can continuously collect vast amounts of data on the crop's performance in terms of soil conditions, weather patterns, health, and livestock behavior. Blockchain heavily relies on trust due to the way it protects information and provides a permanent platform for verifying data. By doing so, stakeholders can collaborateo achieve maximum output [17].

One of the most apparent features of integrating blockchain and the Internet of Things in agriculture is the capability to track the supply chain. The capture of all data along the course of the product from the farm to the fork by storing data from the Internet of Things devices in the blockchain ledger. Thus, we get the product to be original; it should be superior and mindful. A sample sensed all this information regarding planting, irrigation, and harvesting through sensors positioned in the fields and transmitted it. This information is further compiled and then recorded in the blockchain. Transparency enables shoppers to verify the origin and journey of food, which builds trust and confidence in the supply chain.

However, the integration of the Internet of Things and blockchain technology will enable the development of smart contracts in the agricultural sector. Hence, transactions involving parties will be carried out in an automated manner, based on real-time events. Intelligent contracts can be helpful in farming activities by automating many tasks, such as purchasing inputs, logistics, and payments. As a result, the likelihood of delays, errors, and conflicts in transactions is minimized.

Thus, it is possible to avoid situations where manual invoicing and reclaiming are used. Instead, smart contracts would automatically trigger the payments to the farmers when the Internet of Things sensors receive the location of the supplied crops. It enables automated invoicing and reconciliation, thereby centralizing the process [18].

Furthermore, the participation of blockchain technology in the Internet of Things interaction between agribusiness stakeholders provides them with a platform to share information and collaborate. Platforms based on algorithms, such as distributed data processing systems, enable farmers, researchers, agronomists, and policymakers to share and access data collected from Internet of Things devices. Such collaboration will be able to spur activity, creativity, and knowledge. Data can be assessed jointly through this, enabling predictive analytics relevant to farming purposes, suitable crop management practices can be developed, and risks related to climate change and the environment can be minimized.

Moreover, powering up blockchain in IoT systems could be an option for decentralizing agricultural marketplaces and arranging supply chain financing. Farmers can utilize blockchain systems to establish direct relationships with buyers, thereby eliminating intermediaries and reducing transaction costs. IoT data, such as crop production analysis and quality control, can drive advanced payment and financial planning through intelligent contract platforms. This helps the farmers elude a vital dimension of the banking network where they can get the required money and credit.

When taken as a whole, combining blockchain technology and the Internet of Things can completely transform agriculture by bringing about more openness, efficiency, and sustainability in the food supply chain. Several critical difficulties in agriculture, including food traceability, supply chain inefficiencies, and access to funding, can be addressed by stakeholders by utilizing Internet of Things (IoT) devices and blockchain technology. This will ultimately lead to increased resilience and innovation within the agricultural sector [19].

CASE STUDIES OF IOT AND BLOCKCHAIN IMPLEMENTATION IN AGRICULTURE

A couple of case studies that show the effective use of blockchain technology and the Internet of Things in agriculture are as follows:

Case Study 1: Smart Farming with IoT and Blockchain

Smart farming involves automating agricultural processes and enhancing productivity through improved resource utilization. Technology can help meet the needs of an expanding population. It also helps reduce the negative environmental impact, and farmer income improves. The revolutionary technologies of blockchain and IoT automate and enhance fairness by improving integrity and security. The following use case shows the use of cutting-edge technology to contribute to the agriculture field and optimize farming operations and the sustainability of the environment. In this scenario, a group of farmers is attempting to enhance crop productivity by optimizing resource utilization and minimizing negative environmental impacts. They are adapting their farming methods by utilizing blockchain and IoT technology to achieve their goals.

Data Collection using Internet of Things

Farmers install numerous sensors in their fields to collect data on crops and soil. IoT devices help monitor soil moisture and crop quality. They also inform about physical damage, such as introduction, fire, or climate change. These devices record vital elements for production, like temperature, soil moisture, and humidity. These sensors continuously collect data and transmit it to the control server *via* a gateway, where it can be analyzed and used to inform better decisions.

Data Processing and Analysis

Cleaning and normalization are performed on the gathered data to ensure it is accurate and valuable. Adding extra information like metadata to store the data with relevant fields for feature use. Algorithms are used to process this data to get insight into the collected data. Two types of data include analysis and alarming data, where immediate action should be taken. AI or ML algorithms are used to store and process analysis data, enabling the collection of information about crop quality, yield optimization, and demand for soil fertilizers. By gaining insight into processed data, farmers increase their efficiency and make decisions based on accurate information.

Secure Storage on Blockchain

Processed data and gained information must be stored safely on blockchain networks using decentralized storage services such as IPFS. This ensures data integrity and transparency; the immutable ledger makes the data accessible to all stakeholders and prevents unauthorized modification. Real-time data helps farmers optimize their resources and increase productivity. It is analyzed and accurately used to make better decisions. These technologies benefit farmers through improved resource utilization and increased productivity.

Environmental Sustainability

In the agricultural field, efficient resource management reduces the use of chemicals, preserves soil and water quality, and has a lower environmental impact. A blockchain-based supply chain ensures the timely ordering and delivery of products, while also reducing food waste. Farmers can ensure that they receive fair pricing for their products and maintain financial stability. The collected data is from IoT devices and is used for environment, soil, and water quality and requirements study, and processing this data; insight into the environment, like soil, air, and water, helps to understand the environment and helps to maintain a secure environment by making the best decisions based on data [20].

Case Study 2: Blockchain-based Food Traceability System

Good-quality agricultural products, including vegetables, fruits, and dairy products, are essential to a healthy life. They are susceptible to the environment and can be preserved for less time. Therefore, the timely delivery of high-quality products is essential, and customers must be able to track the origin and supply chain of these products. Blockchain helps to trace the food supply with security and integrity [21]. The supply chain is old technology, making it very difficult to verify and check the quality and origin of agricultural products. Blockchain-based food supply chains make them transparent and efficient.

Challenges in the Management of the Food Supply Chain at present

The food supply chain is a vital component of daily life. The system must be transparent and able to verify the food's origin and the product's quality. Many types of food fraud exist, such as counterfeiting and mislabeling. The supply chain has traceability issues; descriptions and labels can be altered.

The Solution from Blockchain

A decentralized system removes the need for a central authority and can guarantee transparency, integrity, security, and confidence among stakeholders. Using blockchain technology, stakeholders can ensure confidence and transparency, thereby reducing food fraud and enhancing traceability.

Step 1: Internet of Things sensors generate data, or farmers store data on crop quality, type of seed, and meteorological conditions. The data addresses are stored in the blockchain, and the data is saved on a distributed storage platform, such as IPFS.

Step 2: Distribute the crops grown to food processing companies. On a bidding platform, organizations that process food submit bids for various types of crops.

Plants are transported by Internet of Things-enabled vehicles, which record the temperature conditions. The blockchain is used to store data from processing companies, guaranteeing both quality and compliance with regulations.

Step 3: The third step involves distributing processed food to wholesalers and retailers. When it comes to processed food goods, wholesalers and retailers compete for bids. IoT-enabled cars are used to distribute food goods, ensuring they can be traced. Blockchain technology makes it easier to perform investigations or recalls promptly.

Step 4: Consumers can trace the supply chain backward in this step. The facts of the farm's origin, shipping, batch numbers, and other information can be traced back to the consumer. Transparency is made possible by blockchain technology, which also helps identify the origins of contamination.

Real-time bidding platform architecture

The bidding platform powered by blockchain technology offers a chance for interested stakeholders to bid for processed foodstuffs and crops. The features include setting a bidding parameter, putting up and running the ads, paying for the ads, and monitoring campaign results. Google App Engine is a platform that offers campaign applications, such as managing dashboards and reporting. Two-part bidding, also known as double-clicking or using an ad exchange, combines the two parts used to place an ad. Such bids are then sent to the Bidding Service to find the corresponding bids. As for direct interaction with the blockchain, the ads are accommodated and kept in storage. On the other hand, if the user requests an advertisement, the ad server will be responsible for fulfilling it. The output of ad efforts is being considered through modulations and analytics. In contrast to the Big Query data querying and loading process, the prediction API has implemented machine learning methods. Proof that the food supply chain is managed with precision and autonomy will no longer affect the trust of food producers and consumers. By integrating blockchain technology, stakeholders can disrupt fraudulent acts such as food adulteration, ensure transparency, and fortify the food safety issue for all actors along the value chain.

Case Study 3: IoT-enabled Agricultural Finance Monitoring and Management

The main problem faced by small-scale farmers, primarily those residing in developing countries, is the limited access to various financial services to which they are challenged. We must better structure public infrastructure with more installment plans and a clear line of credit. The public sector also has the matter of complying with contract law enforcement. These constraints indeed reduce agricultural productivity by hampering smooth operations and effective investment in the business sectors of the agri-business sector. As a result, these dynamics would steer the donors' and the farmers' core measures of performance of agricultural value chains. By the end of this case study, readers will understand why distributed ledger technology is the most effective solution for addressing the issue of limited access that small-scale farmers face when seeking financing and general financial services. Blockchain technology integration ensures that food fraud is reduced, productivity is increased, and payment equity is established, as agricultural activities are efficiently and accurately processed due to the smooth and quick processing of agricultural transactions. This is achieved through the establishment of transparency, traceability, and efficiency across all steps of the supply chain.

Challenges in Agriculture finance Management

Small farmers should be given an ad-hoc fund as they suffer from a natural disaster. Another revenue-generating source is the obstacle. Such crisis resolution of emergency funding from banks and other finance sectors is based on the ability of these transactions to be verified and made transparent. The credit status of small-scale farmers should be part and parcel of the pieces of the transaction to facilitate these small transactions. The resolution of these issues needs more effective contract enforcement. Additionally, incorporating the terms and conditions of the contracts into society's consciousness requires considerable effort.

Blockchain Solutions

The performance of agricultural value chains is impacted by limited access to financial services. These issues can be resolved by using blockchain technology in agricultural finance in two crucial ways:

Information Exchange between Stakeholders at Every Stage of Food Production

Blockchain helps to document each transaction, providing open access to all participants. It improves the quality and maintains beliefs between stakeholders. It provides the required information on time and increases their transparency and trust.

Efficient auditing by auditors

Blockchain technology is the best for maintaining the integrity and security of transactions. Information is permanently stored and guarantees integrity throughout time. Applying blockchain technology in agriculture creates fairness and belief among smallholder farmers in overcoming transaction uncertainty. Any auditor can check the origin of the traction and modification in the transaction. These transactions do not come under the central authorities and improve transparency between stakeholders. It serves the purpose of the farming industry, the achievement of food security, and the country's economic development.

Case Study 4: Controlling Weather Crisis

Farmers in India and worldwide face the challenges of weather conditions and unpredictable behaviors. Indian agriculture is called the gamble of the monsoon and is most affected by climate change. The production and survival of crops may also depend on weather conditions. Timely information can help us face these challenges. Excessive rain can lead to flooding, causing significant damage to crops. Additionally, a lack of transparency in the food supply chain may cause prices to fluctuate based on the fluctuations in crop production. Blockchain technology offers solutions to providers for the traceability and prediction of weather conditions and making decisions according to that. Timely and accurate information, enabled by blockchain technology, allows stakeholders to predict pricing fluctuations and streamline processes such as supply chain management and crop insurance claims.

Objective

The objective of this case study is to determine the impact of weather conditions on farming and how blockchain and IoT technology can help mitigate weather-related problems, inform decision-making to minimize the effects of weather crises, and streamline insurance processes.

Challenges

Unpredictable weather conditions impact crop survival and production, making farmers' lives more challenging. Lack of transparency in the food supply chain leads to uncertainty in the process. Delays in insurance claims and the Landy loan process create problems. Using blockchain technology in controlling whether crises and fast insurance claims involves a three-step process:

- Agricultural weather stations send essential information to the blockchain. Weather information should be provided to farmers as soon as possible. For this purpose, the weather station is deployed in various areas, and information is updated in a timely manner using broadcast or personal messages. Smart agriculture weather stations gather crucial weather data by measuring parameters like rainfall, wind speed, humidity, and atmospheric pressure. All data security is recorded in a blockchain and is transparently accessible to all stakeholders. A personal message or a broadcast alarming message may be sent to farmers. This data should be securely recorded for future use.

- Farmers can take preventive actions: Access to real-time weather data and timely information enables farmers to take suitable actions to prevent damage. Early warning systems allow farmers to take preventive action against crises. Based on weather conditions, proactive action, such as an irrigation schedule, may be taken. The weather information is saved in blockchain storage and can be used in the future for insurance claims.

- Quick application for crop insurance: For the unavoidable situation of weather and crop destruction, there must be a process that farmers can easily apply for insurance claims. Blockchain enables transparency in the process, and insurance companies and authorized parties can access information quickly. Smart contracts automate insurance claims, streamlining the process. Disbursement of insurance money to farmers' wallets and automation using smart contracts and blockchain processes.

Blockchain technology can be utilized in agriculture to mitigate crises and offer numerous other benefits. When combined with IoT technology, it provides real-time monitoring. It speeds up the process and maintains transparency and security. Farmers make informed decisions based on timely information received and mitigate risk. It helps to settle the insurance claim and loan process by storing immutable data, providing integrity and security that builds confidence between participants and stakeholders. This enhances agricultural resilience and fosters trust and efficiency in food supply chains. As the farm sector embraces blockchain solutions, stakeholders can better cope with the challenges posed by unpredictable weather conditions, ensuring sustainable food production and security.

Collaborative Platforms and Data Sharing in Agriculture

Collaborative platforms and programs for exchanging data are the ones that are taking the agricultural landscape into a new shape. These organizational approaches allow the creation of a straighter line to food production concerning openness, honesty, and innovativeness, and they also optimize processes [22]. The platforms that bring together farmers, researchers, agronomists, policymakers, and other stakeholders make information and resources accessible through the participation of all parties, resulting in more recent and sustainable practices.

Information exchange is usually one of the crucial aspects of cooperative platforms in the agricultural industry. Farmers can thus securely transfer information obtained from their plows to scientists and other specialists through these platforms. This data class contains soil moisture levels, crop yields, livestock health, and meteorological conditions. The availability of data for this kind of sharing would enable collaborative analyses and widespread recognition, which can serve as a guide in optimizing crop management techniques, resource allocation, and best practices. Additionally, cross-platforms often utilize blockchain technologies to ensure the integrity and traceability of shared data, enhance user confidence, and extend accountability.

Also, teamwork platforms reduce the need for farmers and other concerned actors to enlighten each other, since they can interact and develop joint work through teamwork [23]. Farmers can sign up for online forums, social networks, and digital communities to discuss various agricultural concerns, including asking for advice and inquiring about rural problems and topics from professionals. These points encompass a range of topics, from farming techniques to pest control strategies. Such channels become the means of forming solid and well-competitive agricultural communities. Besides, they pave the way for researching, creating purchase cooperatives, and launching joint marketing campaigns. On the other hand, there are numerous instances where governmental agencies and bodies create trust platforms and initiatives to share data in agriculture, which is imperative.

Regarding agriculture, government agencies and organizations frequently find it vital to develop collaborative platforms and initiatives to share data. Governments can facilitate the establishment of resilient agricultural ecosystems that use collective intelligence and data-driven innovation by providing money, technical support, and legislative frameworks that encourage open data sharing and interoperability [24].

Collaborative platforms and projects that share data hold tremendous potential for transforming agriculture into a more integrated, knowledge-intensive, and sustainable industry. These platforms can improve productivity, resilience, and inclusivity throughout the agricultural value chain. This will ultimately contribute to global food security and environmental stewardship. This enables farmers and stakeholders to interact, share ideas, and harness collective data.

CONCLUDING REMARKS

It is inevitable that technologies like the Internet of Things (IoT), blockchain, and others that are yet to develop in the future will be the game changers in the industry of agriculture in the sense that they not only reduce the time and the effort needed but they also ensure better sustainability and transparency that the industry has never experienced before. IoT plays a crucial role, as sensors implanted in agricultural equipment, soil, and livestock allow dashboards to retrieve current information on parameters such as humidity levels, temperature, and plant health status instantly from remote locations [25]. Farmers are thus given the option to be aware of resource planning through which they can make optimum use of such resources. To ensure that this information remains accessible only to authorized individuals, the use of blockchain technology will prevent unauthorized changes, making transactions more straightforward and more convenient, while also facilitating trustworthy transactions and supply chain tracking. At the same time, implementing smart contracts on the blockchain can automatically settle agreements between the parties involved and streamline business operations and logistics transactions, including payroll processing or freight management. These improvements will increase yields and reduce waste in the agricultural environment, ultimately resulting in greater trust and cooperation on all agriculture-related issues. Agribusinesses can obtain immensely beneficial innovations through the continuous evolution of these technologies, which provide the sector with new avenues for positive impact. Technological advancements, such as AI and machine learning, are instrumental in modern agriculture. You can use these technologies in several ways that benefit agriculture. Your productivity will increase, your processes will be more sustainable, and your decision-making will become easier. AI technologies could analyze a vast collection of sensor readings, drone videos, satellite imagery, and other measurable data and then produce valuable crop health, soil condition, weather, and pest infestation details. Therefore, with this evaluation, AI algorithms can render significant scraps of facts, which will be substantial. Farmers can take preventive measures by relying on machine learning models that predict risks in advance, resulting in a higher crop yield. The algorithms can also develop suspicious watering plans, detect the earliest signs of diseases and nutritional deficiencies in crops, and predict the optimal planting times.

Edge computing and fog computing are two emerging paradigms that hold tremendous promise for transforming agriculture. These paradigms bring computer capacity and data processing closer to the data collection source, enabling real-time decision-making and enhancing the efficiency of farming operations.

REFERENCES

[1]   D. Davcev, K. Mitreski, S. Trajkovic, V. Nikolovski, and N. Koteli, "IoT agriculture system based on LoRaWAN", *Proc. 14th IEEE Int. Workshop Factory Commun. Syst. (WFCS)*, pp. 1-4, 2018.Imperia, Italy
[http://dx.doi.org/10.1109/WFCS.2018.8402368]

[2]   Z. Cui, F. Xue, S. Zhang, X. Cai, Y. Cao, W. Zhang, and J. Chen, "A hybrid blockchain-based identity authentication scheme for multi-WSN", *IEEE Trans. Serv. Comput.*, vol. 13, no. 2, p. 1, 2020.
[http://dx.doi.org/10.1109/TSC.2020.2964537]

[3]   S. Aheleroff, X. Xu, Y. Lu, M. Aristizabal, J. Pablo Velásquez, B. Joa, and Y. Valencia, "IoT-enabled smart appliances under industry 4.0: A case study", *Adv. Eng. Inform.,* vol. 43, p. 101043, 2020.
[http://dx.doi.org/10.1016/j.aei.2020.101043]

[4]   K. Kansara, V. Zaveri, S. Shah, S. Delwadkar, and K. Jani, "Sensor-based automated irrigation system with IoT: A technical review", *Int. J. Comput. Sci. Inf. Technol.,* vol. 6, no. 6, pp. 5331-5333, 2015.

[5]   W. Lin, X. Huang, H. Fang, V. Wang, Y. Hua, J. Wang, H. Yin, D. Yi, and L. Yau, "Blockchain technology in current agricultural systems: From techniques to applications", *IEEE Access,* vol. 8, pp. 143920-143937, 2020.
[http://dx.doi.org/10.1109/ACCESS.2020.3014522]

[6]   L. García, L. Parra, J.M. Jimenez, J. Lloret, and P. Lorenz, "IoT-based smart irrigation systems: An overview on the recent trends on sensors and IoT systems for irrigation in precision agriculture", *Sensors (Basel),* vol. 20, no. 4, p. 1042, 2020.
[http://dx.doi.org/10.3390/s20041042] [PMID: 32075172]

[7]   D.K. Sreekantha, and A.M. Kavya, "Agricultural crop monitoring using IoT—a study", *Proc. 11th Int. Conf. Intell. Syst. Control (ISCO),* pp. 134-139, 2017.

[8]   S. Neethirajan, and B. Kemp, "Digital livestock farming", *Sens. Biosensing Res.,* vol. 32, p. 100408, 2021.
[http://dx.doi.org/10.1016/j.sbsr.2021.100408]

[9]   T.H. Pranto, A.A. Noman, A. Mahmud, and A.K.M.B. Haque, "Blockchain and smart contract for IoT enabled smart agriculture", *PeerJ Comput. Sci.,* vol. 7, p. e407, 2021.
[http://dx.doi.org/10.7717/peerj-cs.407] [PMID: 33834098]

[10]   O. Elijah, T.A. Rahman, I. Orikumhi, C.Y. Leow, and M.H.D.N. Hindia, "An overview of Internet of Things (IoT) and data analytics in agriculture: Benefits and challenges", *IEEE Internet Things J.,* vol. 5, no. 5, pp. 3758-3773, 2018.
[http://dx.doi.org/10.1109/JIOT.2018.2844296]

[11]   A. Vangala, A.K. Das, N. Kumar, and M. Alazab, "Smart secure sensing for IoT-based agriculture: Blockchain perspective", *IEEE Sens. J.,* vol. 21, no. 16, pp. 17591-17607, 2021.
[http://dx.doi.org/10.1109/JSEN.2020.3012294]

[12]   L. Rempelos, M. Baranski, J. Wang, T.N. Adams, K. Adebusuyi, J.J. Beckman, C.J. Brockbank, B.S. Douglas, T. Feng, J.D. Greenway, M. Gür, E. Iyaremye, C.L. Kong, R. Korkut, S.S. Kumar, J. Kwedibana, J. Masselos, B.N. Mutalemwa, B.S. Nkambule, O.B. Oduwole, A.K. Oladipo, J.O. Olumeh, L. Petrovic, N. Röhrig, S.A. Wyld, L. Xu, Y. Pan, E. Chatzidimitriou, H. Davis, A. Magistrali, E. Sufar, G. Hasanaliyeva, H.H.H.A. Kalee, A. Willson, M. Thapa, P. Davenport, D. Średnicka-Tober, N. Volakakis, A. Watson, C.J. Seal, M. Goltz, P. Kindersley Jr, P.O. Iversen, and C. Leifert, "Integrated soil and crop management in organic agriculture: A logical framework to ensure food quality and human health?", *Agronomy (Basel),* vol. 11, no. 12, p. 2494, 2021.
[http://dx.doi.org/10.3390/agronomy11122494]

[13]   B. McGurk, and S. Reichenbach, "Blockchain and distributed ledger technology", In: *Financial Services Law and Distributed Ledger Technology.* Edward Elgar Publishing: Northampton, MA, USA, 2024, pp. 12-46.
[http://dx.doi.org/10.4337/9781035300884.00009]

[14]   S.N. Khan, F. Loukil, C. Ghedira-Guegan, E. Benkhelifa, and A. Bani-Hani, "Blockchain smart contracts: Applications, challenges, and future trends", *Peer-to-Peer Netw. Appl.,* vol. 14, no. 5, pp. 2901-2925, 2021.
[http://dx.doi.org/10.1007/s12083-021-01127-0] [PMID: 33897937]

[15]   S. Wang, L. Ouyang, Y. Yuan, X. Ni, X. Han, and F.Y. Wang, "Blockchain-enabled smart contracts: Architecture, applications, and future trends", *IEEE Trans. Syst. Man Cybern. Syst.,* vol. 49, no. 11, pp. 2266-2277, 2019.
[http://dx.doi.org/10.1109/TSMC.2019.2895123]

[16]   M. Torky, and A.E. Hassanein, "Integrating blockchain and the internet of things in precision agriculture: Analysis, opportunities, and challenges", *Comput. Electron. Agric.,* vol. 178, p. 105476, 2020.
[http://dx.doi.org/10.1016/j.compag.2020.105476]

[17]   S. Nigam, U. Sugandh, and M. Khari, "The integration of blockchain and IoT edge devices for smart agriculture: Challenges and use cases", In: *Advances in Computers.* vol. Vol. 127. Elsevier: Amsterdam, Netherlands, 2022, pp. 507-537.

[18]   M.D. Borah, "Supply chain management in agriculture using blockchain and IoT", In: *Adv. Appl. Blockchain Technol.* Springer: Singapore, 2020, pp. 227-242.
[http://dx.doi.org/10.1007/978-981-13-8775-3_11]

[19]   R. Goodland, "Environmental sustainability in agriculture: diet matters", *Ecol. Econ.,* vol. 23, no. 3, pp. 189-200, 1997.
[http://dx.doi.org/10.1016/S0921-8009(97)00579-X]

[20]   H. Feng, X. Wang, Y. Duan, J. Zhang, and X. Zhang, "Applying blockchain technology to improve agri-food traceability: A review of development methods, benefits and challenges", *J. Clean. Prod.,* vol. 260, p. 121031, 2020.
[http://dx.doi.org/10.1016/j.jclepro.2020.121031]

[21]   M. Wysel, D. Baker, and W. Billingsley, "Data sharing platforms: How value is created from agricultural data", *Agric. Syst.,* vol. 193, p. 103241, 2021.
[http://dx.doi.org/10.1016/j.agsy.2021.103241]

[22]   L. Wiseman, J. Sanderson, A. Zhang, and E. Jakku, "Farmers and their data: An examination of farmers' reluctance to share their data through the lens of the laws impacting smart farming", *NJAS Wagening. J. Life Sci.,* vol. 90-91, no. 1, pp. 1-10, 2019.
[http://dx.doi.org/10.1016/j.njas.2019.04.007]

[23]   A. Maru *et al.*, "Digital and data-driven agriculture: Harnessing the power of data for smallholders," Global Forum Agric. Res. Innov., 2018.

[24]   K. Spanaki, E. Karafili, and S. Despoudi, "AI applications of data sharing in agriculture 4.0: A framework for role-based data access control", *Int. J. Inf. Manag.,* vol. 59, p. 102350, 2021.
[http://dx.doi.org/10.1016/j.ijinfomgt.2021.102350]

[25]   T. Cropin, *IoT Applications in Agriculture: 5 Best Use Cases to Increase Efficiency and Profitability.*https://www.cropin.com/blogs/iot-applications-in-agriculture.html

Harvesting Innovation: Exploring Challenges, Risks, and Ethical Pathways in the Integration of Smart Technologies with Agriculture

Pawan Kumar Mall[1,*], **Anuj Gupta**[2], **Satyam Kumar Sainy**[1], **Swapnita Srivastava**[1] and **Vipul Narayan**[3]

[1] *GL Bajaj Institute of Technology and Management, Greater Noida, India*

[2] *School of Engineering and Technology, Sharda University, Greater Noida, India*

[3] *Galgotias University, Greater Noida, India*

Abstract: Smart technology integration in agriculture offers a bright path forward for innovation, but it also comes with a lot of risks, problems, and ethical issues. The implementation of advanced technologies and inventions has increased agricultural productivity. Agricultural technical support is provided to farmers to assist with their farming activities, from raising crop yields to cutting back on pesticides, fertilizers, and water use, to enhancing farm workers' working conditions. It's critical to keep in mind that the new technologies are not related to agriculture. By providing sufficient food and other essential commodities and services in a manner that is both profitable and socially responsible, agriculture can ultimately enhance environmental quality, social responsibility, and the overall well-being of people. This is what is meant by a sustainable agricultural system. Depending on the viewpoint taken, the idea under examination has different implications for appropriate technology: at the farm level, at the level of the agri-food industry, or in relation to the larger local or worldwide economy. This chapter will examine the challenging landscape of applying new technologies to agriculture, examining issues such as data privacy, cybersecurity vulnerabilities, and the potential to worsen socioeconomic inequalities. It also examines the ethical implications of labor displacement and automation and emphasizes shared equity and negative impacts. By adopting ethical pathways and successfully navigating these challenges in the agriculture sector, we can fully utilize smart technology to enhance sustainability, production, and resilience.

Keywords: Harvesting, Innovation systems, Precision agriculture, Robotic farming, Smart technology, Sustainable development.

* **Corresponding author Pawan Kumar Mall:** GL Bajaj Institute of Technology and Management, Greater Noida, India; E-mail: Pawankumar.mall@gmail.com

Shefali Arora Chouhanm Nagendra Pratap Singh, Banalaxmi Brahma & Shashank Gupta (Eds.)

INTRODUCTION

Agriculture is the oldest and the most significant business enterprise in the world. The need for jobs and food demand is rising rapidly due to the world's population growth. The traditional methods of farming are insufficient to meet current food requirements while also creating jobs for billions of people globally [1]. Research is ongoing these days on automated methods to meet these demands. Due to a lack of labor, tighter laws, rising global population, and dwindling farming population, farmers are compelled to look for new alternatives such as Artificial Intelligence (AI). The limitations of traditional methods provide an opportunity to the research community- to discover AI-powered systems that have demonstrated superior effectiveness in terms of precision and resilience when compared to other options [2]. Providing universal solutions is a challenging task due to the constantly changing nature of agriculture, as conditions vary widely. Utilizing AI methods to analyze specific details of each situation enables us to deliver customized solutions tailored to address particular challenges [3]. The term "digital agriculture" describes the application of cutting-edge technology that has revolutionized the agriculture industry by improving the intelligence and efficiency of farm operations. Automated techniques like Artificial Intelligence (AI) gather and analyse agricultural data that can help enhance productivity [4]. There are a lot of research papers and inventions that are focused on the use of AI in many different sectors. Domains like agriculture, healthcare, education, economics, government, and other areas have all benefited greatly from AI. Since agriculture is a complicated issue in its own right , this paper aims to highlight studies that employed AI approaches in agriculture. A vital component of the world economy is agriculture. Over the past 21 years, there has been a rise in demand for appropriate and safer farming practices. AI-powered solutions can improve crop quality and output while also creating a model for farming. This essay offers a comprehensive analysis of AI methods applied to agriculture. The application of AI in agriculture is shown in Fig. (**1**).

This chapter provides an overview of the complicated realm of smart agriculture, looking at the developments in technology, possible risks, and ethical decisions that need to be taken for them to be effectively incorporated. The integration of smart technology in agriculture presents a promising avenue to improve work conditions for farm workers. AI can raise crop yields while reducing the need for pesticides, fertilizers, and water. These benefits come with significant risks, challenges, and ethical concerns. This chapter will explore the complex landscape of applying advanced technologies to agriculture, focusing on issues such as data privacy, cybersecurity vulnerabilities. It will also examine the ethical implications of automation and ensure that the benefits of these technologies are shared equitably. While the vast majority of these emerging technologies originate outside the agricultural sector, they hold the potential to drive a more sustainable agricultural system—one that improves environmental quality, social responsibility, and overall well-being. The concept of sustainability in agriculture can be viewed from various perspectives, whether at the farm level, across the agri-food industry, or within the broader local or global economy. Smart agriculture sustainable development involves the use of advanced technologies and environmentally friendly methods to increase productivity while conserving natural resources for generations to come. Through the use of instruments such as precision farming, IoT sensors, artificial intelligence, and data analytics, smart agriculture ensures effective utilization of water, land, and energy, minimizing wastage and harm to the environment. This method not only enhances crop yields and farmer incomes but also improves biodiversity, fights climate change, and provides food security in an increasing global population. In the end, smart agriculture is a prime example of how innovation can propel sustainability in agriculture.

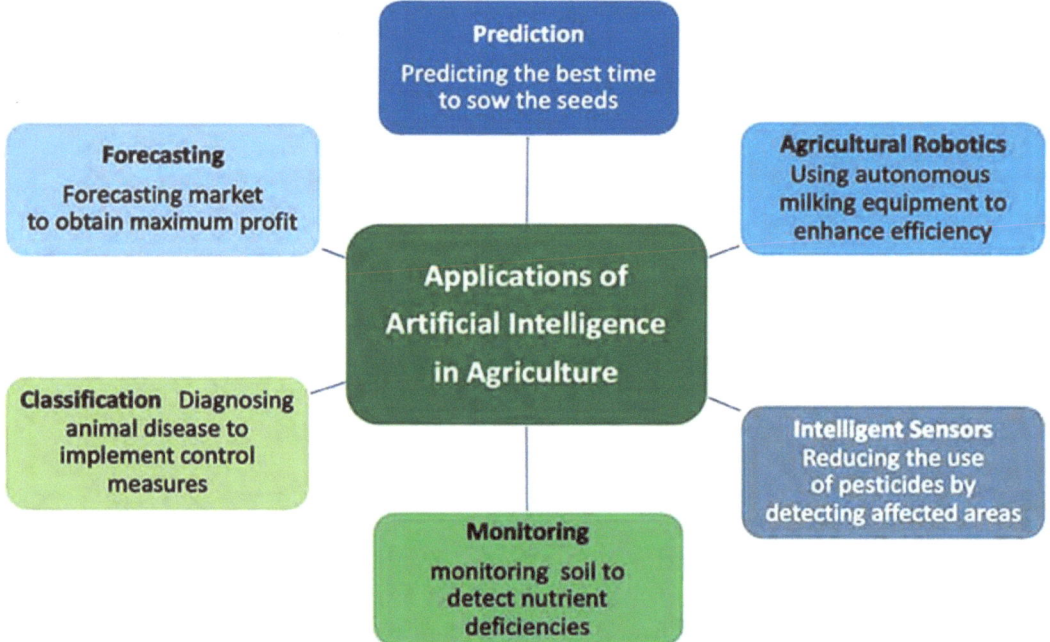

Fig. (1). Different AI applications in the field of agriculture.

In this chapter, our contributions are as follows. The technological innovation in the smart agriculture industry is covered in Section II. Section III discusses the challenges in integrating smart technologies with the agriculture industry; this makes up the majority of this chapter's discussion. It also covers technical complexities and other issues address by researchers in the field of agriculture. The chapter is wrapped up in Section VI, which discusses the risks associated with smart agriculture. Section V presents an overview of ethical pathways for responsible integration. The chapter ends with a conclusion.

TECHNOLOGICAL INNOVATIONS IN SMART AGRICULTURE

Precision Farming

Precision farming (PF) is an agricultural management approach that focuses on observing, measuring, and responding to temporal and spatial variability to enhance agricultural productivity and ensure sustainability [5]. Site-specific crop management is a farming method that uses data to support management choices based on anticipated variability [6, 7]. This covers crop scouting, soil testing, and Variable Rate Technology (VRT). The precision farming working approach is depicted in Fig. (**2**).

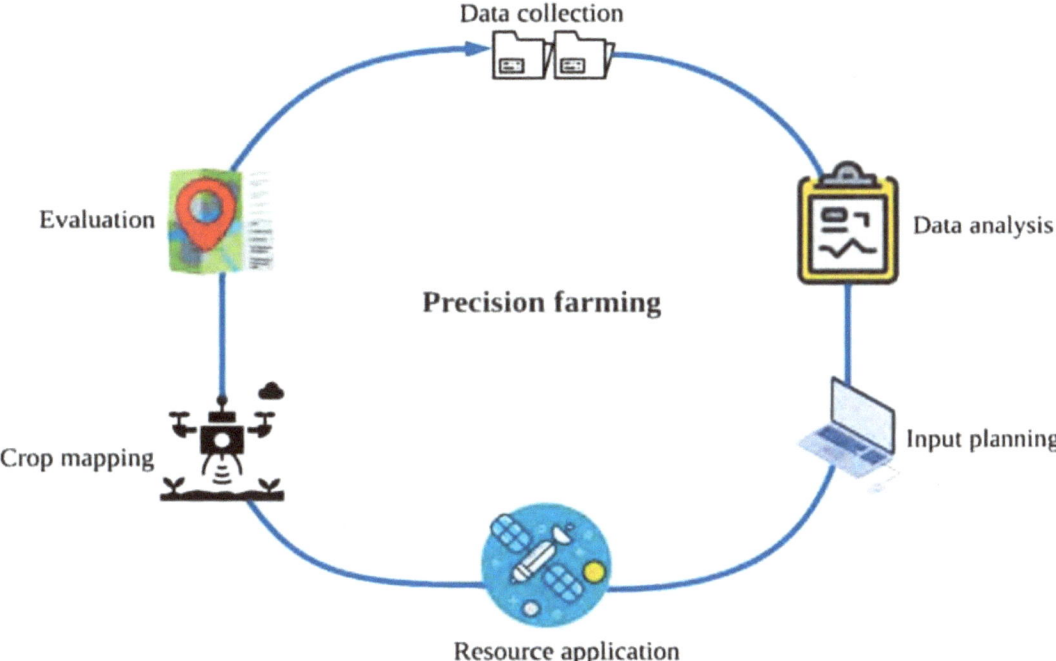

Fig. (2). Precision farming.

The related works include a range of methods for combining IoT and AI in precision agriculture with the goals of increasing sustainability, productivity, and resource efficiency. Ghosh *et al.* [8], discuss deep learning and convolutional neural networks that are used to manage pests in AI-driven management systems for increased agricultural yield and sustainable practices. Hussein *et al.* [9] review the role of AI and IoT in transforming agriculture, focusing on real-time monitoring and data analysis. Karn *et al.* [11] advocate for AIoT-based precision water management to optimize crop yield and address water conservation challenges, demonstrating significant benefits in sustainable farming practices. Collectively, these studies underscore the potential of AI for a growing global population. Table **1** lists the applications of AI in precision farming.

Table 1. Highlights AI applications in precision farming with strength and limitations.

References	Objective	Methodology	Advantages	Limitations
[6]	Enhancing resource management in precision farming through AI-based irrigation optimization.	Overview of precision farming integrated with AI, covering data collection techniques, AI applications in crop monitoring, management, and real-life case studies.	Optimizes resource utilization, promotes sustainable practices, and provides comprehensive coverage of AI applications in farming.	Challenges include data quality, interpretability, and ethical considerations.
[7]	Exploring AI's impact on crop yield prediction and precision farming practices.	Analysis of AI technologies in agriculture, focusing on methodologies, challenges, and outcomes, with policy recommendations.	Enables data-driven decisions, ensures food security, and promotes environmental sustainability.	Requires international collaboration and ethical frameworks for equitable implementation.
[8]	Improving agricultural productivity and sustainability through AI-driven precision agriculture.	Integration of AI-driven management systems with data collection from various sources for crop health and pest management.	Enhances crop productivity, optimizes resource utilization, and maintains agri-ecosystem sustainability.	Conventional techniques have limitations, requiring advanced AI-aided systems.
[9]	Reviewing the role of AI and IoT in transforming modern agriculture for sustainability.	Analysis of AI and IoT applications in precision agriculture, crop yield forecasting, and resource management.	Smarter farming methods, real-time monitoring, enhanced transparency, and data security.	Integration challenges with existing farming practices and technological infrastructure.
[10]	Improving efficiency in precision farming using machine vision techniques in low-cost devices.	Review of AI and IoT technologies, emphasizing real-time monitoring, data analysis, and management of agricultural processes.	Enhanced efficiency, predictive capabilities, and automation of farming operations.	Potential high initial costs and technological barriers for small-scale farmers.

(Table 1) cont.....

References	Objective	Methodology	Advantages	Limitations
[11]	Advocating for AIoT-based precision water management to optimize crop yield and sustainability.	Integration of AI and IoT to automate irrigation with comprehensive analysis of diverse parameters.	Improves crop yield, reduces human intervention, and addresses water conservation challenges.	Requires comprehensive knowledge of crop and soil characteristics, and climate conditions.

Sensor Networks and IoT Devices

These collect real-time data on weather conditions, soil moisture, and crop condition, which helps farmers to make decisions and automate fertilization and irrigation processes. Precision farming, which dramatically increases production and sustainability, is being made possible by the Internet of Things (IoT) and sensor networks, which are transforming the agricultural industry. Accurate irrigation, fertilization, and pest management are made possible by these technologies, which offer real-time data on temperature, soil moisture, humidity, and nutrient levels. They also monitor the livestock, crop health, and weather to help farmers make advised decisions and move swiftly to protect and care for their animals and crops. Through waste reduction, quality assurance, and produce tracking from farm to market, IoT also improves supply chain efficiency. By integrating with robots and automated systems, IoT reduces labor costs and boosts operational efficiency, which eventually leads to more sustainable and ecologically friendly farming practices.

Numerous studies demonstrate how precision agriculture has evolved greatly with the use of IoT and Wireless Sensor Networks (WSN). A scalable WSN architecture has been proposed [12] to improve productivity and water irrigation control in remote agricultural regions. To maximize water utilization, Zulkifli and Noor [13] created an automated irrigation system utilizing Active RFID, WMSN, and ZigBee technologies. Abdollahi *et al.* [14] monitored soil conditions using WSN and IoT to decrease water usage and raise production on small farms. For large-scale fields, Nurellari and Srivastava [15] developed an energy-efficient WSN utilizing LoRaWAN, allowing for long-range communication and adaptive monitoring. Kiani and Seyyedabbasi [16] sought to improve small-scale agricultural production by utilizing WSN and IoT to deliver real-time data on soil conditions. Jaishetty and Patil [17] revolutionized farming practices. Savale *et al.* [18] used precision agriculture with IoT and WSN to maximize crop output while optimizing water and fertilizer consumption. In their study of the use of machine learning approaches in WSN-based precision agriculture, Mekonnen *et al.* [19] emphasized the advantages of better forecasting and data-driven decision-making. When taken as a whole, these studies highlight how IoT and WSN may revolutionize agriculture by increasing sustainability, efficiency, and production. Table **2** highlights the applications of AI in sensor networks and IoT devices.

Table 2. Highlights of AI applications in sensor networks and IoT devices with strengths and limitations.

References	Objective	Methodology	Advantages	Limitations
[12]	Implementing a scalable WSN architecture for precision agriculture in remote areas.	Proposes a WSN architecture for monitoring and control using IoT.	Improved water irrigation management, enhanced productivity.	High initial setup cost, potential connectivity issues in remote areas.
[13]	Developing an automated irrigation system using IoT.	Uses Active RFID, WMSN, and ZigBee technology for real-time irrigation control.	Efficient water use, automated irrigation based on soil moisture.	Dependence on a specific frequency band (2.4 GHz), potential interference.
[14]	Reducing water consumption and increase productivity on small farms	Monitors soil moisture, temperature, and humidity using WSN and IoT	Optimized water use, real-time data, and weather forecasts.	Limited to small farm applications, requires ongoing maintenance.
[15]	Designing energy-efficient WSN for large-scale agricultural fields	Uses LoRaWAN for long-range communication and adaptive sensor nodes.	Extended WSN operational life, large ROI monitoring.	Complexity in network setup, potential data transmission delays.
[16]	Monitoring soil conditions on small farms to increase productivity	Provides architecture using WSN and IoT to monitor soil moisture, temperature, and humidity.	Reduced water usage, increased productivity, and real-time data.	Limited scalability, high maintenance requirements.
[17]	Enhancing energy efficiency and scalability of WSN for agricultural monitoring	Uses fuzzy c-means clustering algorithm for sensor node optimization.	Maximized sensor network lifetime, optimized resource usage.	Complexity in algorithm implementation, potential computational overhead.
[18].	Modernizing farming processes using IoT for soil health monitoring and irrigation control.	Integrates physical sensors with cloud computing for real-time data analysis.	Improved decision-making, real-time monitoring.	High initial setup cost, requires reliable internet connectivity.
[19].	Applying IoT and WSN in precision agriculture for real-time crop and environmental monitoring.	Uses sensor networks to connect agronomists, farmers, and crops.	Optimized water and fertilizer use, maximized crop yield.	Potential connectivity issues, high initial cost.

(Table 2) cont.....

References	Objective	Methodology	Advantages	Limitations
[20].	Applying machine learning techniques in WSN-based precision agriculture.	Analyzes sensor data using machine learning algorithms for better decision-making.	Improved forecasting, reliable sensor management.	High computational requirements, complexity in data analysis.

Drones and Aerial Images

These are equipped with multispectral cameras that provide detailed aerial images that help monitor crop health, detect pests, and assess crop yields. Drones and aerial imaging are transforming agriculture by providing detailed and comprehensive views of fields, which enhance monitoring and management practices—equipped with high-resolution cameras and sensors. Drones can capture images of crop health, soil conditions, and field variability with high precision. This technology enables farmers to identify issues such as pest infestations, disease outbreaks, and nutrient deficiencies early, allowing for targeted interventions. Drones can monitor irrigation systems, evaluate plant development, and provide precise maps for precision farming. Drones offer an aerial perspective that enhances crop yields, reduces expenses, and optimizes resource utilization. This leads to more effective and sustainable farming methods.

Several studies have shown that the use of Unmanned Aerial Vehicles (UAVs) has significantly advanced precision agriculture. Raj *et al.* (2020) [20] highlight how UAVs might improve agricultural management in impoverished nations by offering real-time, high-resolution data on crop and soil conditions. Although initial investment prices continue to be a hurdle. Puri *et al.* (2017) [21] highlight the significance of drones in enhancing crop quality and minimizing field damage with sophisticated monitoring technology. Mahadasa *et al.* (2020) [22] investigate how precision agriculture and data-driven decision-making are made possible by drones. A technical examination of UAV models is given by Marinello *et al.* (2016) [23] emphasizing cost and performance while concentrating on the models' performance in agricultural activities. Tahir *et al.* (2023) [24] address several UAV applications that have been made possible by advances in AI. Drones reduce resource waste by enabling accurate application of agricultural inputs shown by Muraru *et al.* (2019) [25]. Cancela *et al.* (2019) [26] concentrate on enhancing irrigation techniques through the effective use of remote sensing for agricultural water management. De Oca and Flores (2021) [27] provide farmers in underdeveloped countries with an inexpensive alternative to precision agriculture.

A review of several UAV applications is provided by Norasma *et al.* (2019) [28]. They stress the need to choose appropriate sensors and models to satisfy particular agricultural demands, hence encouraging sustainability and yield enhancement. When taken as a whole, these studies highlight the expanding significance and variety of uses of UAVs in modernizing agriculture, despite some obstacles regarding cost, technical specifications, and data processing. Table **3** highlights the applications of AI in aerial imaging.

Table 3. Highlights of AI applications in drones and aerial imaging with strengths and limitations.

References	Objective	Methodology	Advantages	Limitations
[20]	Exploring the potential of precision agriculture using UAVs in developing countries.	Utilizing drone-based sensing and image interpretation for high-resolution data collection.	Provides real-time, high-resolution information on soil and crop conditions for effective farm management.	High costs and technical know-how are required for implementation in developing countries.
[21]]	Highlighting the importance of drones in agriculture and review top agricultural drones.	Review of recent developments in drone technology and its application in agriculture.	Enhances crop quality and prevents field damage through advanced monitoring and observation.	Initial investment and maintenance costs can be high for farmers.
[22]	Investigating the impact of agricultural drones on modern farming practices.	Examination of drones' capabilities in crop monitoring, precision agriculture, and data-driven decision-making.	Transforms traditional farming practices with advanced data and intelligence.	Dependency on technological infrastructure and potential privacy concerns.
[23]	Analyzing the technical performance of various UAV types in agriculture.	Technical analysis of over 250 UAV models considering factors like mass, payload, speed, and cost.	Provides a comprehensive understanding of UAV applicability to agricultural operations.	Performance limitations and high costs of advanced models.
[24]	Discussing various types of UAVs and their agricultural applications.	Review of UAV applications in crop monitoring, yield estimation, pest detection, and more.	Enhances efficiency and safety in complex agricultural environments with AI advancements.	Requires significant investment in AI and sensor technology.
[25]	Researching the use of drones in various agricultural applications.	Compilation and analysis of high-resolution images and data collected by drones.	Facilitates precise application of seeds, fertilizers, and pesticides, reducing resource wastage.	Data processing and interpretation require specialized software and skills.

(Table 3) cont.....

References	Objective	Methodology	Advantages	Limitations
[26]	Providing an overview of using remote sensing for water management in agriculture.	Review of peer-reviewed articles on new equipment and technologies for irrigation efficiency.	Improves irrigation management and accurate assessment of crop water needs.	Limited focus on other aspects of precision agriculture beyond water management.
[27]	Developing a low-cost unmanned aerial system for precision agriculture.	Construction of a drone, vision algorithms, and a multispectral imaging system for crop monitoring.	Provides a cost-effective solution for farmers in developing regions.	Lower performance compared to high-end commercial systems.
[28]	Reviewing the applications of UAVs in agriculture.	A comprehensive review of UAV technology and its various agricultural applications.	Promotes sustainability and increased yield through advanced monitoring.	Need for appropriate sensors and UAV models based on specific agricultural needs.

Robotics and Automation

Agricultural robots assist in planting, weeding, and harvesting, reducing labor costs and increasing efficiency. Automated machinery, such as self-driving tractors, further streamlines farm operations. Robotics and automation play a transformative role in agriculture by enhancing efficiency, productivity, and sustainability. Agricultural robots can perform a wide range of tasks, including planting, weeding, harvesting, and sorting, with high precision and consistency. These robots reduce the reliance on manual labor. It addresses labor shortages and lowers operational costs. Automated systems can also handle repetitive and time-consuming tasks, which allows farmers to focus more on strategic aspects of farming. Robotics integrated with IoT and sensor networks enables real-time monitoring and data collection, which provides leading decision-making and optimized resource use. The use of drones and autonomous vehicles for tasks such as crop spraying and field monitoring further boosts efficiency and precision. Robotics and automation enhance agricultural productivity by minimizing the environmental impact and improving the quality and consistency of agricultural outputs.

Recent studies have extensively explored the integration of robotics and Artificial Intelligence (AI) in agriculture, highlighting various technologies, applications, and challenges. Shvets *et al.* (2024) [29] focus on the impact of robotic systems in agriculture, discussing automation in feeding processes, pasture management, and crop harvesting, while highlighting economic efficiency, sustainability, and challenges such as high initial investments and the need for qualified personnel. Gupta and Gupta (2024) [30] review robotics and AI with an emphasis on food crops. Covering the history and development of precision agriculture and Unmanned Ground Vehicles (UGVs), as well as the cost-effectiveness and prospects of these technologies. Sharma *et al.* (2024) [31] investigate the potential of robotic automation in mitigating climate vulnerability in horticulture and emphasizing the benefits of aligning technological advancements with environmental resilience. Kaliannan and Al Saidi (2024) [32] explore IoT-enabled smart farming and discuss how IoT sensors assist in monitoring crop harvests, soil humidity, rainfall, and livestock. Das (2024) [33] explores the transformative impact of robotics and drones on sustainable farming, highlighting their roles in tasks such as tillage, seeding, crop protection, and harvesting, and discussing the challenges of high costs, regulatory hurdles, and the need for substantial infrastructure and training. Together, these works underscore the transformative potential of robotics and AI in agriculture, while also recognizing significant barriers to their widespread adoption. Table **4** lists the applications of AI in robotics.

Table 4. Highlights of AI applications in robotics and automation with strength and limitations.

References	Objective	Methodology	Advantage	Limitations
[29]	Analyzing the impact of robotic systems on modern agriculture.	Discusses the integration of advanced technologies like the automation of feeding, pasture management, and automated crop harvesting.	Improved working conditions, reduced environmental impact, increased productivity.	High initial investments are needed for qualified personnel, adaptation of old farm structures.
[30]	Reviewing robotics and AI in agriculture with emphasis on food crops.	Comprehensive review of robotics and AI applications, including UGVs and autonomous tractors.	Enhanced precision in planting, plant care, crop management, and post-harvest processes.	High costs, technological complexity, need for controlled conditions.
[31]	Investigating the role of robotic automation in mitigating climate vulnerability in horticulture.	Examines case studies and emerging trends in robotic automation.	Improved resource management, enhanced crop yields, and environmental sustainability.	Technological and economic barriers for strategic alignment.
[32]	Exploring IoT-enabled smart farming for precision agriculture.	Discusses IoT sensors for monitoring crop harvests, soil humidity, rainfall, and livestock.	Enhanced decision-making through real-time data access.	High initial costs, the technological learning curve.

(Table 4) cont.....

References	Objective	Methodology	Advantage	Limitations
[33]	Reviewing the impact of robotics and drones on sustainable farming.	Examines applications, benefits, challenges, and prospects of robotics and drones in agriculture.	Increased productivity, reduced environmental impact, and optimized resource use.	High costs, regulatory hurdles, data security concerns, need for substantial infrastructure and training.

ARTIFICIAL INTELLIGENCE AND MACHINE LEARNING

In order to forecast crop yields, optimize planting schedules, and spot disease outbreaks—all of which contribute to better farm management—AI and machine learning algorithms evaluate data from a variety of sources. Agriculture is undergoing a transformation thanks to Artificial Intelligence (AI) and Machine Learning (ML), which make it possible to make data-driven decisions and optimize different farming techniques. Robust datasets from sensors, drones, and other sources are analyzed by AI and ML to provide information on crop health, soil properties, weather trends, and insect infestations.

Farmers may use this information to forecast yields, schedule planting and harvesting dates more effectively, and choose the ideal crop kinds for a given set of circumstances. Precision farming methods may also be improved and automated with the use of AI-powered technologies. Real-time advice and modifications are provided by this technology. Supply chain management may benefit from AI and ML by decreasing waste, streamlining logistics, and forecasting market demand. The increase in yield quality and quantity is largely dependent on the timely supply of agronomical suggestions. Nevertheless, these suggestions usually include or demand that a certain action be taken. Artificial Intelligence has greatly enhanced the sector of agriculture. A substantial and overwhelming harvest is essential. Uncertain weather circumstances, such as haze, fog, draft, and inappropriate precipitation, create a great deal of crop production misfortune in the horticulture sector. Table **5** lists the strengths and limitations of AI applications.

Table 5. Highlights of AI applications in AI and ML with strengths and limitations.

References	Objective	Methodology	Advantage	Limitations
[34]	Review of applications of artificial neural networks in agriculture.	Literature review of ANN applications.	Wide range of applications (forecasting, disease verification, weed control).	Requires handling large datasets and appropriate software.

(Table 5) cont.....

References	Objective	Methodology	Advantage	Limitations
[35]	Overview of AI and IoT in Agriculture Automation.	Review of recent research from scientific databases.	Real-time monitoring and control of farm operations.	Adoption challenges and technical complexities.
[36]	Integration of nanotechnology and AI for sustainable agriculture.	Coupling nutrient cycling models with nano-informatics	Optimizes targeting, uptake, delivery, and nutrient capture.	Long-term impacts on soil microbial communities are not fully understood
[37]	Evaluation of nitrogen status in wheat crops using AI.	Image-based analysis with GA and ANN for crop classification.	High validation accuracy (97.75%)	May not generalize well to different crops or conditions
[38]	Survey of AI applications in irrigation, weeding, and spraying.	Review of various AI technologies in agriculture.	Reduces water, pesticide, and herbicide usage.	Implementation costs and the need for technical infrastructure
[39]	Review of deep learning-based computer vision for smart agriculture.	Analysis of recent computer vision technologies.	High precision and accuracy in various agricultural activities.	Challenges in real-time implementation and data quality requirements.
[40]	Summarizing AI research projects for precision agriculture.	Comparative analysis of pilot experiments across Europe	Improves decision support and optimizes production	Low replicability and systematic data gathering challenges.
[41]	Development of AIRA system for irrigation recommendation and alerts.	Use of the k-N4 classifier and the APSO algorithm.	Provides optimal recommendations and high data security.	Complexity in system implementation and data management.
[42]	Highlighting IoT and machine learning in precision agriculture.	Proposed model for Apple disease prediction using IoT data analytics.	Enhances production quantity and quality.	Integration challenges with traditional farming methods.

CHALLENGES IN INTEGRATING SMART TECHNOLOGIES

High Initial Costs

The deployment of smart technologies requires significant investment in hardware, software, and training, which can be a barrier for small-scale farmers. Table **6** compares the various aspects of smart agriculture.

Table 6. Comparison of crop production, animal production, and post-harvesting in smart agriculture.

Properties	Crop Production	Animal Production	Post Harvesting
Computational power of the system	X	N/A	✓
Algorithm communication language	X	X	N/A
Counting and crowd control	X	X	N/A
Operated by Batteries	X	✓	X
Psychological effect	X	✓	N/A
Detection speed	✓	X	✓
Demand of market	✓	✓	X
Inventory	✓	✓	✓
Holding cost	X	X	✓
Transportation cost	X	X	✓

Legend: ✓ (Yes), X (No), N/A (Not Applicable)

Technical Complexity

The complexity of managing and maintaining advanced technological systems can be daunting, requiring specialized knowledge and skills. Table 7 compares various sensors in terms of various aspects.

Table 7. Comparison of sensors, Unmanned Aerial Vehicles (UAVs), Internet of Things (IoT), and Artificial Intelligence (AI) in smart agriculture.

Properties	Sensors	UAVs	IOT	AI
High transmission speed	X	✓	N/A	✓
Provide connectivity where no internet is available.	X	✓	X	✓
Cover a long range of distance for data transmission.	X	✓	N/A	✓
Mobility within the farm	X	✓	N/A	N/A
High processing power	X	X	N/A	✓
Analyze data aggregate	X	X	N/A	✓
High security in the transmission of data	X	✓	✓	✓
Capturing of data by direct contact	✓	X	X	X
Run out of power over time.	✓	✓	N/A	N/A
The Psychological Effect on Livestock	✓	✓	N/A	N/A
Low cost of deployment	✓	X	X	X

Legend: ✓ (Yes), X (No), N/A (Not Applicable)

OTHER ISSUES ADDRESS BY RESEARCHERS

The issues in the application of AI in smart agriculture are listed in Table **8**.

Table 8. Comprehensive comparison of AI issues in smart farming.

S.No.	Properties	[53]	[54]	[55]	[56]	[57]	[58]	[59]	[60]	[61]	[62]
1	Security	✗	N/A	✗	✗	N/A	N/A	✗	✗	✗	✗
2	Control actuators	✓	✗	✗	✗	✗	✗	✗	✗	✗	✗
3	Network lifetime	✗	N/A	✗	✗	N/A	N/A	✗	✗	✗	✗
4	Network latency	N/A	N/A	N/A	N/A	N/A	N/A	✗	✗	✗	✗
5	Detection of weather conditions	✗	✓	✗	✗	✗	✗	✓	✓	✗	✗
6	Preventive measures using IoT	✓	✓	✓	✗	✓	✓	✗	✗	✗	✗
7	Architecture	✗	✗	✗	✗	✗	✓	✗	✗	✗	✗
8	Reduce communication cost	✗	✗	✗	✓	✗	✗	✗	✗	✗	✗
9	Quality of Service (QoS)	✗	✗	✓	✓	✓	✗	✗	✗	✗	✗
10	Handle multi-keyword search	✗	✗	✗	✗	✗	✗	✗	✗	✗	✗
11	Increase in computation overhead	N/A	N/A	N/A	N/A	N/A	N/A	✗	✗	✗	✗
12	Lightweight encryption for IIoT	✗	✓	✗	✗	✗	✗	✗	✗	✗	✗
13	Failure detection	✗	✓	✗	✗	✗	✗	✗	✗	✗	✗
14	Prediction for IIoT	✗	✓	✗	✗	✗	✗	✗	✗	✗	✗
15	Data reliability	✗	✓	✗	✗	✗	✗	✗	✗	✗	✗
16	Access control in IIoT	✗	✓	✗	✗	✗	✗	✗	✗	✗	✗
17	Real attacks in IIoT	✗	✓	✗	✗	✗	✗	✗	✗	✗	✗
18	Management of IIoT designs and software	✗	✓	✗	✗	✗	✗	✗	✗	✗	✗
19	Validation of safe trust in IIoT	✗	✓	✗	✗	✗	✗	✗	✗	✗	✗
20	Noise filtering capacity	✓	✗	✗	✗	✗	✗	✓	✗	✗	✗
21	Increased computational time	✗	✗	✗	✗	✗	✗	✗	✗	✗	✗
22	Faster detection rate for crop disease	✓	✓	✗	✗	✗	✗	✓	✓	✗	✗
23	Reduced the time of diagnosis of animal illness	✓	✓	✗	✗	✗	✗	✓	✓	✗	✗
24	Enhanced data transmission	✗	✗	✓	✗	✗	✗	✗	✗	✓	✗
25	Monitor the movement of the animals within and outside the farm	✗	✗	✓	✓	✗	✗	✗	✗	✓	✓
26	Determine the animal's attitude and behavioral pattern	✗	✗	✓	✓	✗	✗	✗	✗	✓	✓
27	Monitor health changes among the animals	N/A	N/A	✓	✓	N/A	N/A	✗	✗	✓	✓
28	Color and shape from 3D sensor	N/A	N/A	N/A	N/A	N/A	N/A	N/A	N/A	N/A	N/A

(Table 8) cont.....

S.No.	Properties	[53]	[54]	[55]	[56]	[57]	[58]	[59]	[60]	[61]	[62]
29	Interactive voice response with farmers	N/A	N/A	N/A	N/A	N/A	N/A	✗	✗	N/A	N/A
30	Determination of soil condition	N/A	N/A	N/A	N/A	N/A	N/A	✗	✗	N/A	N/A
31	Soil conductivity	N/A	N/A	N/A	N/A	N/A	N/A	✗	✗	N/A	N/A
32	Protection of crop disease using IoT	N/A	N/A	N/A	N/A	N/A	N/A	✗	✗	N/A	N/A
33	Monitor the leaf water stress	N/A	N/A	N/A	N/A	N/A	N/A	✗	✗	N/A	N/A

Legend: ✓ (Yes), ✗ (No), N/A (Not Applicable)

RISKS ASSOCIATED WITH SMART AGRICULTURE

The idea that security has no bearing on IoT applications in agriculture is untrue. For farmers to contribute to excellent yields, access and accuracy of data are critical needs. A situational approach, often known as dynamic security, is necessary for an IoT network to be secure. Adaptive security is a cybersecurity-based enhanced security method for enhancing IoT security. A critical component of agricultural growth in a smart farming setting is the absence of security.

Cybersecurity Threats

The related works encompass various approaches to managing cybersecurity and IT risks in the agriculture sector. Wheeler (2015) [43] identifies the critical dependency of the food and agriculture sector on the IT sector through a comprehensive literature review and professional interviews, suggesting further granular-level research to determine specific cybersecurity weaknesses. Chatzipoulidis, Michalopoulos, and Mavridis (2014) [44] propose a Physical Unclonable Function (PUF) based security scheme for IoT devices in agriculture, offering a lightweight and scalable solution to prevent device duplication and unauthorized access.

Sitnicki *et al.* [45] focus on managing IT risks in agriculture through standardized security metrics. Advocating for automated processes that enhance productivity and policy compliance. They also emphasize the role of cyber insurance in Agriculture 4.0., a cooperative algorithm between agricultural companies and insurers to mitigate cyber risks and provide post-incident support. Caviglia *et al.* (2023) [46] developed an SDR-based cybersecurity verification framework for Smart Agricultural Machines (SAMs) to detect vulnerabilities in wireless communication channels.

Peppes *et al.* (2021) [47] evaluate machine learning-based ensemble methods for network threat detection in Agriculture 4.0, demonstrating higher accuracy with ensemble models compared to individual classifiers. Zidi *et al.* (2024) [48] present an intrusion detection system using downsized kernel methods, showing improved accuracy in network traffic classification with ensemble models across different dataset variations. These studies highlight the importance of robust cybersecurity measures and innovative IT solutions to safeguard the agriculture sector in an increasingly digital and interconnected world. Table **9** highlights the risks associated with smart agriculture.

Table 9. Highlights of risks associated with smart agriculture, its strengths and limitations.

References	Objective	Methodology	Advantage	Limitations
[43]	To identify the food and agriculture sector's dependence on the IT sector.	Literature review and interviews with professionals in the food and agriculture sector.	Provides a comprehensive understanding of the dependency on IT in food and agriculture.	Limited to the current classification and lacks granular-level analysis.
[44]	To manage IT risk in the agriculture sector using automated security metrics.	Implementation of a Physical Unclonable Function (PUF) based hardware security primitive for IoT device authentication.	Lightweight, scalable, and robust security scheme.	Potential implementation challenges in diverse agricultural environments.
[45]	To manage IT risk in agriculture through standardized security metrics.	Proposal of specifications for automatic identification, analysis, and reporting on critical assets using Security Content Automation Protocol (SCAP).	Increases productivity, reduces uncertainty, and provides policy guidelines.	Implementation might require an initial investment and an adaptation period.
[45]	To assess and mitigate cyber risks in Agriculture 4.0 using cyber insurance.	Development of a cooperation algorithm between agricultural companies and insurance companies for cyber risk insurance.	Minimizes the likelihood of cyber incidents and provides post-incident support.	Heterogeneous need for cyber insurance in different regions.
[46]	To explore cybersecurity issues in smart agricultural machines.	Development of an SDR-based cybersecurity verification framework and testbed evaluation.	Effective in detecting vulnerabilities in wireless communication channels of SAMs.	Focuses mainly on wireless channels and may not address all types of cyber threats.
[47]	To enhance network threat detection in Agriculture 4.0 using machine learning-based ensemble methods.	Evaluation of various ML classifiers and ensemble models using the NSL-KDD dataset variations.	Ensemble models show higher accuracy in threat detection.	Performance may vary based on the dataset and real-world applicability needs further validation.

(Table 9) cont.....

References	Objective	Methodology	Advantage	Limitations
[48]	To develop an intrusion detection system for smart agriculture using downsized kernel methods.	Evaluation of ML classifiers for network traffic classification on different variations of the NSL-KDD dataset.	Improved accuracy with ensemble models.	Effectiveness depends on the quality and representativeness of the dataset.

Security Aspects of SF and PA

Recent research has highlighted critical security aspects of Smart Farming (SF) and Precision Agriculture (PA), which can be summarized as follows:

- **Privacy:** Essential for preventing unauthorized access to users' information. Physical attacks, replay attacks, and masquerade attacks pose significant threats to privacy. Numerous studies have examined privacy concerns in SF and PA [49].
- **Integrity:** Ensures that information remains unchanged during storage or transmission. The integrity of PA and SF systems has been a focal point in various research projects [49].
- **Confidentiality:** Protects data from unauthorized access. This aspect has been explored by several researchers [50].
- **Availability:** Guarantees continuous service provision. Recent research has focused on the availability of SF and PA systems [51].
- **Non-Repudiation:** Prevents users from denying their actions within the system. Some researchers have noted the importance of non-repudiation in SF and PA [52].
- **Trust:** Prevents users from spoofing identities. Research in this area has focused on the authenticity of SF and PA [53].

Without adequate security measures, SF and PA systems are vulnerable to various attacks that can exploit these environments, leading to harm, unauthorized changes, or destruction.

Classification of Attacks on SF and PA

Attacks on SF and PA can be classified based on their target components:

Attacks on Hardware: Exploits unknown or unprotected vulnerabilities in IoT and cyber-physical devices using specialized tools [53]. Notable examples include:

- Side Channel Attacks: Gather unauthorized information by monitoring physical parameters such as electrical current or voltage, compromising system confidentiality [54].
- RF Jamming Attacks: Exploit the open nature of wireless channels, disrupting system availability in areas like greenhouses [55].

Attacks on Network and Related Equipment: Target network or connected devices, including:

- Issues related to the control of actuators in sensor networks [57, 58] lead to potential security concerns in an architecture.
- Issues related to data transmission in devices have been discussed by authors in [59, 60].
- Denial of Service (DoS): Prevents authorized access to resources by overwhelming the network [61]. Access control issues [62] lead to pertinent problems in the domain of smart agriculture.
- Man-In-The-Middle (MITM) Attacks: Intercept and potentially alter data during transmission, threatening system confidentiality and integrity [6].
- Botnets: Use internet-connected devices for Distributed DoS attacks, information theft, and SPAM dissemination, affecting availability, integrity, and trust [63].
- Cloud Computing Attacks: Misuse cloud resources to spread malware, impacting non-repudiation, trust, and integrity [64].

Attacks on Data: Target data during storage, transmission, or processing, such as:

- Cloud Data Leakage: Exposure of user data, violating privacy [52].
- False Data Injection: Inserts malicious data into the system, compromising integrity [53].
- Ransomware: Encrypts data and demands ransom, affecting privacy, trust, and integrity [54].
- Data Leakage: Unauthorized transmission of data, violating confidentiality [56].
- Misconfiguration: Configures systems incorrectly, leading to disruptive decisions and integrity breaches.

Attacks on Code (Applications): Includes:

- Software Update Attacks: Disrupt the update process, affecting integrity and availability.
- Malware Injection: Infects devices with malicious code, compromising integrity [55].

- Buffer Overflow: Exploits software vulnerabilities, violating availability [56].
- Indirect Attacks (SQL Injection): Misleads database servers to execute malicious SQL code, undermining trust [64].

Attacks on Support Chain: Target components of the support chain, such as:

- Third-Party Attacks: Infiltrate systems *via* external partners, affecting confidentiality and integrity [51].
- Data Fabrication: Creates malicious data or processes, violating system integrity [53].

Misuse Attacks: Exploit SF and PA resources to attack other entities:

- Cyber-Terrorism: Uses IoT systems to attack remotely, damaging trust in SF and PA systems.

ETHICAL PATHWAYS FOR RESPONSIBLE INTEGRATION

Ensuring Inclusivity

Policies and efforts should prioritize granting access to smart technology to all farmers, irrespective of their location or scale, in order to ensure equal benefits. This calls for a number of calculated steps:

- Subsidies and Financial Support: Small and marginal farmers should be able to invest in smart technology through grants, low-interest loans, and subsidies from governments and financial institutions. The gap that exists between larger commercial farms and smaller businesses can be filled in part by this financial assistance.
- Infrastructure Development: It is imperative to provide resilient digital infrastructure in isolated and rural regions. This involves extending cell network coverage and broadband internet access to make smart agricultural technology easier to utilize.
- Tailored Solutions: Small-scale farmer demands should be catered for by technology providers through the development of scalable solutions. This might entail developing more accessible, cost-effective technologies.
- Community-Based Approaches: Promoting the establishment of community organizations and cooperatives can assist small farmers in pooling resources and expertise to adopt smart technology with low costs and risks.

Promoting Data Ethics

Protecting farmers' rights and privacy requires establishing clear policies for data collection, storage, and use. There are the following key components:

- Data Ownership and Consent: Farmers should retain ownership of their data and provide informed consent for its collection and use. Policies must ensure transparency in how data will be used and who will access it.
- Data Security: Protecting critical agricultural information requires the implementation of strong cybersecurity safeguards. This includes encryption, secure storage solutions, and regular security audits.
- Ethical Guidelines: Developing ethical guidelines for data usage that prevent exploitation and misuse. These guidelines should cover aspects such as data anonymization, fair usage policies, and restrictions.
- Regulatory Frameworks: Governments should establish regulatory frameworks that enforce data protection standards and hold organizations accountable for any breaches of these standards.

Sustainable Practices

In order to reduce environmental effects and increase resource efficiency, sustainability for smart technology in agriculture. This may be accomplished by:

- Renewable Energy: Reducing the carbon footprint of agricultural activities by promoting the use of renewable energy sources.
- Waste Reduction: Implementing smart technologies that monitor and manage farm waste effectively can lead to significant reductions in waste production and improved resource recycling.
- Climate-Resilient Practices: Developing and promoting technologies that enhance the resilience of agricultural systems to climate change, such as drought-resistant crops and advanced irrigation systems, is crucial for long-term sustainability.

Fostering Collaboration

Collaboration between various stakeholders, including governments, industry, academia, and farmers, is essential to address challenges and maximize the benefits of smart agriculture.

- Public-Private Partnerships (PPPs): Creating PPPs to leverage the strengths and resources of both sectors can accelerate smart technologies in agriculture.

- Research and Development (R&D): Encouraging collaborative research and development efforts among university establishments, research agencies, and industry participants can stimulate inventive thinking and the development of novel smart farming approaches.
- Knowledge Sharing Platforms: The exchange of knowledge and experiences among stakeholders may be facilitated by setting up venues for best practice dissemination and information sharing.
- Stakeholder Engagement: Engaging farmers and local communities in the decision-making process ensures that their needs and perspectives are considered.

Continuous Education and Training

It is crucial for farmers to use smart technology efficiently. The key actions are as follows:

- Training Programs: Developing comprehensive training programs that cover the use of smart farming technologies, data management, and sustainable practices can enhance farmers' competencies.
- E-Learning Platforms: Creating e-learning platforms and mobile applications that offer accessible, on-demand training resources for farmers.
- Capacity Building: Investing in capacity-building initiatives that empower local agricultural leaders and extension agents to become trainers for smart farming practices within their communities.

CONCLUDING REMARKS

The combination of smart technologies in agriculture offers a transformative perspective to improve productivity, sustainability, and resilience in farming systems. Smart farming is an idea that uses emerging technology like robots, drones, AI, and the Internet of Things to manage and control farms in order to produce more goods of higher quality and with less human work. Given that population numbers are rising sharply on a global scale, these advantages will boost economic development and profitability. The agricultural sector can fully harness the potential of smart technologies by focusing on data ethics, sustainability, collaboration, and education. This comprehensive approach will not only improve productivity and efficiency but also contribute to the overall well-being of farmers and the environment. This chapter has offered comprehensive explanations of AI uses in smart farming. This study will help understand AI applications, risks, and challenges involved in smart farming. There are certain research gaps and challenges that should be taken into account by the scientific community. These present new chances for researchers to pursue novel research directions utilizing reliable, secure data, climate change variables, and weather forecasting to boost productivity. AI can assist us in satisfying the increased demand for agricultural goods. Numerous issues confront agriculture, including crop disease, inadequate irrigation, water management, environmental impact, low yield, and incorrect soil treatment. AI applications have the potential to address this issue. Farmers' issues may be resolved by using AI in crop monitoring, disease control, weeding, and soil management.

REFERENCES

[1]   C.R. Eastwood, J.P. Edwards, and J.A. Turner, "Review: Anticipating alternative trajectories for responsible Agriculture 4.0 innovation in livestock systems", *Animal,* vol. 15, suppl. Suppl. 1, p. 100296, 2021.
        [http://dx.doi.org/10.1016/j.animal.2021.100296] [PMID: 34246598]

[2]   N. C. Eli-Chukwu, "Applications of artificial intelligence in agriculture: A review," Engineering, Technology & Applied Science Research, vol. 9, no. 4, 2019.
        [http://dx.doi.org/10.48084/etasr.2756]

[3]   M. Wakchaure, B.K. Patle, and A.K. Mahindrakar, "Application of AI techniques and robotics in agriculture: A review", *Artif. Intell. Life Sci.,* vol. 3, p. 100057, 2023.
        [http://dx.doi.org/10.1016/j.ailsci.2023.100057]

[4]   M. Javaid, A. Haleem, I.H. Khan, and R. Suman, "Understanding the potential applications of Artificial Intelligence in agriculture sector", *Advanced Agrochem,* vol. 2, no. 1, pp. 15-30, 2023.
        [http://dx.doi.org/10.1016/j.aac.2022.10.001]

[5]   S. Sharma, K. Verma, and P. Hardaha, "Implementation of artificial intelligence in agriculture", *Journal of Computational and Cognitive Engineering,* vol. 2, no. 2, pp. 155-162, 2022.
        [http://dx.doi.org/10.47852/bonviewJCCE2202174]

[6]   S. Adinarayana, "Enhancing resource management in precision farming through AI-based irrigation optimization",
        [http://dx.doi.org/10.1002/9781394214167.ch15]

[7]   W. Jack and S. Bagh, "Revolutionizing agriculture: ai-powered crop yield forecasting and precision farming for optimal harvests," no. 11942, 2024.

[8]   D. Ghosh, M.A. Siddique, and D. Pal, "AI-driven approach to precision agriculture", In: *AI in Agriculture for Sustainable and Economic Management.* CRC Press, 2025, pp. 67-77.

[9]   G. Mgendi, "Unlocking the potential of precision agriculture for sustainable farming", In: *Discover Agriculture* vol. 2. , 2024.
        [http://dx.doi.org/10.1007/s44279-024-00078-3]

[10]   J.F. Jaramillo-Hernández, V. Julian, C. Marco-Detchart, and J.A. Rincón, "Application of machine vision techniques in low-cost devices to improve efficiency in precision farming", *Sensors (Basel),* vol. 24, no. 3, p. 937, 2024.
        [http://dx.doi.org/10.3390/s24030937] [PMID: 38339654]

[11]   S. Karn, R. Kotecha, and R.K. Pandey, "Towards sustainable farming: Leveraging aiot for precision water management and crop yield optimization", *Procedia Comput. Sci.,* vol. 233, pp. 772-781, 2024.
        [http://dx.doi.org/10.1016/j.procs.2024.03.266]

[12]   D.D. Dasig, "Implementing IoT and wireless sensor networks for precision agriculture",
        [http://dx.doi.org/10.1007/978-981-15-0663-5_2]

[13]   C.Z. Zulkifli, and N.N. Noor, "Wireless sensor network and internet of things (IoT) solution in agriculture", *Pertanika J. Sci. Technol.,* vol. 25, no. 1, 2017.

[14] A. Abdollahi, K. Rejeb, A. Rejeb, M.M. Mostafa, and S. Zailani, "Wireless sensor networks in agriculture: Insights from bibliometric analysis", *Sustainability (Basel),* vol. 13, no. 21, p. 12011, 2021.
[http://dx.doi.org/10.3390/su132112011]

[15] E. Nurellari, and S. Srivastava, "A practical implementation of an agriculture field monitoring using wireless sensor networks and IoT enabled", *2018 IEEE International Symposium on Smart Electronic Systems (iSES),* 2018pp. 134-139
[http://dx.doi.org/10.1109/iSES.2018.00037]

[16] F. Kiani, and A. Seyyedabbasi, "Wireless sensor network and internet of things in precision agriculture", *Int. J. Adv. Comput. Sci. Appl.,* vol. 9, no. 6, 2018.
[http://dx.doi.org/10.14569/IJACSA.2018.090614]

[17] S. A. Jaishetty and R. Patil, "IoT sensor network-based approach for agricultural field monitoring and control," IJRET: International Journal of Research in Engineering and Technology, vol. 5, no. 06, pp. 45-48, 2016., p. 12011, 2021.

[18] O. Savale, A. Managave, D. Ambekar, and S. Sathe, "Internet of things in precision agriculture using wireless sensor networks", *International Journal of Advanced Engineering & Innovative Technology,* vol. 2, no. 3, pp. 1-5, 2015.

[19] Y. Mekonnen, S. Namuduri, L. Burton, A. Sarwat, and S. Bhansali, "Machine learning techniques in wireless sensor network-based precision agriculture", *J. Electrochem. Soc.,* vol. 167, no. 3, p. 037522, 2020.
[http://dx.doi.org/10.1149/2.0222003JES]

[20] A. Raj, S. Kar, R. Nandan, and A. Jagarlapudi, "Precision agriculture and Unmanned Aerial Vehicles (UAVs)", *Unmanned Aerial Vehicle: Applications in Agriculture and Environment,* pp. 7-23, 2020.
[http://dx.doi.org/10.1007/978-3-030-27157-2_2]

[21] V. Puri, A. Nayyar, and L. Raja, "Agriculture drones: A modern breakthrough in precision agriculture", *Journal of Statistics and Management Systems,* vol. 20, no. 4, pp. 507-518, 2017.
[http://dx.doi.org/10.1080/09720510.2017.1395171]

[22] R. Mahadasa, P. Surarapu, V.R. Vadiyala, and P.R. Baddam, "Utilization of agricultural drones in farming by harnessing the power of aerial intelligence", *Malaysian Journal of Medical and Biological Research,* vol. 7, no. 2, pp. 135-144, 2020.

[23] F. Marinello, A. Pezzuolo, A. Chiumenti, and L. Sartori, "Technical analysis of unmanned aerial vehicles (drones) for agricultural applications", *Engineering for Rural Development,* vol. 15, no. 2, pp. 870-875, 2016.

[24] M.N. Tahir, Y. Lan, Y. Zhang, H. Wenjiang, Y. Wang, and S.M.Z.A. Naqvi, "Application of unmanned aerial vehicles in precision agriculture", In: *Precision Agriculture.* Academic Press, 2023, pp. 55-70.
[http://dx.doi.org/10.1016/B978-0-443-18953-1.00001-5]

[25] S. L. Muraru, P. Cardei, V. Muraru, R. Sfiru, and P. Condruz, "Researches regarding the use of drones in agriculture", *International Multidisciplinary Scientific GeoConference (SGEM),* vol. 19, no. 6.2, pp. 683-690, 2019.

[26] J.J. Cancela, X.P. González, M. Vilanova, and J.M. Mirás-Avalos, "Water management using drones and satellites in agriculture", *Water,* vol. 11, no. 5, p. 874, 2019.
[http://dx.doi.org/10.3390/w11050874]

[27] A. Montes de Oca, and G. Flores, "The AgriQ: A low-cost unmanned aerial system for precision agriculture", *Expert Syst. Appl.,* vol. 182, p. 115163, 2021.
[http://dx.doi.org/10.1016/j.eswa.2021.115163]

[28] C.Y.N. Norasma, M.A. Fadzilah, N.A. Roslin, Z.W.N. Zanariah, Z. Tarmidi, and F.S. Candra, "Unmanned aerial vehicle applications in agriculture", *IOP Conf. Series Mater. Sci. Eng.,* vol. 506, p.

012063, 2019. IOP Publishing.
[http://dx.doi.org/10.1088/1757-899X/506/1/012063]

[29]   Y. Shvets, D. Morkovkin, M. Basova, A. Yashchenko, and T. Petrusevich, "Robotics in agriculture: Advanced technologies in livestock farming and crop cultivation", In: *E3S Web of Conferences.* vol. 480. EDP Sciences, 2024, p. 03024.
[http://dx.doi.org/10.1051/e3sconf/202448003024]

[30]   N. Gupta, and P. K. Gupta, "Robotics and Artificial Intelligence (AI) in agriculture with major emphasis on food crops", *Digital Agriculture: A Solution for Sustainable Food and Nutritional Security,* pp. 577-605, 2024.

[31]   A. Sharma, S. Kumar, A. Singh, S. Kumar, Saurabh, H.C. Yadav, S. Hazarika, and R. Hasan, "Exploring the role of robotic automation in climate vulnerability mitigation: Towards sustainable horticulture", *International Journal of Environment and Climate Change,* vol. 14, no. 2, pp. 6-13, 2024.
[http://dx.doi.org/10.9734/ijecc/2024/v14i23914]

[32]   V. Kaliannan, and F.K.S. Al Saidi, "Intelligent computing with drones and robotics for precision agriculture", In: *Intelligent Robots and Drones for Precision Agriculture.* Springer Nature Switzerland: Cham, 2024, pp. 1-17.
[http://dx.doi.org/10.1007/978-3-031-51195-0_1]

[33]   S. Das, "Transforming agriculture: Harnessing robotics and drones for sustainable farming solutions", *Journal of Experimental Agriculture International,* vol. 46, no. 7, pp. 219-231, 2024.
[http://dx.doi.org/10.9734/jeai/2024/v46i72577]

[34]   S. Kujawa, and G. Niedbała, "Artificial neural networks in agriculture", *Agriculture,* vol. 11, no. 6, p. 497, 2021.
[http://dx.doi.org/10.3390/agriculture11060497]

[35]   A. Subeesh, and C.R. Mehta, "Automation and digitization of agriculture using artificial intelligence and internet of things", *Artificial Intelligence in Agriculture,* vol. 5, pp. 278-291, 2021.
[http://dx.doi.org/10.1016/j.aiia.2021.11.004]

[36]   P. Zhang, Z. Guo, S. Ullah, G. Melagraki, A. Afantitis, and I. Lynch, "Nanotechnology and artificial intelligence to enable sustainable and precision agriculture", *Nat. Plants,* vol. 7, no. 7, pp. 864-876, 2021.
[http://dx.doi.org/10.1038/s41477-021-00946-6] [PMID: 34168318]

[37]   A. Sharma, M. Georgi, M. Tregubenko, A. Tselykh, and A. Tselykh, "Enabling smart agriculture by implementing artificial intelligence and embedded sensing", *Comput. Ind. Eng.,* vol. 165, p. 107936, 2022.
[http://dx.doi.org/10.1016/j.cie.2022.107936]

[38]   T. Talaviya, D. Shah, N. Patel, H. Yagnik, and M. Shah, "Implementation of artificial intelligence in agriculture for optimisation of irrigation and application of pesticides and herbicides", *Artificial Intelligence in Agriculture,* vol. 4, pp. 58-73, 2020.
[http://dx.doi.org/10.1016/j.aiia.2020.04.002]

[39]   V.G. Dhanya, A. Subeesh, N.L. Kushwaha, D.K. Vishwakarma, T. Nagesh Kumar, G. Ritika, and A.N. Singh, "Deep learning based computer vision approaches for smart agricultural applications", *Artificial Intelligence in Agriculture,* vol. 6, pp. 211-229, 2022.
[http://dx.doi.org/10.1016/j.aiia.2022.09.007]

[40]   M.T. Linaza, J. Posada, J. Bund, P. Eisert, M. Quartulli, and J. Döllner, "Data-driven artificial intelligence applications for sustainable precision agriculture", *Agronomy (Basel),* vol. 11, no. 6, p. 1227, 2021.
[http://dx.doi.org/10.3390/agronomy11061227]

[41]   R. Veerachamy, and R. Ramar, "Agricultural Irrigation Recommendation and Alert (AIRA) system using optimization and machine learning in Hadoop for sustainable agriculture", *Environ. Sci. Pollut.*

Res. Int., vol. 29, no. 14, pp. 19955-19974, 2022.
[http://dx.doi.org/10.1007/s11356-021-13248-3] [PMID: 33788091]

[42]   R. Akhter, and S.A. Sofi, "Precision agriculture using IoT data analytics and machine learning", *Journal of King Saud University - Computer and Information Sciences,* vol. 34, no. 8, pp. 5602-5618, 2022.
[http://dx.doi.org/10.1016/j.jksuci.2021.05.013]

[43]   J.A. Wheeler, Classification of the information technology sector as a dependency for the food and agriculture sector, 2015.

[44]   A. Chatzipoulidis, D. Michalopoulos, and I. Mavridis, "Managing IT risk in the agriculture sector through automated security metrics", *International Workshop on Enterprise Information Systems and Their Applications, May.,* vol. 15, 2014.

[45]   M.W. Sitnicki, N. Prykaziuk, H. Ludmila, O. Pimenowa, F. Imbrea, L. Şmuleac, and R. Paşcalău, "Regional perspective of using cyber insurance as a tool for protection of Agriculture 4.0", *Agriculture,* vol. 14, no. 2, p. 320, 2024.
[http://dx.doi.org/10.3390/agriculture14020320]

[46]   R. Caviglia, G. Gaggero, G. Portomauro, F. Patrone, and M. Marchese, "An SDR-based cybersecurity verification framework for smart agricultural machines", *IEEE Access,* vol. 11, pp. 54210-54220, 2023.
[http://dx.doi.org/10.1109/ACCESS.2023.3282169]

[47]   N. Peppes, E. Daskalakis, T. Alexakis, E. Adamopoulou, and K. Demestichas, "Performance of machine learning-based multi-model voting ensemble methods for network threat detection in Agriculture 4.0", *Sensors (Basel),* vol. 21, no. 22, p. 7475, 2021.
[http://dx.doi.org/10.3390/s21227475] [PMID: 34833551]

[48]   K. Zidi, K. Ben Abdellafou, A. Aljuhani, O. Taouali, and M.F. Harkat, "Novel intrusion detection system based on a downsized kernel method for cybersecurity in smart agriculture", *Eng. Appl. Artif. Intell.,* vol. 133, p. 108579, 2024.
[http://dx.doi.org/10.1016/j.engappai.2024.108579]

[49]   L. Barreto, and A. Amaral, "Smart farming: Cyber security challenges", In: *International Conference on Intelligent Systems (IS).* IEEE., 2018, pp. 870-876.
[http://dx.doi.org/10.1109/IS.2018.8710531]

[50]   A. Kulkarni, Y. Wang, M. Gopinath, D. Sobien, A. Rahman, and F. A. Batarseh, "A review of cybersecurity incidents in the food and agriculture sector", *2403.08036,* 2024.
[http://dx.doi.org/10.48550/arXiv.2403.08036]

[51]   J. Nikander, O. Manninen, and M. Laajalahti, "Requirements for cybersecurity in agricultural communication networks", *Comput. Electron. Agric.,* vol. 179, p. 105776, 2020.
[http://dx.doi.org/10.1016/j.compag.2020.105776]

[52]   S. Sontowski, M. Gupta, S. Sree, M. Abdelsalam, S. Mittal, A. Joshi, and R. Sandhu, "Cyber attacks on smart farming infrastructure", *Proc. IEEE Conf. on Communications and Information Security (CIC).,* 2020.
[http://dx.doi.org/10.1109/CIC50333.2020.00025]

[53]   E. Kristen, R. Kloibhofer, V.H. Díaz, and P. Castillejo, "Security assessment of agriculture IoT (AIoT) applications", *Appl. Sci. (Basel),* vol. 11, no. 13, p. 5841, 2021.
[http://dx.doi.org/10.3390/app11135841]

[54]   M. A. Ferrag, L. Shu, O. Friha, and X. Yang, "Cybersecurity intrusion detection for agriculture 4.0: Machine learning-based solutions, datasets, and future directions", *IEEE/CAA Journal of Automatica Sinica,* vol. 9, no. 3, pp. 407-436, 2021.

[55]   SP, "Unmanned aerial vehicle in the smart farming systems: Types, applications, and cyber-security threats", *2022 International Conference on Innovative Computing, Intelligent Communication, and*

Smart Electrical Systems (ICSES), IEEE., pp. 1-9, 2022.

[56] M.A. Usmani, K.A. Usmani, A. Kaleem, and M. Samiuddin, "Cyber threat migration: Perpetuating in the healthcare sector and agriculture and food industries", In: *Advances in Cyberology and the Advent of the Next-Gen Information Revolution.* IGI Global, 2023, pp. 62-85.
[http://dx.doi.org/10.4018/978-1-6684-8133-2.ch004]

[57] T.H.H. Aldhyani, and H. Alkahtani, "Cybersecurity for detecting distributed denial of service attacks in agriculture 4.0: Deep learning model", *Mathematics,* vol. 11, no. 1, p. 233, 2023.
[http://dx.doi.org/10.3390/math11010233]

[58] R. Prodanović, D. Rančić, I. Vulić, N. Zorić, D. Bogićević, G. Ostojić, S. Sarang, and S. Stankovski, "Wireless sensor network in agriculture: Model of cybersecurity", *Sensors (Basel),* vol. 20, no. 23, p. 6747, 2020.
[http://dx.doi.org/10.3390/s20236747] [PMID: 33255859]

[59] K.J.D. Vatn, Cybersecurity in agriculture: A threat analysis of cyber-enabled dairy farm systems, 2023.

[60] E. Symeonaki, K.G. Arvanitis, D. Loukatos, and D. Piromalis, "Enabling IoT wireless technologies in sustainable livestock farming toward agriculture 4.0. In IoT-Based Intelligent Modelling for Environmental and Ecological Engineering: IoT Next Generation EcoAgro Systems", *Cham: Springer International Publishing,* pp. 213-232, 2021.
[http://dx.doi.org/10.1007/978-3-030-71172-6_9]

[61] X. Bai, X. Li, Z. Fu, X. Lv, and L. Zhang, "A fuzzy clustering segmentation method based on neighborhood grayscale information for defining cucumber leaf spot disease images", *Comput. Electron. Agric.,* vol. 136, pp. 157-165, 2017.
[http://dx.doi.org/10.1016/j.compag.2017.03.004]

[62] E. Tullo, I. Fontana, A. Diana, T. Norton, D. Berckmans, and M. Guarino, "Application note: Labelling, a methodology to develop reliable algorithm in PLF", *Comput. Electron. Agric.,* vol. 142, pp. 424-428, 2017.
[http://dx.doi.org/10.1016/j.compag.2017.09.030]

[63] D. Berckmans, "Precision livestock farming technologies for welfare management in intensive livestock systems", *Rev. Sci. Tech.,* vol. 33, no. 1, pp. 189-196, 2014.
[http://dx.doi.org/10.20506/rst.33.1.2273] [PMID: 25000791]

[64] Z. Angyalos, S. Botos, and R. Szilágyi, "The importance of cybersecurity in modern agriculture. Agrárinformatika", *Agrárinform. F.,* vol. 12, no. 2, pp. 1-8, 2021.
[http://dx.doi.org/10.17700/jai.2021.12.2.604]

CHAPTER 3

Revolutionizing Crop Disease Detection with Computational Deep Learning-based Techniques

Ajaypal Singh[1]**, Sukhdeep Singh**[1] **and Kanu Goel**[1,*]

[1] *Department of Computer Science and Engineering, Punjab Engineering College (Deemed to be) University, Chandigarh-160012, India*

Abstract: The early detection and classification of crop diseases is crucial in sustainable agriculture. Traditional inspection methods involve a lot of labor and are prone to errors. Therefore, the need for automated solutions for the detection of crop diseases has emerged. Deep learning techniques, especially Convolutional Neural Networks (CNNs), use image analysis to automate disease detection and classification. In this chapter, we analyze the performance of pre-trained deep learning models (DenseNet, MobileNet, EfficientNetB7) on a public benchmark encompassing annotated images of crops with diseases. The chapter discusses the role of transfer learning and fine-tuning of models to classify several diseases. The experimentation performed on the CCMT dataset is evaluated using accuracy, precision, recall, and F1 score metrics. Results indicated that MobileNet exhibited superior accuracy and balanced performance, making it a promising model for automated crop disease classification. However, addressing challenges in distinguishing visually similar diseases remains a priority for future research. The chapter discusses potential avenues for enhancing model performance, incorporating domain knowledge, improving data diversity, exploring advanced architectures, and ensuring model interpretability. Deep learning models show immense potential in revolutionizing crop disease detection, contributing to sustainable agricultural practices and global food security.

Keywords: CNN, Crop disease, Deep learning, Smart farming, Transfer learning.

INTRODUCTION

One of the critical challenges in modern agriculture is the early detection of crop diseases, with far-reaching implications for global food security and sustainable farming practices [1, 2]. Crop diseases can lead to yield losses and reduced crop quality, thereby threatening the farmers' livelihood. Traditionally, crop disease detection depended on expert manual inspection, which was time-intensive and vulnerable to inconsistencies [3]. In recent years, the emergence of deep learning

* **Corresponding author Kanu Goel:** Department of Computer Science and Engineering, Punjab Engineering College (Deemed to be) University, Chandigarh-160012, India; E-mail: kanugoel@pec.edu.in

Shefali Arora Chouhanm Nagendra Pratap Singh, Banalaxmi Brahma & Shashank Gupta (Eds.)

techniques, particularly in computer vision, has paved the way for the automated detection and classification of crop disease. CNNs are robust architectures for extracting intricate visual features from plant images, enabling accurate identification of various disease symptoms [4, 5].

The chapter provides insightful information on using deep learning models for effectively diagnosing crop diseases as well as the challenges and drawbacks, such as biases in the dataset or the model's generalizability. The chapter also provides directions for future research. The chapter also presents a comprehensive approach that employs pre-trained deep-learning architectures for crop disease detection. For this purpose, we use the open-source CCMT plant dataset, which consists of a diverse range of crop images annotated with disease labels [6]. The transfer learning approach involves fine-tuning pre-trained deep-learning models for crop disease detection [7]. It leverages the knowledge learned by models trained on large-scale image datasets, such as ImageNet, and adapts it to our target domain with relatively few annotated examples. This approach enables efficient utilization of computational resources and accelerates the model training process, making it feasible to explore multiple architectures and experimental settings.

Improving agricultural productivity and sustainability could be significantly impacted by the effective use of deep learning models in crop disease detection [8, 9]. Farmers can reduce output losses and slow the spread of illnesses by applying appropriate treatments, including targeted pesticide application or crop management techniques, when crop diseases are reliably identified and diagnosed early. Additionally, deep learning-based automated disease detection systems can reduce the need for chemical pesticides. Furthermore, by guaranteeing the production of robust and healthy crops, incorporating these cutting-edge technologies into agricultural systems may help improve global food security [10 - 12].

Our practical approach is based on designing training procedures and evaluation metrics to ensure adequate performance assessment. The experimentation involves standard protocols for dataset partitioning, including train-validation-test splits.

The experimentation revealed promising performance across different deep-learning architectures. Specifically, DenseNet achieved an accuracy of 92% with an F1 score of 91.3%, while MobileNet demonstrated an accuracy of 93.4% with an F1 score of 92.8%. EfficientNetB7 exhibited slightly lower accuracy at 89% but achieved a commendable F1 score of 88.6%. While DenseNet and EfficientNetB7 also showed strong performance, MobileNet emerged as the most effective solution for automated crop disease detection tasks. These results underscore the potential of deep learning models in automating crop disease detection tasks, providing accurate and efficient solutions to address critical challenges in modern agriculture.

BACKGROUND

Overview of Crop Diseases

Crop diseases can be categorized into the following three main types, as shown in Fig. (**1**):

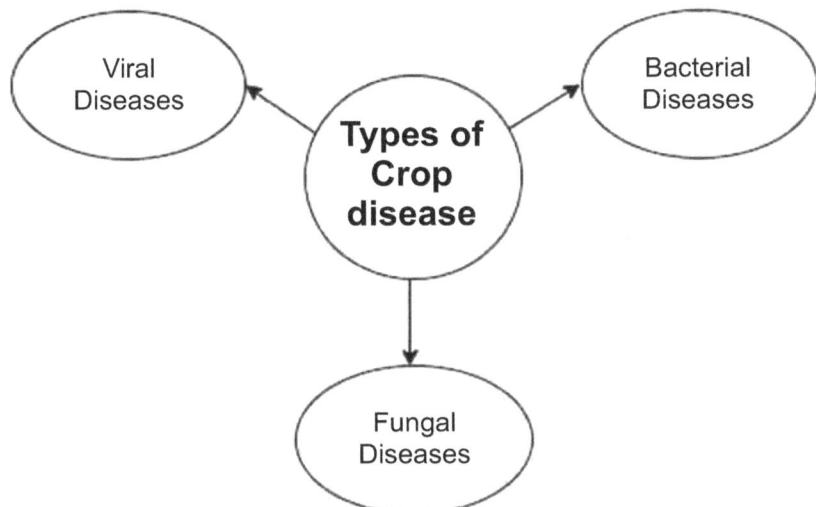

Fig. (1). Classification of crop diseases.

- **Fungal Diseases:** One of the most frequent causes of plant illnesses is fungus. Anthracnose, leaf spot, rust, and powdery mildew are a few examples of fungal infections.
- **Bacterial Diseases:** Bacterial infections have the potential to seriously harm crops. Under ideal environmental circumstances, they can spread quickly and frequently infect plants through wounds or natural openings. Citrus canker, bacterial wilt, and bacterial blight are a few types of bacterial illnesses.
- **Viral Diseases:** Viruses are microscopic pathogens that can produce a variety of symptoms in plants, such as deformation, stunting, and leaf mottling. Vectors like insects, nematodes, or contaminated seeds or plant material are frequently used to spread viral infections. Necrosis viruses, mosaic viruses, and leaf curl viruses are a few types of viral illnesses.

Fig. (**1**) depicts the various types of diseases in crops.

Table **1** describes the causes and symptoms of various diseases that crops are susceptible to. The diseases related to cashew are explored in a study by Monteiro *et al* [13]. Another study by Legg *et al.* explored the viruses responsible for causing diseases in plants [14]. Whereas, fungal diseases are explored by Rehman *et al* [15].

Table 1. Causes and symptoms of various crop diseases.

S.No.	Crop disease	Causes	Symptoms
1.	Cashew Anthracnose	Fungal infection	Dark lesions on leaves, stems, and fruits; defoliation; yield reduction
2.	Cashew Leaf Miner	Larvae of certain insects tunneling into cashew leaves	Characteristic tunneling patterns on leaves; leaf damage
3.	Cashew Red Rust	Fungal infection	Reddish-brown lesions on leaves; defoliation if severe
4.	Cassava Bacterial Blight	Bacterial pathogens	Necrotic lesions on leaves, stems, and tubers; reduced yield
5.	Cassava Brown Spot	Fungal infection	Dark brown lesions on leaves; premature leaf drop
6.	Cassava Green Mite	Infestation by spider mites	Yellowing; stippling; leaf curling
7.	Cassava Mosaic	Virus transmitted by white flies	Reduced tuber output; stunted development; mosaic patterns on leaves
8.	Maize Leaf Blight	Fungal infection	Large, irregular lesions on leaves; reduced yield
9.	Maize Leaf Spot	Fungal infection	Small, dark lesions on leaves; premature leaf drop
10.	Maize Streak Virus	Virus transmitted by leafhoppers	Yellow streaks and mottling on leaves; stunted growth; reduced grain quality
11.	Tomato Leaf Blight	Fungal infection	Dark lesions on leaves, stems, and fruits; defoliation
12.	Tomato Leaf Curl	Virus transmitted by white flies	Curling and distortion of leaves; stunted growth; reduced fruit production
13.	Tomato Septoria Leaf Spot	Fungal infection	Small, dark lesions with a lighter center on leaves; defoliation
14.	Tomato Verticillium Wilt	Fungal infection	Wilting and yellowing of leaves; vascular discoloration; plant death

LITERATURE REVIEW

DL-based Approaches

Recent advancements in Deep Learning (DL) have revolutionized plant disease detection by enabling automated and accurate diagnosis through image analysis. Ferentinos utilized a sizeable public dataset (PlantVillage) to train deep Convolutional Neural Networks (CNNs), achieving an impressive accuracy of 99.35% in identifying 26 diseases across 14 crop species [16]. DL methods hold much potential for smartphone-assisted diagnosis, particularly in areas with limited agricultural infrastructure [17]. Kulkarni compared the performance of Deep Learning (DL) models with Machine Learning (ML) algorithms for citrus plant disease detection [18]. Pre-trained models, such as VGG-16 and Inception-v3, performed better than ML algorithms, achieving accuracies ranging from 86.5% to 89.5%. The findings show that DL methods perform better in early disease detection, yielding better results for crop management and yield preservation. Saleem *et al.* presented a study using a public leaf image dataset that used deep learning models for disease detection [19]. The research demonstrated the success of both MobileNet and InceptionV3 architectures, achieving a performance of 99% in terms of accuracy.

Another study by Yingchun *et al.* [20] investigated the application of deep learning techniques in plant disease detection and classification, highlighting the benefits over traditional machine learning approaches. Their study explored a range of DL architectures, demonstrating effectiveness in analyzing visual and hyperspectral image data. Mohameth *et al.* conducted a comparative survey of fine-tuning deep learning models for plant disease identification, utilizing the PlantVillage dataset [21]. Dubey and Jalal explored plant disease detection using deep learning and traditional feature extraction techniques with the PlantVillage dataset [22]. They utilized CNN architectures, transfer learning, and deep feature extraction methods, and classified features using SVM and KNN algorithms. CNN-based approaches have shown promise despite data imbalances.

The research underscores the potential of DL methods for early disease detection, even before visible symptoms appear. These studies collectively highlight the transformative potential of deep learning in revolutionizing plant disease detection and diagnosis, offering efficient and accurate solutions for crop health management.

ML-based Approaches

In the realm of agricultural disease detection, Al-Hiary *et al.* [23] delve into the evolution from traditional Machine Learning (ML) methods to the transformative power of Deep Learning (DL) techniques, particularly in potato disease detection. Their research demonstrates the advancement from Support Vector Machines (SVMs) and Random Forests (RFs) to Convolutional Neural Networks (CNNs), which have an astounding accuracy of up to 98.33%. This study highlights the importance of ML and DL in developing precision agriculture. Al-Hiary *et al.* advanced the profession by improving the accuracy and computational efficiency of existing automated disease detection systems [23]. They increase processing speed by 20% and achieve a noteworthy 94% accuracy improvement through strategic advancements in image processing techniques. The work of Al Bashish *et al.* [24] provides a strong framework for identifying and categorizing plant leaf and stem diseases. Leveraging K-Means image segmentation and statistical classification models, they achieve a precision of approximately 93%, with further enhancements leading to an impressive 99.66% accuracy using Hyperspectral Imaging (HSI).

Dandawate and Kokare [25] presented an automated approach tailored explicitly for soybean leaf disease classification. Utilizing image processing techniques and Support Vector Machine (SVM) classifiers, they attain an average accuracy of 93.79%, paving the way for the development of mobile-based Decision Support Systems (DSS) for farmers. Dubey and Jalal [26] evaluated different feature extraction methods and utilized K-means clustering for picture segmentation to detect and classify apple fruit diseases. Up to 93% classification accuracy is attained using their Multi-class Support Vector Machine, and Local Binary Patterns (LBP) stand out as a particularly successful feature extraction technique. In a thorough investigation by Zamani *et al.* [27], the emphasis shifts to machine learning and image processing methods for detecting leaf diseases. Their suggested architecture starts by capturing leaf images and then uses a mean filter to reduce noise, followed by histogram equalization to improve contrast. They use Principal Component Analysis (PCA) to extract features and segment images using K-means clustering. Various machine learning techniques, such as RBF-SVM, SVM, random forest, and ID3, are employed.

Hybrid Approaches

A recent study by Sood and Singh [28] introduced a robust hybrid system for detecting and classifying capsicum plant diseases, emphasizing the significance of early identification for crop protection. Leveraging image processing techniques, including K-means clustering and GLCM texture feature extraction, their method achieved a remarkable 100% accuracy rate when classifying healthy and diseased capsicum images, with SVM and KNN demonstrating superior performance among classifiers. Furthermore, Yağ and Altan [29] introduced a novel hybrid plant disease classification model that combines a CNN classifier with wrapper-based feature selection, designed for real-time deployment in agricultural contexts. By combining a CNN and a Convolutional Autoencoder, Bedi and Gole [30] presented a novel hybrid model for plant disease identification that demonstrated great accuracy while drastically lowering training parameters. Similarly, Chug *et al.* [31] explored a new Hybrid Deep Learning framework for image-based plant disease diagnosis by combining several machine learning classifiers with pre-trained EfficientNet architectures, attaining 87.55-100% accuracy across datasets. Together, these findings demonstrate the expanding significance of hybrid approaches, which effectively bridge the gap between deep learning and classical machine learning techniques to handle agricultural challenges. The accuracy findings of previous research, which employed various datasets, such as PlantVillage and custom datasets, are shown in Table **2**.

Table 2. Result description of existing studies.

Reference	Dataset	Accuracy(in%)
[16]	PlantVillage	99.35
[21]	PlantVillage	99.75
[22]	PlantVillage	80.6
[24]	Custom	99.66
[25]	Custom	93.79
[28]	Custom	100

In conclusion, the literature review underscores the dynamic landscape of agricultural disease detection, where Deep Learning (DL), Machine Learning (ML), and hybrid approaches play crucial roles in advancing precision agriculture. DL-based methods exhibit remarkable accuracy in early disease detection, offering efficient solutions for crop health management. ML-based approaches, while evolving, continue to make a significant contribution to disease classification and identification, particularly in scenarios where computational resources are limited. Furthermore, the emergence of hybrid approaches represents a promising direction, combining the strengths of DL and ML to enhance accuracy, computational efficiency, and real-time applicability in agricultural settings.

PRACTICAL APPLICATION: CROP DISEASE CLASSIFICATION

The proposed experiment performed on the open-source CCMT dataset is depicted in the image below (Fig. **2**). It involves various stages, such as data preprocessing, data augmentation, training of pre-trained deep learning models using transfer learning, and then comparison of the results based on certain evaluation metrics.

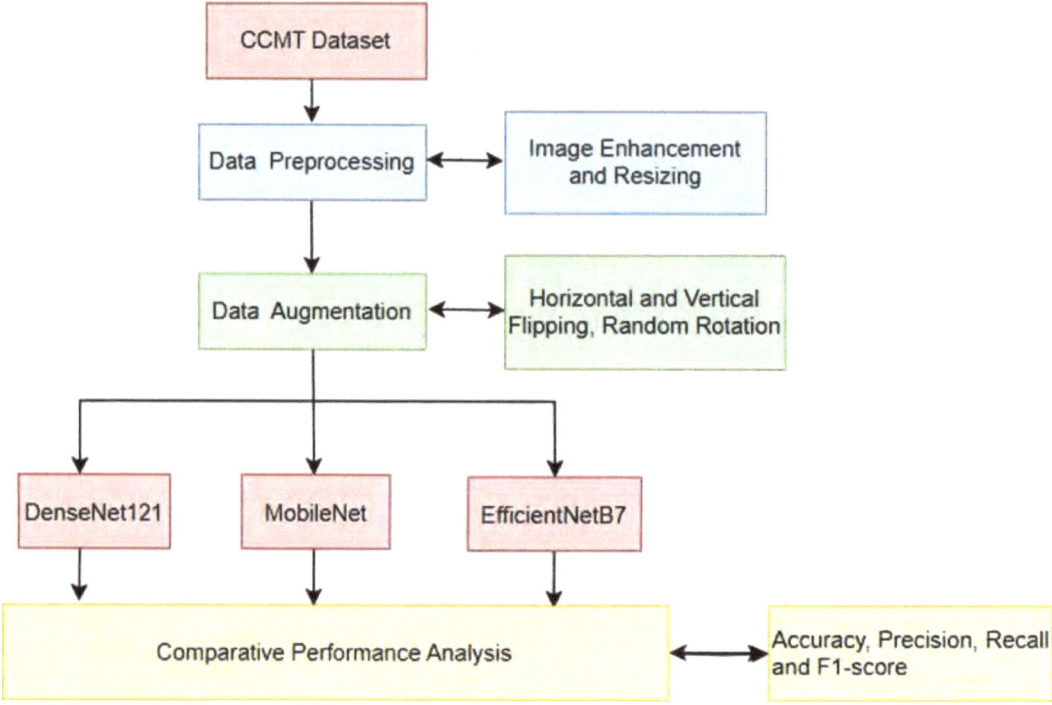

Fig. (2). Proposed methodology.

Dataset Description

The Cashew, Cassava, Maize, and Tomato (CCMT) dataset [6] comprises a diverse collection of 24,881 images across twenty-two classes, aimed at facilitating deep learning tasks, such as multi-classification, detection, and recognition in agricultural contexts. The overall crop-wise distribution of the images is depicted in Fig. (3), while a more detailed breakdown by crop and its associated diseases is provided in Table 3. This dataset is structured into subfolders corresponding to each crop type, namely Cashew, Cassava, Maize, and Tomato, with each subfolder containing images representing specific classes related to plant diseases, pest infestations, and overall crop health assessment.

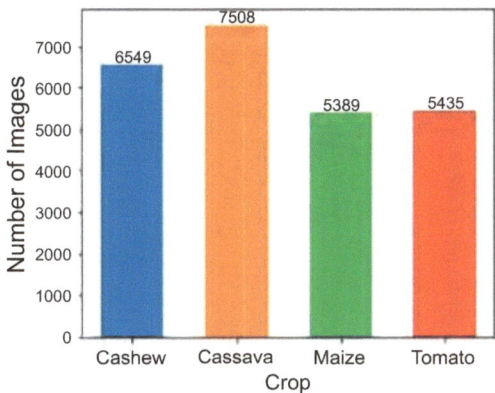

Fig. (3). Cropwise distribution of CCMT dataset.

One of the significant aspects of the CCMT dataset is the presence of class imbalances within each crop category. Class imbalance refers to the unequal distribution of images among different classes, which can impact the performance of ML models. For instance, in the Cashew subfolder, the "Anthracnose" class is heavily represented with 1701 images, while the "Gummosis" class has a much lower representation with only 392 images. Similarly, in the Cassava subfolder, the "Bacterial blight" class dominates with 2614 images, whereas the "Green mite" class has a comparatively smaller representation with 1015 images. These imbalances pose challenges during model training and evaluation, requiring strategies to mitigate their effects.

Furthermore, the CCMT dataset exhibits variations in image sizes, ranging from (400 × 400) to (4032 × 3024), reflecting real-world scenarios where images captured for analysis may vary significantly in resolution and aspect ratio. These variations can introduce challenges in data preprocessing, feature extraction, and model training, necessitating careful handling to ensure model robustness and performance consistency across different image sizes.

High-quality, annotated datasets are essential for crop disease detection, predictive analysis, and model training. In this field, a number of publicly accessible datasets have established themselves as standards, allowing researchers to create, evaluate, and compare deep learning and machine learning models. Some of the most popular datasets for crop health monitoring are shown in Table 2a.

Table 2a. Summary of widely used crop disease datasets.

Sr. No.	Dataset Name	Source / Institution	Crops Covered	Diseases Included	Image Count	Highlights
1	PlantVillage	Penn State University	Tomato, Apple, Potato, Maize, etc.	38 diseases (fungal, bacterial, viral)	~54,000	Widely used benchmark; images under controlled conditions
2	IP102	Chinese Academy of Sciences	Multiple	102 pest species	~75,000	Large-scale pest dataset; useful for insect classification
3	CropDoc	China Agricultural University	Wheat, Maize, Tomato	27 diseases	~9,000	Field-acquired images; useful for real-world generalization
4	DeepWeeds	CSIRO Australia	Weeds in pastures	8 weed species	~17,000	High-resolution images of weeds in natural settings

Table 3. Numerical distribution of CCMT dataset classes.

Sr. No.	Crop	Disease	Image Count
1.	Cashew	Healthy	1368
		Gummosis	392
		Anthracnose	1701
		Leaf Miner	1358
		Res rust	1682
2.	Cassava	Healthy	1193
		Bacterial blight	2614
		Brown spot	1481
		Green mite	1015
		Mosaic	1205
3.	Maize	Healthy	208
		Fall armyworm	285
		Grasshopper	673
		Leaf beetle	948
		Leaf blight	1006
		Leaf spot	1259
		Streak virus	1010

(Table 3) cont.....

Sr. No.	Crop	Disease	Image Count
4.	Tomato	Healthy	500
		Leaf blight	1301
		Leaf curl	518
		Septoria leaf spot	2343
		Verticillium wilt	773
Total No. of Images			24881

In the subsequent section 3.2 of this chapter, we delve into the techniques employed to address the class imbalance and image size issues within the CCMT dataset. These techniques may include data augmentation methods, class weighting strategies, preprocessing steps, such as resizing and normalization, and specialized model architectures designed to handle varying image resolutions effectively. By implementing these techniques, we aim to enhance the dataset's usability, improve model generalization across different classes and image sizes, and ultimately facilitate more accurate and reliable predictions in agricultural tasks such as crop disease diagnosis and pest detection.

Dataset Preprocessing

Optimizing deep learning models for complex tasks like crop disease detection heavily relies on effective dataset preprocessing, particularly for enhancing feature extraction capabilities. Making use of Contrast Limited Adaptive Histogram Equalization (CLAHE) for image enhancement [32], image resizing for standardization, and various augmentation techniques, our goal extends beyond merely improving the diversity and quality of the training data. In this section, we delve into the pivotal role of dataset preprocessing and the techniques Reza [32] applied to enrich the CCMT dataset for training deep learning models. These preprocessing steps were performed to tackle critical challenges like class imbalances and overfitting, ensuring that the models are adept at navigating real-world variations and complexities.

Image Enhancement

To improve the image quality of the CCMT dataset, we used Contrast Limited Adaptive Histogram Equalization (CLAHE) [32]. This adaptive approach enhances local contrast while preserving image characteristics. By limiting contrast amplification, CLAHE prevents noise over-amplification, resulting in improved image quality and detail preservation.

As illustrated in Fig. (**4**), CLAHE can significantly improve the visibility of features within an image. For instance, details like veins in a plant leaf become more pronounced after CLAHE enhancement.

Fig. (4). Sample images before and after CLAHE enhancement.

Image Augmentation

Image augmentation [33] was crucial for diversifying the dataset and mitigating overfitting while addressing class imbalances. We applied horizontal and vertical flipping, as well as random rotation, to introduce variations in orientation and perspective. These techniques enable the models to learn more invariant features, improving their generalization ability to different viewing angles and transformations. By augmenting the dataset with diverse variations of the original images, we aimed to improve the models' performance and adaptability to real-world scenarios. The original image is displayed alongside its horizontally flipped, vertically flipped, and randomly rotated counterparts in Fig. (**5**).

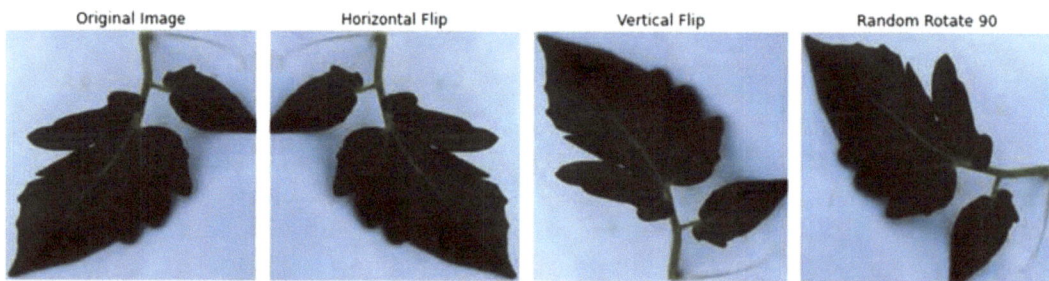

Fig. (5). Samples of augmented images.

MODEL ARCHITECTURES

For the crop disease classification task, we explored several state-of-the-art deep learning architectures, each with its unique characteristics and capabilities. The following architectures were considered:

DenseNet121

DenseNet stands for Dense Convolutional Network, and DenseNet121 refers explicitly to a variant with 121 layers [34]. DenseNet has densely connected layers, where each layer is connected directly to other layers in a feed-forward manner. This pattern facilitates feature reuse, allowing each layer to receive direct gradients from the loss function. DenseNet alleviates the vanishing gradient problem and encourages feature propagation, leading to better utilization of parameters and feature learning. In DenseNet121, the network consists of multiple dense blocks, each containing convolutional layers with batch normalization and ReLU activation. Transition layers with pooling operations reduce the spatial dimensions between dense blocks, helping to control the model's growth in complexity. DenseNet121 strikes an intermediate between model capacity and computational efficiency, making it suitable for a wide range of tasks related to image classification, including crop disease classification. Fig. (**6**) depicts the DenseNet121 architecture with its characteristic dense block connections.

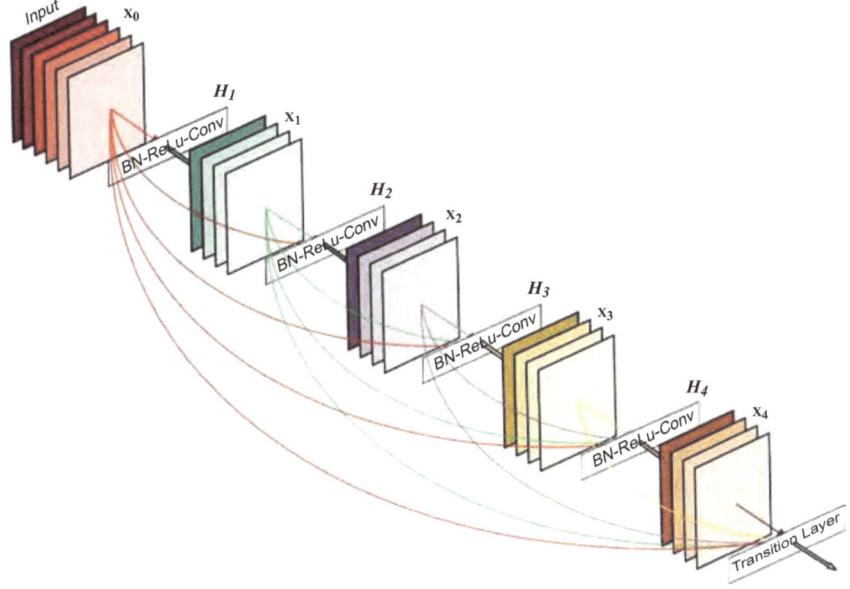

Fig. (6). DenseNet121 architecture [34].

MobileNet

MobileNet is a lightweight convolutional neural network architecture suited for mobile and embedded vision [35]. MobileNet solves the issue of using deep neural networks on resource-constrained devices by significantly reducing the number of parameters and computations without sacrificing accuracy. The key innovation in MobileNet is the use of depth-wise separable convolutions and point-wise convolutions. Depth-wise convolutions use a single convolutional filter per input channel, capturing spatial information independently for each channel. Point-wise convolutions then combine the channel-wise features using 1x1 convolutions, allowing for cross-channel interactions. This factorization drastically reduces the computational cost while maintaining expressive power. MobileNet architectures are characterized by a depth multiplier parameter, which controls the model's width, enabling trade-offs between accuracy and efficiency.

Fig. (**7**) showcases MobileNet's core building block.

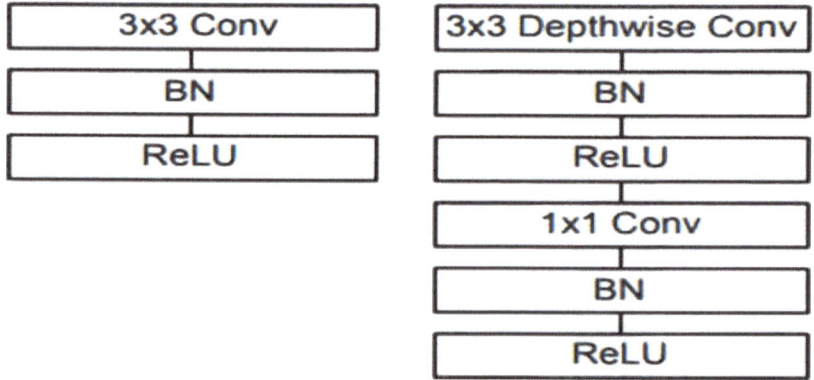

Fig. (7). MobileNet layer architecture [35].

EfficientNetB7

EfficientNet is a family of convolutional neural network architectures proposed by Tan and Le, known for achieving state-of-the-art performance with significantly fewer parameters and computations compared to previous architectures [36]. The key insight behind EfficientNet is systematic scaling of network width, depth, and resolution in a principled manner. EfficientNet architectures are composed of a baseline network that is scaled up uniformly across width, depth, and resolution dimensions. This baseline architecture is then optimized by applying compound scaling coefficients to each dimension. EfficientNetB7 represents one of the largest variants in the EfficientNet family, offering high accuracy while being computationally efficient. It is characterized by a deeper and wider network compared to smaller variants. Despite its increased size, EfficientNetB7 maintains computational efficiency by carefully balancing model parameters and computations through compound scaling. EfficientNetB7 is well-suited for demanding tasks, such as crop disease classification, where both accuracy and efficiency are crucial considerations. Fig. (**8**) illustrates the scaling architecture of EfficientNetB7.

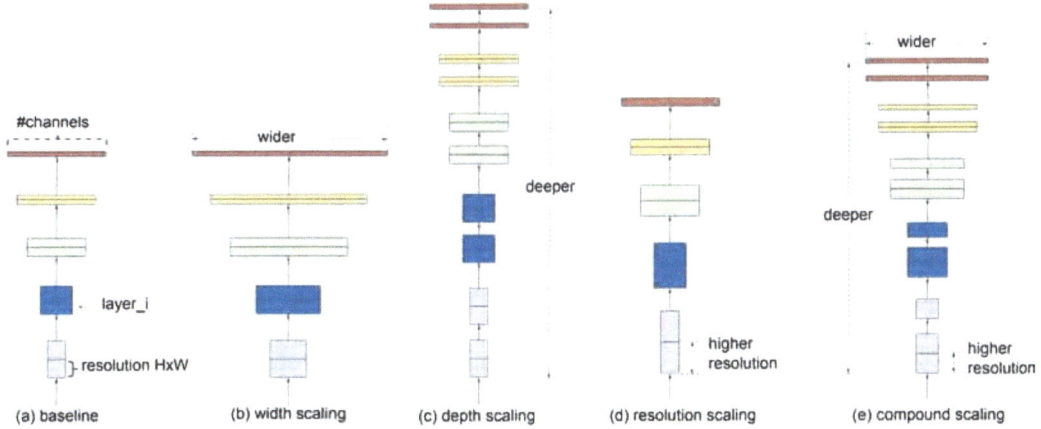

Fig. (8). Scaling architecture of EfficientNetB7 [36].

Training Procedures

To optimize the performance of the selected deep learning models, we meticulously crafted a training procedure encompassing essential elements. Here's how we approached it:

- **Data Split:** The CCMT dataset was partitioned into three subsets:
  - **Training Set (70%):** Utilized to train the models, learn patterns, and adjust model weights.
  - **Validation Set (15%):** Employed to monitor performance during training, tune hyperparameters, and prevent overfitting.
  - **Testing Set (15%):** Reserved solely for unbiased final evaluation of the trained models on unseen data.

- **Optimizer:** We selected the Adam optimizer, renowned for its adaptive learning rate adjustments and computational efficiency. Adam is well-suited for large datasets and often yields superior convergence compared to other gradient descent variants.
- **Loss Function:** Categorical cross-entropy loss was the function of choice due to the multi-class classification nature of the task. This loss function effectively penalizes incorrect predictions, aiding in model learning.
- **Learning Rate:** We adopted an adaptive learning rate strategy to optimize

convergence. An initial learning rate of 0.001 was set, which decayed by a factor of 0.1 upon reaching a performance plateau on the validation set, ensuring continual improvement while mitigating the risk of oscillations.

- **Batch Size:** We selected a batch size of 32, which leads to a balance between computational efficiency and gradient estimation stability.
- **Epochs:** Models were trained for a maximum of 50 epochs. An early stopping mechanism was implemented to terminate training if the validation loss failed to improve for 5 epochs consecutively, preventing overfitting and conserving computational resources.
- **Overfitting Mitigation:** We used L2 regularization (also known as weight decay) to penalize overly complex models and encourage generalization. This encourages the model to learn smaller weights, which often leads to simpler and more generalizable models.

Evaluation Metrics

To assess the performance of the deep learning models for crop disease classification, we employed a range of evaluation metrics designed to provide comprehensive insights into their effectiveness. The evaluation metrics used and their formulas are shown in Fig. (**9**). The following evaluation metrics were utilized:

Evaluation Metric	Mathematical Formula
Accuracy	$\dfrac{TP + TN}{TP + TN + FP + FN}$
Precision (P)	$\dfrac{TP}{TP + FP}$
Recall (R)	$\dfrac{TP}{FN + TP}$
F1 Score	$\dfrac{2PR}{P + R}$

Fig. (9). Evaluation metrics.

- **Accuracy:** The percentage of correctly categorized samples relative to all samples in the evaluation dataset is known as accuracy. It is a commonly used statistic in machine learning applications for healthcare. A perfect categorization of all positive and negative samples is represented by an accuracy of 1, while no accurate predictions are made by a value of 0 [37].

- **Precision:** It is computed as the ratio of correctly identified samples to all samples allocated to a specific class, and it assesses the relevance of retrieved samples. It has a range of 0 to 1, where 1 means that every sample in the class was correctly predicted and 0 means that none of the samples were correctly predicted [37].

- **Recall:** Recall is the percentage of correctly categorized positive samples. It is often referred to as sensitivity, also called the True Positive Rate (TPR). It is computed as the proportion of all samples assigned to the positive class that are correctly categorized as positive samples. A recall value of 1 indicates that the positive class was perfectly predicted, whereas a recall value of 0 indicates that all positive class samples were incorrectly predicted [37].

- **F1 Score:** The F1 score, which penalizes extreme values of either metric, is a balanced metric that is calculated as the harmonic mean of precision and recall. Depending on whether a class is classified as positive or negative, it is asymmetrical between them. Maximum accuracy and recall values are represented by an F1 score of 1, whereas zero precision and/or recall are represented by a score of 0 [37].

RESULTS AND DISCUSSION

Performance Evaluation

The confusion matrix provides a detailed overview of the model's classification performance across different crop diseases. As observed from the confusion matrix for MobileNet shown in Fig. (**10**), the model demonstrates a high level of accuracy, with most diseases being classified correctly. However, there are some notable misclassifications, particularly between visually similar diseases.

Analyzing the training and validation curves (Figs. **11a, 11b, 12a, 12b, 13a, 13b**), we observe a consistent decrease in loss and a corresponding increase in accuracy over epochs for both training and validation datasets. The validation curves also show that the model has not overfit the training data, as the validation loss and accuracy do not diverge significantly from their training counterparts.

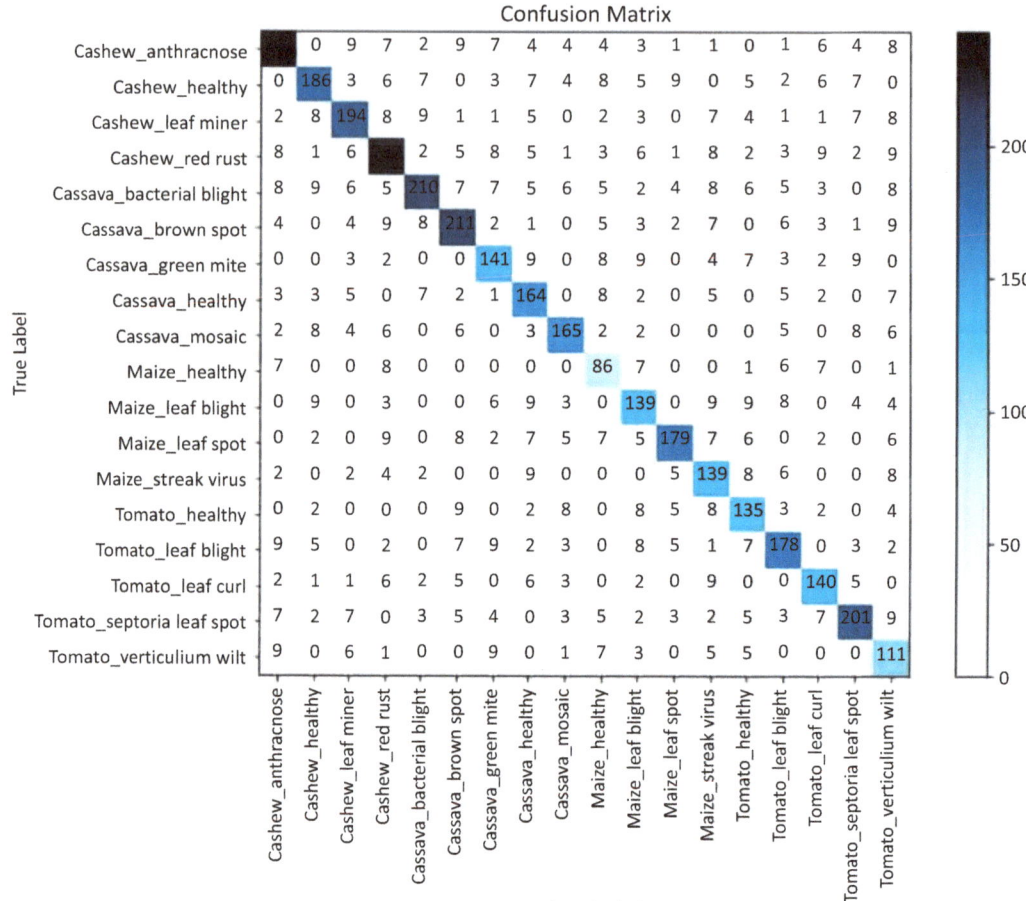

Fig. (10). Confusion matrix for MobileNet.

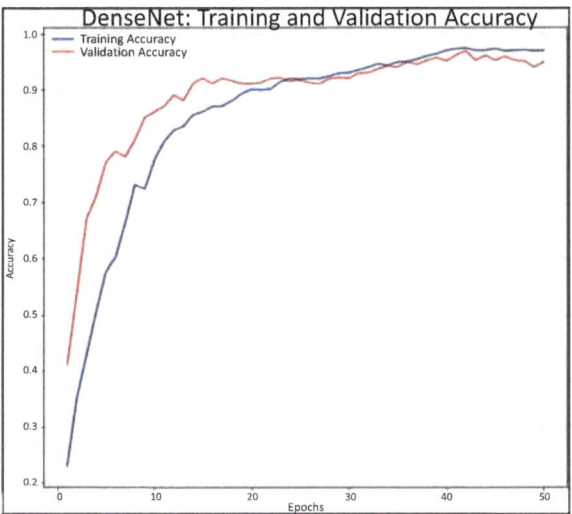

Fig. (11a). Accuracy curve depicting training and validation of DenseNet121.

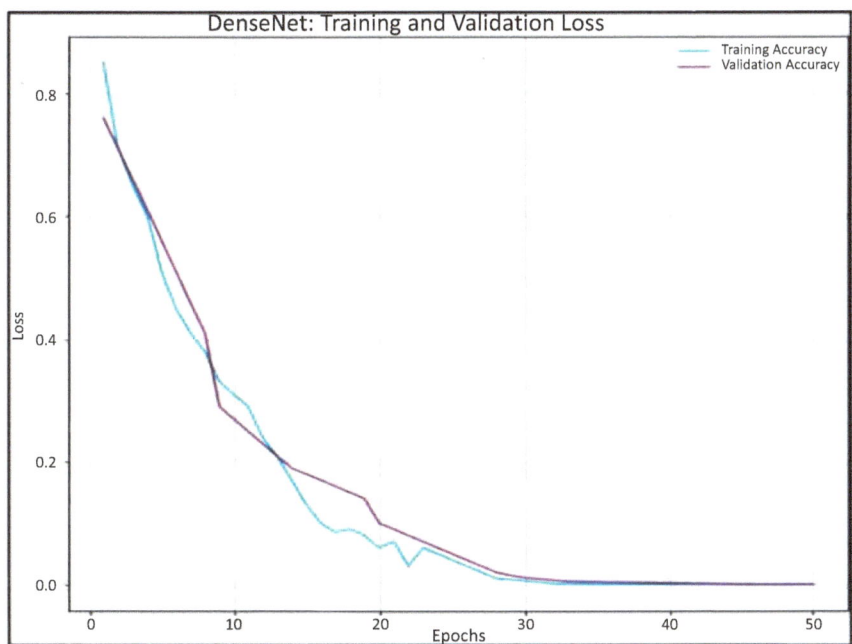

Fig. (11b). Loss curve for training and validation of DenseNet121.

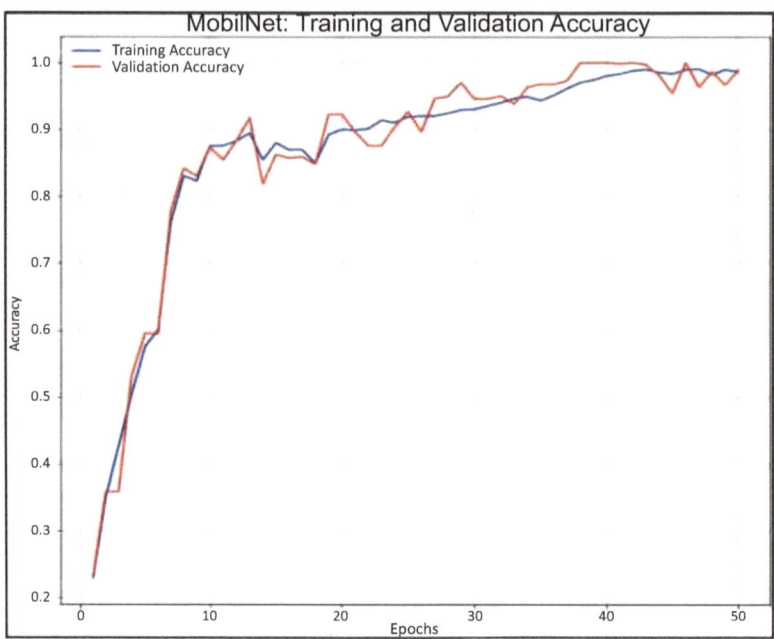

Fig. (12a). Accuracy curve for training and validation of MobileNet.

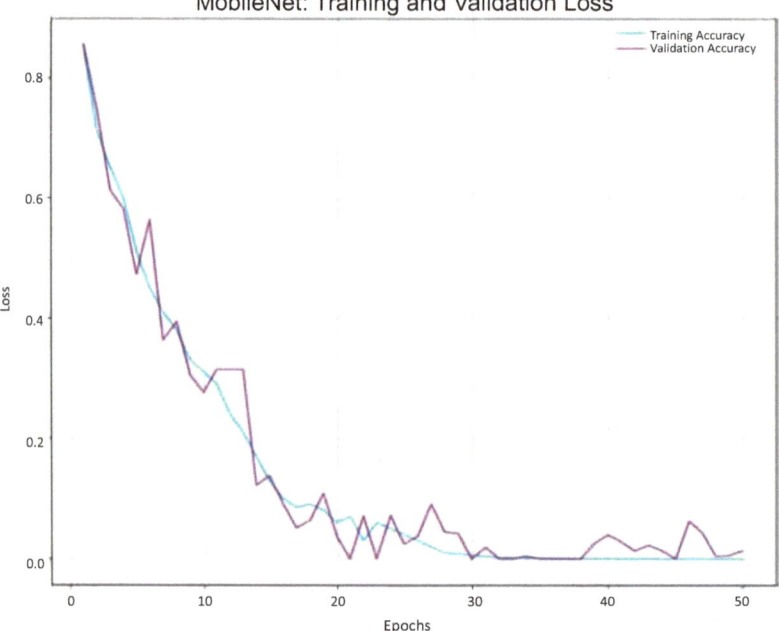

Fig. (12b). Loss curve for training and validation of MobileNet.

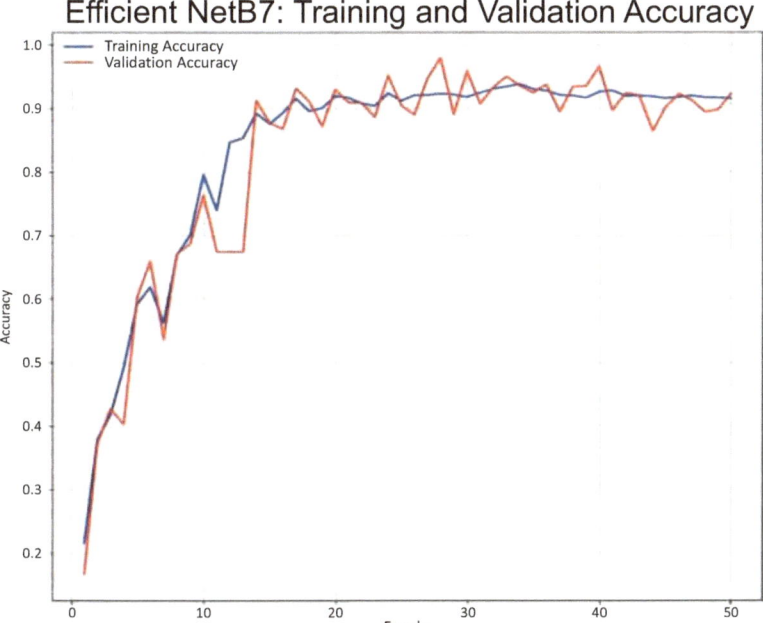

Fig. (13a). Accuracy curve for training and validation of EfficientNetB7.

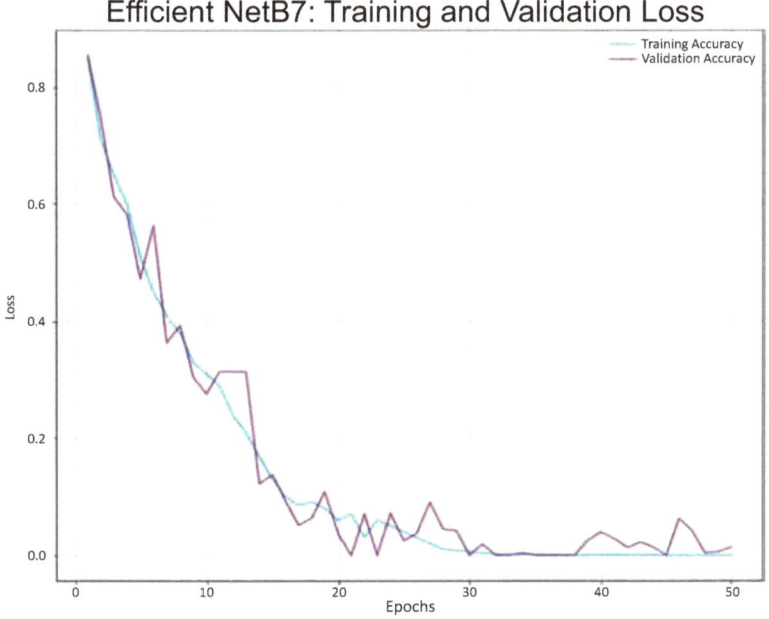

Fig. (13b). Loss curve for training and validation of EfficientNetB7.

Comparative Analysis

The comparative analysis of the three deep learning models—DenseNet, MobileNet, and EfficientNetB7—reveals varying performances in terms of accuracy and F1 score, as shown in Table **4**.

Table 4. Comparison of results

Model	Accuracy	F1 Score
DenseNet	0.92	0.913
MobileNet	0.934	0.928
EfficientNetB7	0.89	0.886

These findings demonstrate MobileNet's promise as a crop disease classification model because of its excellent accuracy and well-balanced precision and recall performance. The needs and limitations of the application, such as available computing power and the desired balance between model complexity and accuracy, will ultimately determine which model is best.

DISCUSSION

The findings in this section demonstrate how deep learning models can be used to classify agricultural diseases. The model's ability to extract pertinent characteristics from images and generalize well to new data is demonstrated by its excellent overall accuracy and steady learning curves. The confusion matrix reveals some limitations in the model's ability to differentiate between illnesses that have similar visual characteristics, nevertheless.

This implies that future studies should focus on creating methods to increase the discriminatory strength of the model in these situations. Potential approaches could include incorporating domain-specific knowledge, utilizing more diverse and representative training data, and exploring advanced model architectures that can capture subtle differences in disease symptoms.

Additionally, the comparative analysis with DenseNet, MobileNet, and EfficientNetB7 provides valuable insights into the relative strengths and weaknesses of different deep learning models for crop disease classification. Predictive analysis frequently encounters class imbalance, particularly when dealing with multi-class classification problems such as crop disease detection. There are notable differences in the number of samples per class in the CCMT dataset, which includes 24,881 photos of four crops (tomato, corn, cassava, and cashew). This can result in learning outcomes that are skewed. To counteract the impacts of imbalance and increase of model resilience, data augmentation techniques like flipping and rotation have been used.

CONCLUDING REMARKS

The use of deep learning models for crop disease classification has been examined in this work, and DenseNet, MobileNet, and EfficientNetB7 have been assessed using a variety of measures, such as accuracy, precision, recall, F1 score, and a confusion matrix. Our findings show that deep learning models—particularly MobileNet—can categorize crop illnesses with high accuracy, providing a promising tool for early diagnosis and intervention in agricultural practices. The results of the confusion matrix analysis showed difficulties differentiating between diseases that are visually similar, underscoring the need for more studies to improve the discriminatory power of these models by incorporating domain knowledge, better data diversity, and sophisticated model architectures. Although MobileNet was the best model in terms of accuracy and F1 score, selecting the best model depends on specific requirements and constraints, such as computational resources and desired trade-offs between accuracy and complexity.

The findings of this study open up several avenues for future research in crop disease classification using deep learning. Potential directions include incorporating domain-specific knowledge to enhance model performance and interpretability, improving data diversity to make models more robust and generalizable, and investigating advanced model architectures like attention-based or hybrid models. Additionally, developing techniques for explainable AI can make models more transparent, enabling better decision-making by farmers and agronomists. Exploring the feasibility of real-time deployment on edge devices, such as smartphones or drones, can also facilitate the real-time crop disease detection and monitoring in the field.

REFERENCES

[1]   S. Chakraborty, and A.C. Newton, "Climate change, plant diseases and food security: an overview", *Plant Pathol.,* vol. 60, no. 1, pp. 2-14, 2011.
[http://dx.doi.org/10.1111/j.1365-3059.2010.02411.x]

[2]   M.A. John, I. Bankole, O. Ajayi-Moses, T. Ijila, T. Jeje, and P. Lalit, "Relevance of advanced plant disease detection techniques in disease and pest management for ensuring food security and their implication: A review", *Am. J. Plant Sci.,* vol. 14, no. 11, pp. 1260-1295, 2023.
[http://dx.doi.org/10.4236/ajps.2023.1411086]

[3]   Y. He, B. Fan, L. Sun, X. Fan, J. Zhang, Y. Li, and X. Suo, "Rapid appearance quality of rice based on machine vision and convolutional neural network research on automatic detection system", *Front. Plant Sci.,* vol. 14, p. 1190591, 2023.
[http://dx.doi.org/10.3389/fpls.2023.1190591] [PMID: 37662147]

[4]   A. Abade, P.A. Ferreira, and F. de Barros Vidal, "Plant diseases recognition on images using convolutional neural networks: A systematic review", *Comput. Electron. Agric.,* vol. 185, p. 106125,

2021.
[http://dx.doi.org/10.1016/j.compag.2021.106125]

[5]   L.C. Ngugi, M. Abelwahab, and M. Abo-Zahhad, "Recent advances in image processing techniques for automated leaf pest and disease recognition – A review", *Inf. Process. Agric.,* vol. 8, no. 1, pp. 27-51, 2021.
[http://dx.doi.org/10.1016/j.inpa.2020.04.004]

[6]   P.K. Mensah, V. Akoto-Adjepong, K. Adu, M.A. Ayidzoe, E.A. Bediako, O. Nyarko-Boateng, S. Boateng, E.F. Donkor, F.U. Bawah, N.S. Awarayi, P. Nimbe, I.K. Nti, M. Abdulai, R.R. Adjei, M. Opoku, S. Abdulai, and F. Amu-Mensah, "CCMT: Dataset for crop pest and disease detection", *Data Brief,* vol. 49, p. 109306, 2023.
[http://dx.doi.org/10.1016/j.dib.2023.109306] [PMID: 37360671]

[7]   F. Zhuang, Z. Qi, K. Duan, D. Xi, Y. Zhu, H. Zhu, H. Xiong, and Q. He, "A comprehensive survey on transfer learning", *Proc. IEEE,* vol. 109, no. 1, pp. 43-76, 2021.
[http://dx.doi.org/10.1109/JPROC.2020.3004555]

[8]   M. Shoaib, B. Shah, S. EI-Sappagh, A. Ali, A. Ullah, F. Alenezi, T. Gechev, T. Hussain, and F. Ali, "An advanced deep learning models-based plant disease detection: A review of recent research", *Front. Plant Sci.,* vol. 14, p. 1158933, 2023.
[http://dx.doi.org/10.3389/fpls.2023.1158933] [PMID: 37025141]

[9]   R. Sharma, S.S. Kamble, A. Gunasekaran, V. Kumar, and A. Kumar, "A systematic literature review on machine learning applications for sustainable agriculture supply chain performance", *Comput. Oper. Res.,* vol. 119, p. 104926, 2020.
[http://dx.doi.org/10.1016/j.cor.2020.104926]

[10]   U. Sekaran, L. Lai, D. A. N. Ussiri, S. Kumar, and S. Clay, "Role of integrated crop-livestock systems in improving agriculture production and addressing food security–A review," Journal of Agriculture and Food Research, vol. 5, Art. no. 100190, 2021.
[http://dx.doi.org/10.1016/j.jafr.2021.100190]

[11]   A.A. Adenle, K. Wedig, and H. Azadi, "Sustainable agriculture and food security in Africa: The role of innovative technologies and international organizations", *Technol. Soc.,* vol. 58, p. 101143, 2019.
[http://dx.doi.org/10.1016/j.techsoc.2019.05.007]

[12]   S.P. Mohanty, D.P. Hughes, and M. Salathé, "Using deep learning for image-based plant disease detection", *Front. Plant Sci.,* vol. 7, p. 1419, 2016.
[http://dx.doi.org/10.3389/fpls.2016.01419] [PMID: 27713752]

[13]   F. Monteiro, M.M. Romeiras, J. Barnabé, S. Catarino, D. Batista, and M. Sebastiana, "Disease-causing agents in cashew: A review in a tropical cash crop", *Agronomy (Basel),* vol. 12, no. 10, p. 2553, 2022.
[http://dx.doi.org/10.3390/agronomy12102553]

[14]   J.P. Legg, P. Lava Kumar, T. Makeshkumar, L. Tripathi, M. Ferguson, E. Kanju, P. Ntawuruhunga, and W. Cuellar, "Cassava virus diseases: Biology, epidemiology, and management", *Adv. Virus Res.,* vol. 91, pp. 85-142, 2015.
[http://dx.doi.org/10.1016/bs.aivir.2014.10.001] [PMID: 25591878]

[15]   F. ur Rehman, M. Adnan, M. Kalsoom, N. Naz, M. G. Husnain, H. Ilahi, M. A. Ilyas, G. Yousaf, R. Tahir, and U. Ahmad, "Seed-borne fungal diseases of maize (*Zea mays L.*): A review", *Agrinula J. Agroteknologi Perkebunan,* vol. 4, no. 1, pp. 43-60, 2021.

[16]   K.P. Ferentinos, "Deep learning models for plant disease detection and diagnosis", *Comput. Electron. Agric.,* vol. 145, pp. 311-318, 2018.
[http://dx.doi.org/10.1016/j.compag.2018.01.009]

[17]   R. Sujatha, J.M. Chatterjee, N.Z. Jhanjhi, and S.N. Brohi, "Performance of deep learning *vs* machine learning in plant leaf disease detection", *Microprocess. Microsyst.,* vol. 80, p. 103615, 2021.
[http://dx.doi.org/10.1016/j.micpro.2020.103615]

[18]   O. Kulkarni, "Crop disease detection using deep learning", *2018 Fourth International Conference on Computing Communication Control and Automation (ICCUBEA),* IEEE, pp. 1-4, 2018.

[19]   M.H. Saleem, J. Potgieter, and K.M. Arif, "Plant disease detection and classification by deep learning", *Plants,* vol. 8, no. 11, p. 468, 2019.
[http://dx.doi.org/10.3390/plants8110468] [PMID: 31683734]

[20]   E.C. Too, L. Yujian, S. Njuki, and L. Yingchun, "A comparative study of fine-tuning deep learning models for plant disease identification", *Comput. Electron. Agric.,* vol. 161, pp. 272-279, 2019.
[http://dx.doi.org/10.1016/j.compag.2018.03.032]

[21]   F. Mohameth, C. Bingcai, and K.A. Sada, "Plant disease detection with deep learning and feature extraction using plant village", *Journal of Computer and Communications,* vol. 8, no. 6, pp. 10-22, 2020.
[http://dx.doi.org/10.4236/jcc.2020.86002]

[22]   J.A. Wani, S. Sharma, M. Muzamil, S. Ahmed, S. Sharma, and S. Singh, "Machine learning and deep learning-based computational techniques in automatic agricultural diseases detection: Methodologies, applications, and challenges", *Arch. Comput. Methods Eng.,* vol. 29, no. 1, pp. 641-677, 2022.
[http://dx.doi.org/10.1007/s11831-021-09588-5]

[23]   H. Al Hiary, S. Bani Ahmad, M. Reyalat, M. Braik, and Z. ALRahamneh, "Fast and accurate detection and classification of plant diseases", *Int. J. Comput. Appl.,* vol. 17, no. 1, pp. 31-38, 2011.
[http://dx.doi.org/10.5120/2183-2754]

[24]   D. Al Bashish, M. Braik, and S. Bani-Ahmad, "A framework for detection and classification of plant leaf and stem diseases", *Proc. 2010 Int. Conf. Signal Image Process.,* pp. 113-118, 2010.
[http://dx.doi.org/10.1109/ICSIP.2010.5697452]

[25]   Y. Dandawate and R. Kokare, "An automated approach for classification of plant diseases towards development of futuristic decision support system in Indian perspective," in Proc. 2015 Int. Conf. Advances Comput., Commun., Inf. (ICACCI), pp. 794–799, 2015.
[http://dx.doi.org/10.1109/ICACCI.2015.7275707]

[26]   S. R. Dubey and A. S. Jalal, "Detection and classification of apple fruit diseases using complete local binary patterns," in Proc. 2012 3rd Int. Conf. Comput. Commun. Technol., pp. 346–351, 2012.
[http://dx.doi.org/10.1109/ICCCT.2012.76]

[27]   A.S. Zamani, L. Anand, K.P. Rane, P. Prabhu, A.M. Buttar, H. Pallathadka, A. Raghuvanshi, and B.N. Dugbakie, "Performance of machine learning and image processing in plant leaf disease detection", *J. Food Qual.,* vol. 2022, pp. 1-7, 2022.
[http://dx.doi.org/10.1155/2022/1598796]

[28]   Anjna, M. Sood, and P.K. Singh, "Hybrid system for detection and classification of plant disease using qualitative texture features analysis", *Procedia Comput. Sci.,* vol. 167, pp. 1056-1065, 2020.
[http://dx.doi.org/10.1016/j.procs.2020.03.404]

[29]   İ. Yağ, and A. Altan, "Artificial intelligence-based robust hybrid algorithm design and implementation for real-time detection of plant diseases in agricultural environments", *Biology (Basel),* vol. 11, no. 12, p. 1732, 2022.
[http://dx.doi.org/10.3390/biology11121732] [PMID: 36552243]

[30]   P. Bedi, and P. Gole, "Plant disease detection using hybrid model based on convolutional autoencoder and convolutional neural network", *Artificial Intelligence in Agriculture,* vol. 5, pp. 90-101, 2021.
[http://dx.doi.org/10.1016/j.aiia.2021.05.002]

[31]   A. Chug, A. Bhatia, A.P. Singh, and D. Singh, "A novel framework for image-based plant disease detection using hybrid deep learning approach", *Soft Comput.,* vol. 27, no. 18, pp. 13613-13638, 2023.
[http://dx.doi.org/10.1007/s00500-022-07177-7]

[32]   A.M. Reza, "Realization of the Contrast Limited Adaptive Histogram Equalization (CLAHE) for real-time image enhancement", *J. VLSI Signal Process.,* vol. 38, no. 1, pp. 35-44, 2004.

[http://dx.doi.org/10.1023/B:VLSI.0000028532.53893.82]

[33] C. Shorten, and T.M. Khoshgoftaar, "A survey on image data augmentation for deep learning", *J. Big Data,* vol. 6, no. 1, p. 60, 2019.
[http://dx.doi.org/10.1186/s40537-019-0197-0]

[34] G. Huang, Z. Liu, L. Van Der Maaten, and K. Q. Weinberger, "Densely connected convolutional networks," in Proc. IEEE Conf. Comput. Vis. Pattern Recognit., pp. 4700–4708, 2017.
[http://dx.doi.org/10.1109/CVPR.2017.243]

[35] A. G. Howard, M. Zhu, B. Chen, D. Kalenichenko, W. Wang, T. Weyand, M. Andreetto, and H. Adam, "Mobilenets: Efficient convolutional neural networks for mobile vision applications," arXiv preprint arXiv:1704.04861, 2017.

[36] M. Tan, and Q. Le, "Efficientnet: Rethinking model scaling for convolutional neural networks", *Proc. Int. Conf. Mach. Learn.,* pp. 6105-6114, 2019.

[37] S.A. Hicks, I. Strümke, V. Thambawita, M. Hammou, M.A. Riegler, P. Halvorsen, and S. Parasa, "On evaluation metrics for medical applications of artificial intelligence", *Sci. Rep.,* vol. 12, no. 1, p. 5979, 2022.
[http://dx.doi.org/10.1038/s41598-022-09954-8] [PMID: 35395867]

CHAPTER 4

Nanotechnology in Agriculture: A New Frontier

Neeraj Dhariwal[1], **Meenu Chahar**[2], **Preety Yadav**[1], **Akanksha**[1] and **Vinod Kumar**[1,*]

[1] *Materials Analysis & Research Laboratory, Department of Physics, NSUT, Dwarka Sec-3, New Delhi-110078, India*

[2] *Department of Physics, Chaudhary Ranbir Singh University, Jind, Haryana-126102, India*

Abstract: The integration of nanotechnology in smart agriculture presents a transformative approach to addressing global food security challenges and sustainable farming practices. Nanotechnology offers innovative solutions, including nanosensors, nanofertilizers, and nanopesticides, that enhance crop yield, reduce resource consumption, and minimize environmental impact. Nanosensors enable precise monitoring of soil conditions, crop health, and environmental factors, facilitating data-driven decisions that optimize agricultural inputs. Nanofertilizers and nanopesticides ensure targeted delivery of nutrients and crop protection agents, reducing waste and preventing pollution. Additionally, nanomaterials in smart agricultural systems can improve water management, enhance the efficiency of photosynthesis, and promote sustainable farming practices. Thus, this chapter examines the current advancements and potential future applications of nanotechnology in agriculture, highlighting its role in advancing precision agriculture, enhancing food security, and promoting sustainable agricultural practices.

Keywords: Nanotechnology, Nanoparticles, Sensors, Smart agriculture.

INTRODUCTION

Recent advances in microtechnology and Micro-electro-mechanical Systems (MEMS) have necessitated the elucidation of flow and transport processes in small dimensions. This is also the case with several other industrial applications, which rely on low-pressure conditions.

Sustainable agricultural techniques are essential to meet global food demand without compromising the environment and human health. Growing crop diseases, pest problems, and the use of pesticides have aggravated the decline in crop production, and land degradation in agriculture has become a huge global

* **Corresponding author Vinod Kumar:** Materials Analysis & Research Laboratory, Department of Physics, NSUT, Dwarka Sec-3, New-Delhi-110078, India; E-mail: vinod@nsut.ac.in

Shefali Arora Chouhanm Nagendra Pratap Singh, Banalaxmi Brahma & Shashank Gupta (Eds.)

challenge [1]. Annual losses in crop production, such as potatoes, corn, peanuts, and soybeans, due to pathogen contamination are estimated to be 10–25% [2]. Nowadays, nano-based systems are proving beneficial for enhancing crop yield and providing more nutritional value while minimizing inputs. Nanotechnology is an interdisciplinary field that studies materials at the nanoscale, allowing for the development of nanomaterials with innovative physical, chemical, and mechanical characteristics by transforming bulk materials [3]. This emerging technology has the potential to address several limitations found in conventional products, including cost, functionality, fabrication methods, and overall performance. Consequently, it presents vast opportunities across various sectors, including food processing, medicine, materials science, agriculture, pharmaceuticals, energy technologies, and electronic devices [4, 5].

Nanoparticles enhance the capabilities of bio-based nanosensors, nanopesticides, and nanofertilizers by providing larger reaction sites, elevating adsorption capacity, and increasing the surface-to-volume ratio [6]. Nano-biosensors or nano-based delivery systems have the potential to impact production without using toxic chemicals. With nanotechnology, it is easier to reduce the bulk volume of chemical fertilizers while improving agricultural growth [7, 8]. While these technological advancements have been crucial for human development, their rapid adoption has brought crop production close to its maximum potential.

Nanoparticle (NP) fertilization and pesticides are crucial techniques used to reduce soil pollution caused by the overuse of chemical-based fertilizers [9]. This approach enables the controlled release of key nutrients while minimizing both biotic and abiotic stresses on plants. The Indian government's launch of nano-sized urea and sulfur-coated urea (Urea Gold) has improved urea release, enhancing nitrogen absorption by 40%. Urea Gold also increases soil sulfur content, which improves plant growth, seed yield (especially in oilseeds), and overall quality. Nanofertilizers offer a promising route toward more sustainable and efficient agriculture [10].

The role of Nanoparticles (NPs) in seed germination is currently under investigation. Since nutrients are essential for plant growth, nanomaterials can enhance seed germination [11]. NPs can also reduce bacterial effects in fields, helping to prevent biotic stress in plants. Several application methods have been discussed in the literature, including seed priming and foliar spraying [12]. Most applications of nanomaterials focus on improving efficiency and productivity in agriculture, aiming to reduce reliance on chemical plant protection additives while enhancing overall crop yield.

Smart agriculture is a farming approach that leverages modern technologies to improve both the quantity and quality of agricultural produce while minimizing environmental degradation [13]. Technologies such as remote sensing, satellite systems, effective yet safe pesticides, and advanced biosensors for soil health monitoring should be utilized. This review focuses on recent advancements and future prospects of nanoparticles, nanofertilizers, nanopesticides, and nanosensors in the field of agriculture.

NANOTECHNOLOGY AND SMART AGRICULTURE

To meet increasing agricultural demands, the advancement and application of innovative techniques are essential. Nanotechnology, a rapidly expanding field, is being integrated into various sectors, including agriculture, to enable precision farming [14]. Applications include the development of nanoparticles, nano/biosensors, nanopesticides, nanofertilizers, and the genetic modification of crops and livestock (see Fig. **1**).

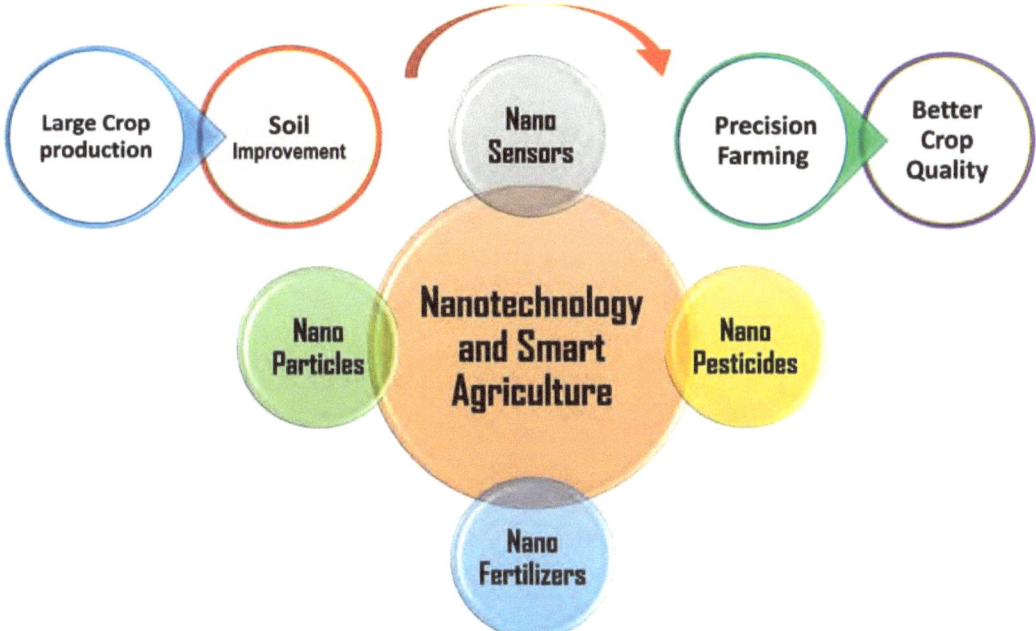

Fig. (1).   Smart agriculture applications including nanoparticles, nanosensors, nanopesticides, and nanofertilizers.

Nanomaterials play diverse roles, including improving farm management, enhancing plant nutrition, and protecting against pests and diseases. The concentration of nanoparticles can significantly influence plant germination and growth [15]. Nanoparticles used in agriculture can be categorized into three main types: organic, inorganic, and carbon-based, with biologically synthesized nanomaterials emerging as a sustainable alternative [16]. Examples and uses of these nanoparticles in precision agriculture are outlined below:

Zinc Oxide Nanoparticles

Zinc is a crucial micronutrient, and its deficiency can negatively impact agricultural productivity, particularly in alkaline soils where its availability and solubility are limited by high pH levels [17]. Common zinc fertilizers include zinc oxide and zinc sulfate, but their effectiveness is often hindered in such soils. The application of zinc oxide nanoparticles, which are smaller than 100 nm and possess a high surface-to-volume ratio, can enhance the solubility and availability of zinc [18]. These nanoparticles can be biosynthesized using plant leaf extracts combined with zinc acetate or zinc sulfate in solvents like water, ethanol, or methanol. Additionally, zinc nanoparticles have been shown to induce oxidative stress in wheat, leading to increased malondialdehyde and decreased levels of glutathione and chlorophyll [19, 20].

Silver Nanoparticles

Silver nanoparticles can be synthesized from various sources, including fungi, bacteria, and plants, and are effective against harmful microorganisms affecting plants [21]. Their antibacterial efficacy surpasses that of bulk silver due to their increased surface area. Recently, the production of silver nanoparticles by white radish has been reported, yielding particles with diameters ranging from 6 to 38 nm. In experiments, 20 nm silver nanoparticles enhanced fenugreek seed performance, achieving a germination rate of 76.11%, root lengths of 76.94 mm, and improved fresh and dry weights at a concentration of 10 g/mL [22].

Silica Nanoparticles

Silica nanoparticles are synthesized using surfactants, such as cetyltrimethyl-ammonium bromide, as templates alongside silica precursors, including tetraethyl orthosilicate or sodium metasilicate (Na_2SiO_3) [23]. These nanoparticles can serve as delivery agents for proteins, nucleotides, and other chemicals in plants. Additionally, the combination of nano zeolite and nanosensors, incorporating silica nanoparticles, can enhance soil water retention and facilitate soil monitoring. A novel nano-silica fungicide has been developed to combat late blight by inducing intracellular oxidative damage in Phytophthora Infestans, resulting in a 98.02% inhibition [24].

Titanium Dioxide

Titanium dioxide is commonly used in pigment production and as an effective photocatalyst, capable of degrading pesticides through a process known as photocatalysis. In a study, spherical titanium dioxide nanoparticles, averaging 32.58 nm in diameter, were synthesized using an aqueous leaf extract of *Psidium guajava* [25]. These nanoparticles demonstrated enhanced antibacterial properties compared to tetracycline, reducing the risk of bacterial resistance [26]. Additionally, leaf extract from *Ecliptaprostrata* was used to create polydisperse titanium dioxide nanoparticles with diameters ranging from 36 to 68 nm, which showed significant bioactivity against *R. solanacearum* at concentrations of 0.01–0.1 mg/mL. As the concentration of TiO_2 nanoparticles increased, so did the damage to bacterial membranes [27, 28].

NANO SENSORS

A nanosensor is a device created at the nanoscale, designed to provide atomic-level data that can be easily analyzed.

Key advantages of nanosensors include their compact size, which leads to lower power requirements, as well as superior sensitivity and specificity compared to conventional sensors [29, 30]. Due to the growing interest in nanotechnology, nanosensors have found widespread use in numerous applications, as shown in Fig. (**2**). Nanosensors provide crucial information about optimal agricultural practices, such as when to water plants, apply pesticides, or harvest, based on soil and climate conditions [31]. They enable early detection of plant diseases before visible symptoms appear, maintaining crop health. Moreover, nano sensors target treatment to specific areas rather than the entire plant, minimizing the use of pesticides and reducing residue, keeping plants healthier. Nano biosensors, a type of nano sensor, feature immobilized bioreceptors that selectively detect target analytes for precise monitoring.

The fundamental workflow involves the specific interaction of a nano sensor with both the analyte and bio-elements, which leads to the transduction and conversion of signals into useful outputs (see Fig. **3**). The behavior of nano sensors varies depending on the type of nanoparticles used; for instance, semiconductor quantum dots operate based on fluorescence measurements, while Carbon Nanotube (CNT) nano sensors function similarly to field-effect transistors due to their heightened sensitivity to electrical changes. This approach differs significantly from traditional methods, such as chromatography and spectroscopy [32, 33]. In contrast, bio-nano sensors can assist in preserving genetic purity by detecting pollen contamination and distinguishing genetically modified crops from non-modified ones. When deployed in agricultural fields, these nano-sensors enable precision farming by providing crucial data, thereby conserving resources and enhancing crop yields.

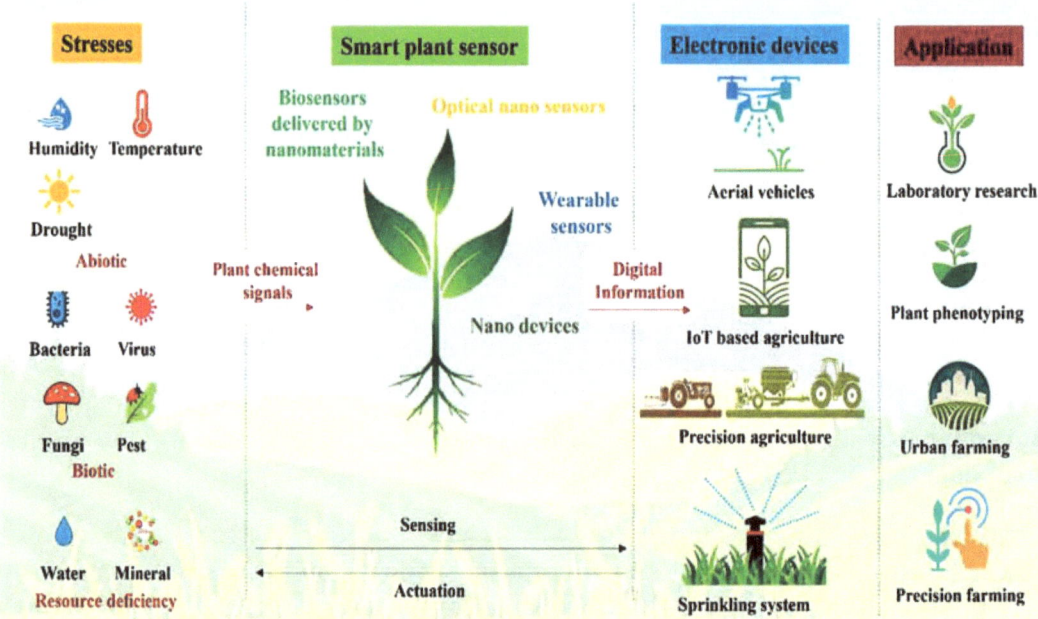

Fig. (2). Schematic illustration of a nanosensor application to tackle plant stress.

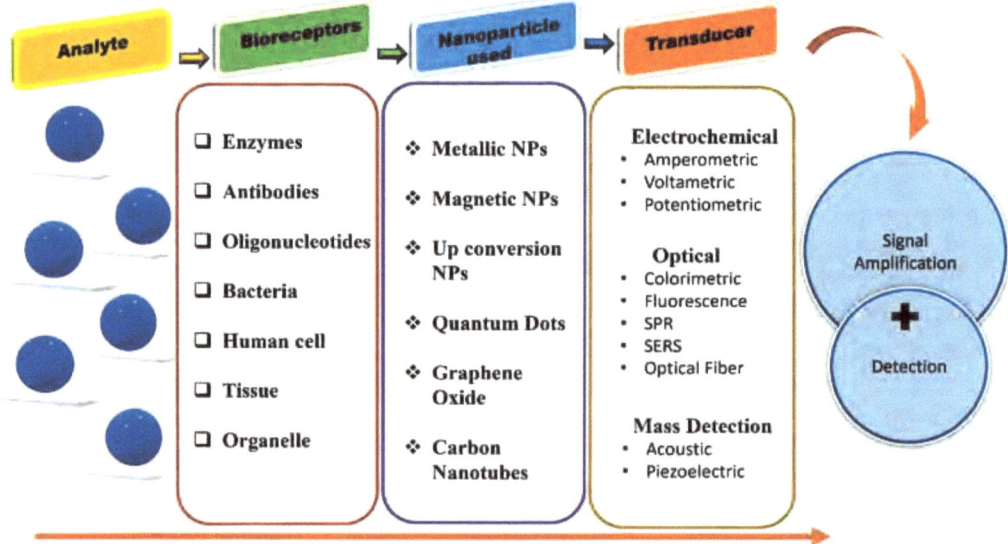

Fig. (3). Essential components and basic workflow of nanosensors.

Electrochemical Sensor

Electrochemical sensors are widely utilized due to their reliance on electrochemical principles. They generate electrochemical signals based on the electrons consumed or produced during interactions with biological elements [34]. These nano sensors function through chemical reactions involving nanostructured materials and target analytes, resulting in measurable changes in voltage, current, or impedance. Their high sensitivity, compatibility with miniaturization technologies, low power needs, durability, affordability, rapid response, and ease of use make them ideal for sensing applications. Electrochemical nano sensors can be categorized into amperometry, voltammetry, and potentiometry based on their operational principles.

Amperometric sensors are a type of electrochemical sensor that continuously monitor the current generated by the redox reactions of electroactive species. By maintaining a fixed potential, the Faradaic current is measured to ascertain the concentration of these species. The peak current observed correlates directly with the concentration of electroactive analytes. Initially applied in healthcare for developing ATP sensors and pregnancy tests, advances in nanofabrication have made amperometric biosensors more reliable and cost-effective, broadening their use in environmental monitoring, food safety, and agriculture, and examples include detecting organophosphates and hydrogen peroxide [35].

Voltammetry involves measuring current by systematically varying the potential applied to an electrochemical cell. Cyclic voltammetry, a specific technique within this method, is used to determine redox potentials and reaction kinetics by measuring the current between a working electrode and a counter electrode as the voltage from a reference electrode changes. This technique has applications in agriculture and food safety, such as detecting carbosulfan in rice, identifying *Salmonella typhi*, and monitoring heavy metal contamination in food samples [36].

Potentiometric sensors, on the other hand, measure the electric potential on the working electrode relative to a reference electrode. The output signal results from ion accumulation at ion-selective electrodes, enabling the detection of ions such as Na^+, K^+, and Ca^{2+} in complex biological matrices. Electrochemical nanosensors have significant implications for identifying various analytes, including preservatives, antibiotics, pesticides, and heavy metals, in food and agricultural contexts [37 - 43].

Optical Sensor

Optical biosensors detect changes in optical signals, making them highly compatible with other spectroscopic techniques, including fluorescence, absorption, phosphorescence, and Raman spectroscopy. These biosensors utilize changes in light properties such as wavelength, phase, intensity, and polarization. Luminescence involves fluorescence and phosphorescence, where excited electrons emit photons upon returning to their ground state [44, 45]. Fluorescence-based nano sensors offer high sensitivity and rapid response times, with applications in detecting nitrite, reactive oxygen species, and pathogenic bacteria. Quantum dots, which are nanoclusters with unique fluorescence properties, enhance bioimaging, biomolecular assays, and other applications through their size-dependent emission wavelengths. Surface Plasmon Resonance (SPR) is a sensitive optical sensing technique that detects changes in the refractive index near a metal-dielectric interface, where free electron oscillations occur. These oscillations create an evanescent field, making it highly responsive to even minor index fluctuations. Various nanomaterials, such as metallic and carbon-based nanoparticles, enhance SPR for detecting analytes like concanavalin A and pathogens [46]. Similarly, Surface-enhanced Raman Scattering (SERS) amplifies signals through interactions with metallic nanoparticles, significantly increasing detection sensitivity at "hot spots" where analyte molecules accumulate [47 - 49].

E-NOSE AND E-TONGUE

Electronic noses and tongues mimic human senses of smell and taste, making them valuable for quality assessment in food, agriculture, and related industries. An electronic nose consists of a sampling system, a data acquisition system, a sensor array, and pattern recognition software, utilizing sensors, such as metal oxides, conductive polymers, and quartz crystals. Data are processed by algorithms such as PCA or ANN. Electronic tongues work similarly, but they analyze liquid samples to assess qualities such as bitterness and saltiness. Both devices are highly sensitive and suitable for evaluating food quality and storage conditions [50, 51].

NANO FERTILIZERS

Nanofertilizers offer various benefits for sustainable agriculture, particularly by reducing nutrient values in soil compared to traditional fertilizers as described in Fig. (**4**). This reduction leads to decreased reliance on inorganic fertilizers, ultimately improving farming efficiency [52]. Gradual-release fertilizers are commonly used in traditional agriculture due to concerns about nutrient depletion and water drainage, which can cause environmental issues like eutrophication in nearby water systems. Nanofertilizers address these challenges effectively with their controlled release properties, making a significant contribution to sustainable agricultural practices [53 - 58].

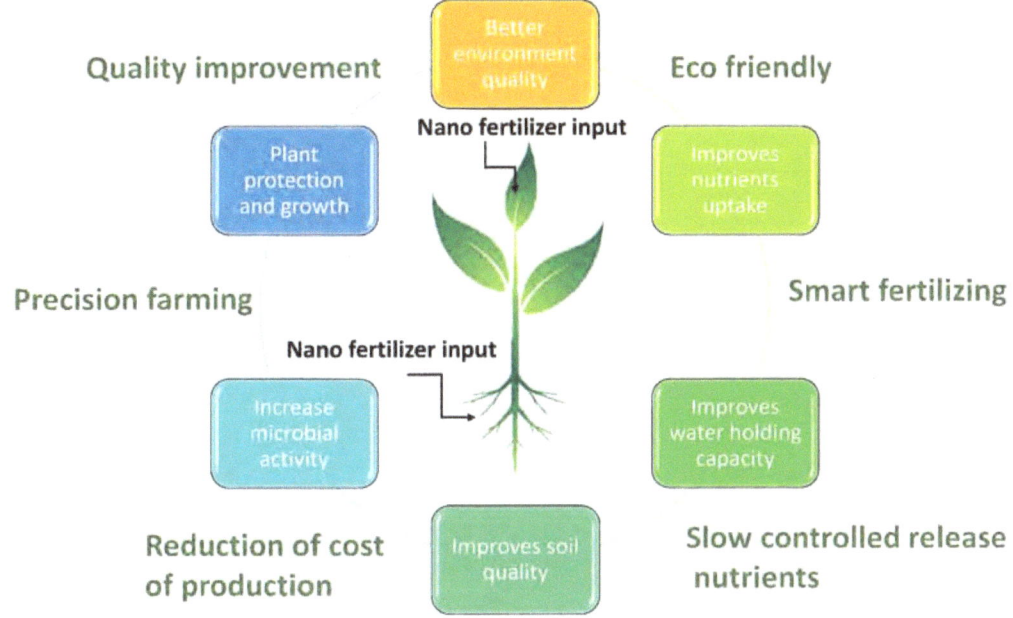

Fig. (4). Benefits of nanofertilizer in plant growth and a sustainable future.

Compared to traditional fertilizers, nanofertilizers are generally less harmful to the environment and human health, while also exhibiting a greater ability to retain water, which helps mitigate soil erosion. They are cost-effective, increase profitability, and improve crop quality, yield, and soil nutrient richness, leading to healthier crops. Carmona *et al.* [59] highlighted that post-synthesis modifications of amorphous calcium phosphate nanofertilizers, rather than synthesizing them in a single step, have significantly reduced manufacturing costs. This innovative method is now being implemented for large-scale nanofertilizer production.

In contrast, chemical-based fertilizers, which are synthetic and derived from non-organic agricultural components, are often applied in large quantities to boost crop yields. They tend to act more quickly than organic fertilizers due to their lower cost and their availability in easily soluble granular or liquid forms. However, phosphorus fertilizers can be challenging to dissolve in water due to the presence of insoluble compounds, such as diammonium phosphate, triple superphosphate, and monoammonium phosphate [60, 61].

Mineral nutrients are essential for plant growth and metabolism, and nanofertilizers are used to optimize nutrient delivery. These are categorized into two types (see Fig. **5**):

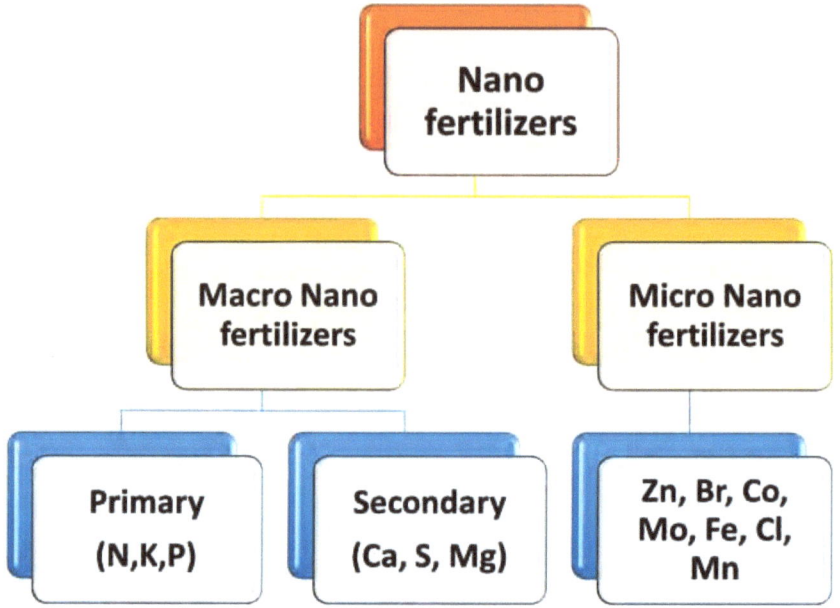

Fig. (5). Divisions of nano-fertilizers into their subgroups.

- Macro nanofertilizers
- Micro nanofertilizers

Macro Nanofertilizers

Nanomaterials are being integrated with essential macronutrients, including nitrogen (N), potassium (K), phosphorus (P), calcium (Ca), magnesium (Mg), and sulfur (S), to create nanofertilizers that ensure precise nutrient delivery to crops. These fertilizers encapsulate one or more macronutrients within nanomaterials, enhancing nutrient efficiency. As the purchase of NPK fertilizers for crops is expected to rise, ongoing research is crucial for developing eco-friendly alternatives with higher nutrient efficiency to replace conventional fertilizers [62].

Micronutrient Nanofertilizers

Micronutrient nanofertilizers are crucial for delivering small amounts of essential elements, such as zinc (Zn), boron (B), iron (Fe), and manganese (Mn), to plants, which are vital for key metabolic functions. Zinc is vital for plant defense, growth regulation, and protein metabolism, while boron aids cell wall synthesis. Studies show that using zinc (Zn) and boron (B) nanofertilizers significantly boosts fruit yields in crops, such as pomegranate and pearl millet. Zinc oxide nanoparticles (Zn NPs) have also improved yields in crops, such as sunflower, rice, and wheat. Stabilized maghemite NPs promote growth in *Brassica napus*. Iron and manganese are vital for photosynthesis, with manganese acting as a cofactor for various enzymes. Studies using Zn, Cu, Mn, and iron oxide nanoparticles at low concentrations have shown enhanced seed germination and seedling growth in lettuce [63].

Nanofertilizers have the potential to significantly boost agricultural yields while reducing costs and environmental emissions. Their enhanced solubility and reactivity allow for deeper penetration through plant cuticles, enabling more targeted nutrient delivery [64, 65]. This can lead to improved crop production, quality, and nutritional value, while also mitigating abiotic stress and the toxicity of heavy metal ions. Consequently, the integration of nanotechnology in agriculture presents promising opportunities for advancing agronomy and environmental risk assessment, thereby promoting sustainable development in the agricultural sector [66 - 68].

Nano Pesticides

Worldwide research efforts have focused on reducing pesticide use by approximately 42% without compromising productivity and profitability on the majority of arable farms, as observed in about 59% of 946 non-organic commercial farms analyzed [69]. In various agricultural settings, it is advisable to adopt a controlled approach to the application of pesticides and fertilizers using eco-friendly methods. This approach maximizes effectiveness, minimizes the use of Active Ingredients (AIs), and ensures precise, targeted application [70].

Advanced technologies, such as nanotechnology, which deals with materials at the nanoscale, offer promising solutions by introducing unique physicochemical properties. Nanotechnology has the potential to transform agriculture by optimizing crop nutrient levels, monitoring water quality, enhancing seed treatments, controlling pests, facilitating the efficient delivery of pesticides and fertilizers, detecting harmful agrochemicals, and reducing the toxic effects of crop protection products, as demonstrated in Fig. (**6**).

Additionally, nanotechnology offers numerous applications in the agri-food sector, including food packaging, animal husbandry (such as the removal of toxicants and the use of nanomedicine), and environmental solutions like water purification and pollutant remediation.

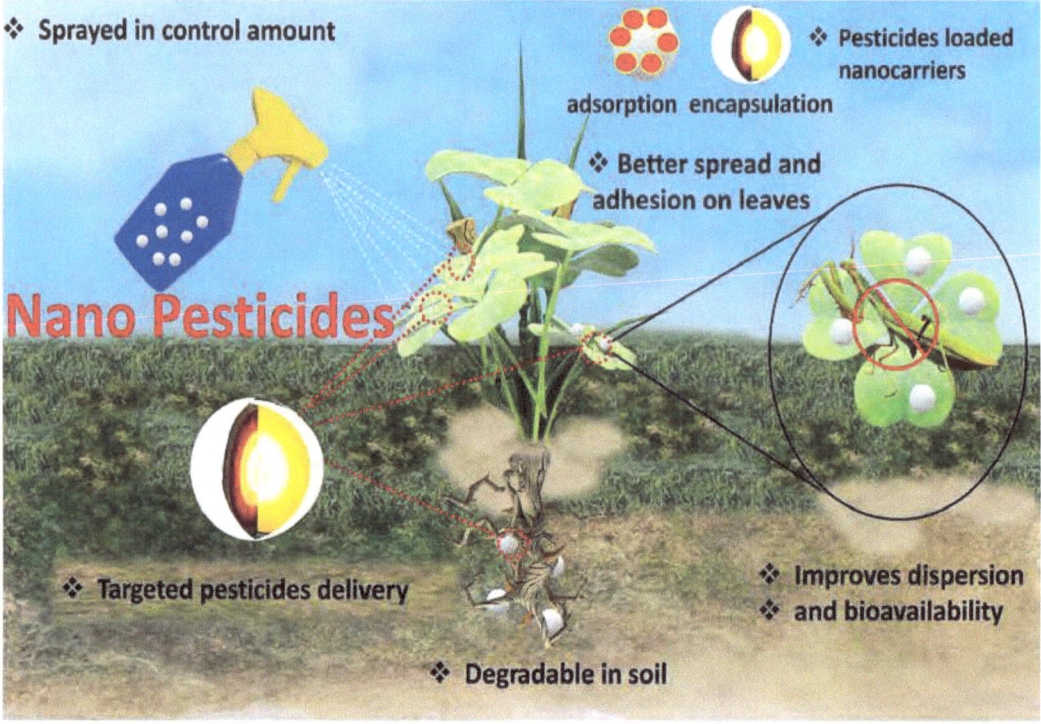

Fig. (6). Nanoparticles attached with the pesticides.

Research is underway to develop nano-sized Active Ingredients (AIs) for pesticides that offer high effectiveness at lower volumes while also enhancing crop yields. Nano-formulations of pesticides, or nanopesticides, are expected to provide several advantages, including improved efficacy and longevity, efficient distribution and adhesion, environmental biodegradability, low toxicity, and photogenerated properties, all while reducing the required concentration of active ingredients [71]. These features enable effective protection of crops against pests and diseases. Rapid advancements in nanopesticide research have led to the development of formulations that are both environmentally friendly and target-specific, without compromising performance [72, 73].

Nanomaterials as Active Ingredients

In addition to their role as nanocarriers, nanomaterials are being explored as Active Ingredients (AIs) for crop protection, although this research is still in its early stages. Nanoparticles demonstrate a broad spectrum of antifungal and antibacterial properties, supporting their potential use as pesticides. For instance, silver nanoparticles exhibit antimicrobial activity against pathogens and are nontoxic [74], while zinc nanoparticles are effective in combating plant fungal pathogens [75, 76], offering promising solutions for environmental challenges, including pollution control and crop disease management. Nanomaterials can address some limitations of conventional Active Ingredients (AIs), such as microbial resistance development over time [77, 78]. Among inorganic nanomaterials, copper nanoparticles have been widely studied for agricultural use. They function as insecticides—providing resistance in Bt cotton [79]—as well as fungicides effective against pathogens such as *Drechslera oryzae* [80], *Alternaria alternata*, and *Curvularia lunata* in paddy seeds. They also serve as herbicides [81] and powerful disinfectants in animal husbandry. Their versatility makes them valuable for enhancing agricultural practices while reducing environmental risks. Kanhedet *et al.* [82] highlighted the antifungal activity of copper Nanoparticles (NPs) against fungi like *Curvularia lunata*, *Phoma destructiva*, and *Alternaria alternata*. These enhanced effects are largely attributed to the high surface area-to-volume ratio of the nanoparticles.

However, concerns regarding copper accumulation in soil have led to efforts aimed at reducing its usage or improving its bioavailability. As an alternative, zinc oxide (ZnO) nanomaterials have been explored for pest control, particularly due to their strong antibacterial action against *Xanthomonas citri*, without inducing phototoxic effects [83, 84]. ZnO nano-formulations have also shown promising results in field trials.

Nanoparticles as Biopesticides

Target-specific nanosized pesticides are designed to minimize harm to non-target plants and reduce environmental release. From an environmental protection standpoint, using low-toxicity and eco-friendly compounds for crop protection—particularly biopesticides—is highly advantageous. These alternatives are generally more effective than synthetic, non-organic pesticides in reducing negative impacts on biodiversity, living organisms, and human health. Biopesticides can be broadly classified into two categories: (i) plant-derived biopesticides [85], and (ii) biocontrol organisms [86, 87]. Nano-formulations derived from plants have shown significant effectiveness against insects, although they tend to be less effective against fungi [88].

Microbial-based formulations are gaining popularity for addressing fungal and insect-related issues. Approved biopesticides by the U.S. Environmental Protection Agency (EPA) include herbicides such as thaxtomin A (from Streptomyces species), fungicides like glycerol monocaprate (derived from fats), and insecticides such as citronellol (from plant oils) and 4-allylanisole (from basil oil) [89]. Huang *et al.* [90] reported the effectiveness of rhizosphere bacteria against *Phytophthora nicotianae, Meloidogyne incognita*, and root-knot black shank in tobacco, demonstrating target specificity, low non-target toxicity, and minimal environmental impact.

However, the use of multiple biocontrol agents can be complex, especially when managing disease complexes, due to challenges related to production costs and ease of application. Furthermore, various environmental factors, such as soil quality and climatic conditions, can affect the stability of bio-based pesticides, potentially leading to premature degradation. As a result, substantial research has focused on developing nanocarriers to ensure the controlled and targeted delivery of biopesticides [91].

Nanoparticles as Fungicides

Fungal diseases pose significant challenges for farmers, leading to substantial crop losses. Although numerous chemical fungicides are available, many of them have detrimental effects on food crops [92]. Silver nanoparticles have demonstrated superior antifungal properties at minimal concentrations compared to ZnO and TiO_2 nanoparticles. In studies involving nano-silica (20–40 nm), maize treated with these particles showed increased resistance to phytopathogens, with higher levels of phenolic compounds and reduced activity of stress-responsive enzymes. Therefore, silica nanoparticles can serve as effective antifungal agents against these pathogens [93].

Additionally, utilizing nanomaterials as Active Ingredients (AIs) in biopesticides and nanofungicides can lead to highly effective management techniques that outperform traditional chemical-based pesticides in various aspects, such as improved water solubility, prevention of premature degradation, and reduced development of plant resistance. The implementation of new pesticidal nano-formulations should follow a circular approach that includes pest identification, development of targeted nano-formulations, and monitoring of any potential collateral effects.

These nano-formulations represent innovative and efficient pest control solutions aimed at addressing urgent issues such as environmental pollution and unsustainable land use practices. Nanotechnology offers a promising path to revolutionize crop production by enhancing nutrient efficiency, boosting resistance to diseases, and increasing overall crop yields.

CONCLUDING REMARKS

In this chapter, we have summarized the potential use of nanotechnology leading to smart agriculture with the efficient and sustainable utilization of nanoparticles.

Nanotechnology-based applications, including nano fertilizers, nano pesticides, and nano sensors, present efficient solutions for emerging agricultural and environmental challenges, primarily related to increasing crop production, food demand, and sustainability. Innovation based on nanotechnology helps to provide better agricultural productivity and also addresses immense issues like the energy crisis, land degradation, and lack of water resources. The present developments in nanotechnology have boosted crop growth and production. Nanoparticles used in agriculture can act as carriers for macro and micronutrients by improving soil quality.

According to collected reports, NP-based nano pesticides and fertilizers help in targeted delivery with much less harmful effect on non-target plants, as they are highly reactive, easily soluble, and can penetrate the cuticle more deeply. Meanwhile, nanosensors can help determine the nutrient, moisture, and physiological status of crops. In addition, nanosensors can also detect environmental factors, such as humidity, temperature, and soil quality, ensuring better crop yield without land deterioration. While much of the research on nanotechnology has been conducted in laboratory settings, there is a need to emphasize its application under field conditions with various environmental factors. To achieve this, increased collaboration among plant biologists, data scientists, and global regulatory authorities is crucial. Their critical evaluation will help ensure the sustainable use of nanotechnology in future agricultural practices.

REFERENCES

[1]   M. Tudi, H. Daniel Ruan, L. Wang, J. Lyu, R. Sadler, D. Connell, C. Chu, and D.T. Phung, "Agriculture development, pesticide application and its impact on the environment", *Int. J. Environ. Res. Public Health,* vol. 18, no. 3, p. 1112, 2021.
[http://dx.doi.org/10.3390/ijerph18031112] [PMID: 33513796]

[2]   S. Savary, L. Willocquet, S.J. Pethybridge, P. Esker, N. McRoberts, and A. Nelson, "The global burden of pathogens and pests on major food crops", *Nat. Ecol. Evol.,* vol. 3, no. 3, pp. 430-439, 2019.
[http://dx.doi.org/10.1038/s41559-018-0793-y] [PMID: 30718852]

[3]   C. Parisi, M. Vigani, and E. Rodríguez-Cerezo, "Agricultural nanotechnologies: What are the current possibilities?", *Nano Today,* vol. 10, no. 2, pp. 124-127, 2015.
[http://dx.doi.org/10.1016/j.nantod.2014.09.009]

[4]   H. Zhang, G.S. Demirer, H. Zhang, T. Ye, N.S. Goh, A.J. Aditham, F.J. Cunningham, C. Fan, and M.P. Landry, "DNA nanostructures coordinate gene silencing in mature plants", *Proc. Natl. Acad. Sci. USA,* vol. 116, no. 15, pp. 7543-7548, 2019.
[http://dx.doi.org/10.1073/pnas.1818290116] [PMID: 30910954]

[5]   A. Hassoun, S. Jagtap, H. Trollman, G. Garcia-Garcia, N.A. Abdullah, G. Goksen, F. Bader, F. Ozogul, F.J. Barba, J. Cropotova, P.E.S. Munekata, and J.M. Lorenzo, "Food processing 4.0: Current and future developments spurred by the fourth industrial revolution", *Food Control,* vol. 145, p. 109507, 2023.
[http://dx.doi.org/10.1016/j.foodcont.2022.109507]

[6]   D. Kumar, and P. Kalita, "Reducing postharvest losses during storage of grain crops to strengthen food security in developing countries", *Foods,* vol. 6, no. 1, p. 8, 2017.

[http://dx.doi.org/10.3390/foods6010008] [PMID: 28231087]

[7]   A.A. Keller, H. Wang, D. Zhou, H.S. Lenihan, G. Cherr, B.J. Cardinale, R. Miller, and Z. Ji, "Stability and aggregation of metal oxide nanoparticles in natural aqueous matrices", *Environ. Sci. Technol.,* vol. 44, no. 6, pp. 1962-1967, 2010.
        [http://dx.doi.org/10.1021/es902987d] [PMID: 20151631]

[8]   A. Ahangari, P. Mahmoodi, and A. Mohammadzadeh, "Advanced nano biosensors for rapid detection of zoonotic bacteria", *Biotechnol. Bioeng.,* vol. 120, no. 1, pp. 41-56, 2023.
        [http://dx.doi.org/10.1002/bit.28266] [PMID: 36253878]

[9]   M. Faizan, A. Singh, A. Eren, H. Sultan, M. Sharma, I. Djalovic, and G. Trivan, "Small molecule, big impacts: Nano-nutrients for sustainable agriculture and food security", *J. Plant Physiol.,* vol. 301, p. 154305, 2024.
        [http://dx.doi.org/10.1016/j.jplph.2024.154305] [PMID: 39002339]

[10]   M. Faizan, F. Karabulut, I. Khan, M.S. Akhtar, and P. Alam, "Emergence of nanotechnology in efficient fertilizer management in soil", *S. Afr. J. Bot.,* vol. 164, pp. 242-249, 2024.
        [http://dx.doi.org/10.1016/j.sajb.2023.12.004]

[11]   A. Yadav, K. Yadav, and K. Abd-Elsalam, "Nanofertilizers: Types, delivery and advantages in agricultural sustainability", *Agrochemicals,* vol. 2, no. 2, pp. 296-336, 2023.
        [http://dx.doi.org/10.3390/agrochemicals2020019]

[12]   S.M. El-Bialy, M.E. El-Mahrouk, T. Elesawy, A.E.D. Omara, F. Elbehiry, H. El-Ramady, B. Áron, J. Prokisch, E.C. Brevik, and S.Ø. Solberg, "Biological nanofertilizers to enhance growth potential of strawberry seedlings by boosting photosynthetic pigments, plant enzymatic antioxidants, and nutritional status", *Plants,* vol. 12, no. 2, p. 302, 2023.
        [http://dx.doi.org/10.3390/plants12020302] [PMID: 36679014]

[13]   R.G. Moulick, S. Das, N. Debnath, and K. Bandyopadhyay, "Potential use of nanotechnology in sustainable and 'smart' agriculture: Advancements made in the last decade", *Plant Biotechnol. Rep.,* vol. 14, no. 5, pp. 505-513, 2020.
        [http://dx.doi.org/10.1007/s11816-020-00636-3]

[14]   D. Singh, and B.R. Gurjar, "Nanotechnology for agricultural applications: Facts, issues, knowledge gaps, and challenges in environmental risk assessment", *J. Environ. Manage.,* vol. 322, p. 116033, 2022.
        [http://dx.doi.org/10.1016/j.jenvman.2022.116033]

[15]   M. Sajid, and J. Płotka-Wasylka, "Nanoparticles: Synthesis, characteristics, and applications in analytical and other sciences", *Microchem. J.,* vol. 154, p. 104623, 2020.
        [http://dx.doi.org/10.1016/j.microc.2020.104623]

[16]   B. Pooja, S.D. Joginder, and K.G. Suresh, "Biogenesis of nanoparticles: A review", *Afr. J. Biotechnol.,* vol. 13, no. 28, pp. 2778-2785, 2014.
        [http://dx.doi.org/10.5897/AJB2013.13458]

[17]   P.N. Takkar, and C.D. Walker, "The distribution and correction of zinc deficiency", In: *Zinc in Soils and Plants.* Springer Netherlands: Dordrecht, 1993, pp. 151-165.
        [http://dx.doi.org/10.1007/978-94-011-0878-2_11]

[18]   J.J. Mortvedt, "Crop response to level of water-soluble zinc in granular zinc fertilizers", *Fert. Res.,* vol. 33, no. 3, pp. 249-255, 1992.
        [http://dx.doi.org/10.1007/BF01050880]

[19]   Y. Xie, Y. He, P.L. Irwin, T. Jin, and X. Shi, "Antibacterial activity and mechanism of action of zinc oxide nanoparticles against *Campylobacter jejuni*", *Appl. Environ. Microbiol.,* vol. 77, no. 7, pp. 2325-2331, 2011.
        [http://dx.doi.org/10.1128/AEM.02149-10] [PMID: 21296935]

[20]   J.S. Duhan, R. Kumar, N. Kumar, P. Kaur, K. Nehra, and S. Duhan, "Nanotechnology: The new

perspective in precision agriculture", *Biotechnol. Rep. (Amst.),* vol. 15, pp. 11-23, 2017.
[http://dx.doi.org/10.1016/j.btre.2017.03.002] [PMID: 28603692]

[21]   K.H. Cho, J.E. Park, T. Osaka, and S.G. Park, "The study of antimicrobial activity and preservative effects of nanosilver ingredient", *Electrochim. Acta,* vol. 51, no. 5, pp. 956-960, 2005.
[http://dx.doi.org/10.1016/j.electacta.2005.04.071]

[22]   S.M. Ali, N.M.H. Yousef, and N.A. Nafady, "Application of biosynthesized silver nanoparticles for the control of land snail *Eobania vermiculata* and some plant pathogenic fungi", *J. Nanomater.,* vol. 2015, no. 1, p. 218904, 2015.
[http://dx.doi.org/10.1155/2015/218904]

[23]   A. Rastogi et al., "Application of silicon nanoparticles in agriculture," 3 Biotech, vol. 9, no. 3, p. 90, Mar. 2019.
[http://dx.doi.org/10.1007/s13205-019-1626-7]

[24]   S. Chen, X. Guo, B. Zhang, D. Nie, W. Rao, D. Zhang, J. Lü, X. Guan, Z. Chen, and X. Pan, "Mesoporous silica nanoparticles induce intracellular peroxidation damage of *Phytophthora infestans*: A new type of green fungicide for late blight control", *Environ. Sci. Technol.,* vol. 57, no. 9, pp. 3980-3989, 2023.
[http://dx.doi.org/10.1021/acs.est.2c07182] [PMID: 36808949]

[25]   L. Sang, Y. Zhao, and C. Burda, "TiO$_2$ nanoparticles as functional building blocks", *Chem. Rev.,* vol. 114, no. 19, pp. 9283-9318, 2014.
[http://dx.doi.org/10.1021/cr400629p] [PMID: 25294395]

[26]   M. Pelaez, N.T. Nolan, S.C. Pillai, M.K. Seery, P. Falaras, A.G. Kontos, P.S.M. Dunlop, J.W.J. Hamilton, J.A. Byrne, K. O'Shea, M.H. Entezari, and D.D. Dionysiou, "A review on the visible light active titanium dioxide photocatalysts for environmental applications", *Appl. Catal. B,* vol. 125, pp. 331-349, 2012.
[http://dx.doi.org/10.1016/j.apcatb.2012.05.036]

[27]   T. Santhoshkumar, A.A. Rahuman, C. Jayaseelan, G. Rajakumar, S. Marimuthu, A.V. Kirthi, K. Velayutham, J. Thomas, J. Venkatesan, and S.K. Kim, "Green synthesis of titanium dioxide nanoparticles using *Psidium guajava* extract and its antibacterial and antioxidant properties", *Asian Pac. J. Trop. Med.,* vol. 7, no. 12, pp. 968-976, 2014.
[http://dx.doi.org/10.1016/S1995-7645(14)60171-1] [PMID: 25479626]

[28]   X. Pan, D. Nie, X. Guo, S. Xu, D. Zhang, F. Cao, and X. Guan, "Effective control of the tomato wilt pathogen using TiO$_2$ nanoparticles as a green nanopesticide", *Environ. Sci. Nano,* vol. 10, no. 5, pp. 1441-1452, 2023.
[http://dx.doi.org/10.1039/D3EN00059A]

[29]   M. Tubaishat, and S. Madria, "Sensor networks: An overview", *IEEE Potentials,* vol. 22, no. 2, pp. 20-23, 2003.
[http://dx.doi.org/10.1109/MP.2003.1197877]

[30]   L. Ruiz-Garcia, L. Lunadei, P. Barreiro, and I. Robla, "A review of wireless sensor technologies and applications in agriculture and food industry: State of the art and current trends", *Sensors (Basel),* vol. 9, no. 6, pp. 4728-4750, 2009.
[http://dx.doi.org/10.3390/s90604728] [PMID: 22408551]

[31]   T.C. Lim, and S. Ramakrishna, "A conceptual review of nanosensors", *Z. Naturforsch. A,* vol. 61, no. 7-8, pp. 402-412, 2006.
[http://dx.doi.org/10.1515/zna-2006-7-815]

[32]   D.G. Panpatte, Y.K. Jhala, H.N. Shelat, and R.V. Vyas, "Nanoparticles: The next generation technology for sustainable agriculture", In: *Microbial Inoculants in Sustainable Agricultural Productivity.* Springer India: New Delhi, 2016, pp. 289-300.
[http://dx.doi.org/10.1007/978-81-322-2644-4_18]

[33]   M. Sharon, A. K. Choudhary, and R. Kumar, Madhuri Sharon et al. "Nanotechnology in agricultural

diseases and food safety," Journal of Phytology, vol. 2010, no. 4, pp. 83–92, 2010, [Online]. Available: https://www.researchgate.net/publication/284063192

[34]   A. Chaubey, and B.D. Malhotra, "Mediated biosensors", *Biosens. Bioelectron.,* vol. 17, no. 6-7, pp. 441-456, 2002.
[http://dx.doi.org/10.1016/S0956-5663(01)00313-X] [PMID: 11959464]

[35]   A. Kueng, C. Kranz, and B. Mizaikoff, "Amperometric ATP biosensor based on polymer entrapped enzymes", *Biosens. Bioelectron.,* vol. 19, no. 10, pp. 1301-1307, 2004.
[http://dx.doi.org/10.1016/j.bios.2003.11.023] [PMID: 15046763]

[36]   J. Yan, H. Guan, J. Yu, and D. Chi, "Acetylcholinesterase biosensor based on assembly of multiwall carbon nanotubes onto liposome bioreactors for detection of organophosphates pesticides", *Pestic. Biochem. Physiol.,* vol. 105, no. 3, pp. 197-202, 2013.
[http://dx.doi.org/10.1016/j.pestbp.2013.02.003]

[37]   Y. Xu, J. Ding, H. Chen, Q. Zhao, J. Hou, J. Yan, H. Wang, L. Ding, and N. Ren, "Fast determination of sulfonamides from egg samples using magnetic multiwalled carbon nanotubes as adsorbents followed by liquid chromatography–tandem mass spectrometry", *Food Chem.,* vol. 140, no. 1-2, pp. 83-90, 2013.
[http://dx.doi.org/10.1016/j.foodchem.2013.02.078] [PMID: 23578618]

[38]   K.C. Lin, C.P. Hong, and S.M. Chen, "Simultaneous determination for toxic ractopamine and salbutamol in pork sample using hybrid carbon nanotubes", *Sens. Actuators B Chem.,* vol. 177, pp. 428-436, 2013.
[http://dx.doi.org/10.1016/j.snb.2012.11.052]

[39]   X. Lin, Y. Ni, and S. Kokot, "Glassy carbon electrodes modified with gold nanoparticles for the simultaneous determination of three food antioxidants", *Anal. Chim. Acta,* vol. 765, pp. 54-62, 2013.
[http://dx.doi.org/10.1016/j.aca.2012.12.036] [PMID: 23410626]

[40]   R. Antiochia, G. Vinci, and L. Gorton, "Rapid and direct determination of fructose in food: A new osmium-polymer mediated biosensor", *Food Chem.,* vol. 140, no. 4, pp. 742-747, 2013.
[http://dx.doi.org/10.1016/j.foodchem.2012.11.023] [PMID: 23692761]

[41]   R.Y.A. Hassan, "Advances in electrochemical nano-biosensors for biomedical and environmental applications: From current work to future perspectives", *Sensors (Basel),* vol. 22, no. 19, p. 7539, 2022.
[http://dx.doi.org/10.3390/s22197539] [PMID: 36236638]

[42]   J.P. Giraldo, M.P. Landry, S.M. Faltermeier, T.P. McNicholas, N.M. Iverson, A.A. Boghossian, N.F. Reuel, A.J. Hilmer, F. Sen, J.A. Brew, and M.S. Strano, "Plant nanobionics approach to augment photosynthesis and biochemical sensing", *Nat. Mater.,* vol. 13, no. 4, pp. 400-408, 2014.
[http://dx.doi.org/10.1038/nmat3890] [PMID: 24633343]

[43]   J.P. Giraldo, M.P. Landry, S.Y. Kwak, R.M. Jain, M.H. Wong, N.M. Iverson, M. Ben-Naim, and M.S. Strano, "A ratiometric sensor using single chirality near-infrared fluorescent carbon nanotubes: Application to *in vivo* monitoring", *Small,* vol. 11, no. 32, pp. 3973-3984, 2015.
[http://dx.doi.org/10.1002/smll.201403276] [PMID: 25981520]

[44]   H. Geng, S. Vilms Pedersen, Y. Ma, T. Haghighi, H. Dai, P.D. Howes, and M.M. Stevens, "Noble metal nanoparticle biosensors: from fundamental studies toward point-of-care diagnostics", *Acc. Chem. Res.,* vol. 55, no. 5, pp. 593-604, 2022.
[http://dx.doi.org/10.1021/acs.accounts.1c00598] [PMID: 35138817]

[45]   J. Li, H. Wu, I. Santana, M. Fahlgren, and J.P. Giraldo, "Standoff optical glucose sensing in photosynthetic organisms by a quantum dot fluorescent probe", *ACS Appl. Mater. Interfaces,* vol. 10, no. 34, pp. 28279-28289, 2018.
[http://dx.doi.org/10.1021/acsami.8b07179] [PMID: 30058800]

[46]   S. Singh, A. Numan, and S. Cinti, "Electrochemical nano biosensors for the detection of extracellular vesicles exosomes: From the benchtop to everywhere?", *Biosens. Bioelectron.,* vol. 216, p. 114635,

2022.
[http://dx.doi.org/10.1016/j.bios.2022.114635] [PMID: 35988430]

[47]   S. Huang, W. Yan, M. Liu, and J. Hu, "Detection of difenoconazole pesticides in pak choi by surface-enhanced Raman scattering spectroscopy coupled with gold nanoparticles", *Anal. Methods,* vol. 8, no. 23, pp. 4755-4761, 2016.
[http://dx.doi.org/10.1039/C6AY00513F]

[48]   S. Huang, J. Hu, P. Guo, M. Liu, and R. Wu, "Rapid detection of chlorpyriphos residue in rice by surface-enhanced Raman scattering", *Anal. Methods,* vol. 7, no. 10, pp. 4334-4339, 2015.
[http://dx.doi.org/10.1039/C5AY00381D]

[49]   T. Dong, L. Lin, Y. He, P. Nie, F. Qu, and S. Xiao, "Density functional theory analysis of deltamethrin and its determination in strawberry by surface enhanced raman spectroscopy", *Molecules,* vol. 23, no. 6, p. 1458, 2018.
[http://dx.doi.org/10.3390/molecules23061458] [PMID: 29914118]

[50]   M. Hegde, P. Pai, M.G. Shetty, and K.S. Babitha, "Gold nanoparticle based biosensors for rapid pathogen detection: A review", *Environ. Nanotechnol. Monit. Manag.,* vol. 18, p. 100756, 2022.
[http://dx.doi.org/10.1016/j.enmm.2022.100756]

[51]   M. Rezayi, M. Khazaei, M. Darroudi, and K. Ghasemi, "Toward early diagnosis of colorectal cancer: focus on optical nano biosensors", *Mini Rev. Med. Chem.,* vol. 23, no. 9, pp. 1033-1049, 2023.
[http://dx.doi.org/10.2174/1389557522666220512142842] [PMID: 35549882]

[52]   B. Nandini, K. S. Mawale, and P. Giridhar, "Nanomaterials in agriculture for plant health and food safety: A comprehensive review on the current state of agro-nanoscience," 3 Biotech, vol. 13, no. 3, p. 73, Mar. 2023.
[http://dx.doi.org/10.1007/s13205-023-03470-w]

[53]   J. Hong, C. Wang, D.C. Wagner, J.L. Gardea-Torresdey, F. He, and C.M. Rico, "Foliar application of nanoparticles: Mechanisms of absorption, transfer, and multiple impacts", *Environ. Sci. Nano,* vol. 8, no. 5, pp. 1196-1210, 2021.
[http://dx.doi.org/10.1039/D0EN01129K]

[54]   O.S. Devika, S. Singh, D. Sarkar, P. Barnwal, J. Suman, and A. Rakshit, "Seed priming: A potential supplement in integrated resource management under fragile intensive ecosystems", *Front. Sustain. Food Syst.,* vol. 5, p. 654001, 2021.
[http://dx.doi.org/10.3389/fsufs.2021.654001]

[55]   D. Ghosh, M.M. Sarkar, and S. Roy, *Smart Fertilizers: The Prospect of Slow Release Nanofertilizers in Modern Agricultural Practices*, 2024.
[http://dx.doi.org/10.1007/978-3-031-41329-2_13]

[56]   S.K. Ghosh, and T. Bera, "Molecular mechanism of nano-fertilizer in plant growth and development: A recent account", In: *Advances in Nano-Fertilizers and Nano-Pesticides in Agriculture.* Elsevier, 2021, pp. 535-560.
[http://dx.doi.org/10.1016/B978-0-12-820092-6.00022-7]

[57]   A.S.M. Ghumman, R. Shamsuddin, M.M. Nasef, W.Z.N. Yahya, A. Abbasi, and H. Almohamadi, "Sulfur enriched slow-release coated urea produced from inverse vulcanized copolymer", *Sci. Total Environ.,* vol. 846, p. 157417, 2022.
[http://dx.doi.org/10.1016/j.scitotenv.2022.157417] [PMID: 35850358]

[58]   Y. Ding, W. Zhao, G. Zhu, Q. Wang, P. Zhang, and Y. Rui, "Recent trends in foliar nanofertilizers: A review", *Nanomaterials (Basel),* vol. 13, no. 21, p. 2906, 2023.
[http://dx.doi.org/10.3390/nano13212906] [PMID: 37947750]

[59]   F.J. Carmona, G. Dal Sasso, G.B. Ramírez-Rodríguez, Y. Pii, J.M. Delgado-López, A. Guagliardi, and N. Masciocchi, "Urea-functionalized amorphous calcium phosphate nanofertilizers: optimizing the synthetic strategy towards environmental sustainability and manufacturing costs", *Sci. Rep.,* vol. 11, no. 1, p. 3419, 2021.

[http://dx.doi.org/10.1038/s41598-021-83048-9] [PMID: 33564033]

[60]   G.B. Ramírez-Rodríguez, G. Dal Sasso, F.J. Carmona, C. Miguel-Rojas, A. Pérez-de-Luque, N. Masciocchi, A. Guagliardi, and J.M. Delgado-López, "Engineering biomimetic calcium phosphate nanoparticles: a green synthesis of slow-release multinutrient (npk) nanofertilizers", *ACS Appl. Bio Mater.,* vol. 3, no. 3, pp. 1344-1353, 2020.
[http://dx.doi.org/10.1021/acsabm.9b00937] [PMID: 35021628]

[61]   F. Zulfiqar, M. Navarro, M. Ashraf, N.A. Akram, and S. Munné-Bosch, "Nanofertilizer use for sustainable agriculture: Advantages and limitations", *Plant Sci.,* vol. 289, p. 110270, 2019.
[http://dx.doi.org/10.1016/j.plantsci.2019.110270] [PMID: 31623775]

[62]   A. Ditta, and M. Arshad, "Applications and perspectives of using nanomaterials for sustainable plant nutrition", *Nanotechnol. Rev.,* vol. 5, no. 2, 2016.
[http://dx.doi.org/10.1515/ntrev-2015-0060]

[63]   S. S. Dhaliwal, V. Sharma, and A. K. Shukla, "Impact of micronutrients in mitigation of abiotic stresses in soils and plants—A progressive step toward crop security and nutritional quality," in Advances in Agronomy, vol. 173, D. L. Sparks, Ed. Academic Press, 2022, pp. 1–78.
[http://dx.doi.org/10.1016/bs.agron.2022.02.001]

[64]   M. Hosny, M. Fawzy, E.M. El-Fakharany, A.M. Omer, E.M.A. El-Monaem, R.E. Khalifa, and A.S. Eltaweil, "Biogenic synthesis, characterization, antimicrobial, antioxidant, antidiabetic, and catalytic applications of platinum nanoparticles synthesized from Polygonum salicifolium leaves", *J. Environ. Chem. Eng.,* vol. 10, no. 1, p. 106806, 2022.
[http://dx.doi.org/10.1016/j.jece.2021.106806]

[65]   H.M. Abdelmigid, M.M. Morsi, N.A. Hussien, A.A. Alyamani, N.A. Alhuthal, and S. Albukhaty, "Green synthesis of phosphorous-containing hydroxyapatite nanoparticles (nhap) as a novel nano-fertilizer: Preliminary assessment on pomegranate (Punica granatum L.)", *Nanomaterials (Basel),* vol. 12, no. 9, p. 1527, 2022.
[http://dx.doi.org/10.3390/nano12091527] [PMID: 35564235]

[66]   Z. Abideen, M. Hanif, N. Munir, and B.L. Nielsen, "Impact of nanomaterials on the regulation of gene expression and metabolomics of plants under salt stress", *Plants,* vol. 11, no. 5, p. 691, 2022.
[http://dx.doi.org/10.3390/plants11050691] [PMID: 35270161]

[67]   Haseeb-ur-Rehman, M.G. Asghar, R.M. Ikram, S. Hashim, S. Hussain, M. Irfan, K. Mubeen, M. Ali, M. Alam, M. Ali, I. Haider, M. Shakir, M. Skalicky, S.A. Alharbi, and S. Alfarraj, "Sulphur coated urea improves morphological and yield characteristics of transplanted rice (Oryza sativa L.) through enhanced nitrogen uptake", *J. King Saud Univ. Sci.,* vol. 34, no. 1, p. 101664, 2022.
[http://dx.doi.org/10.1016/j.jksus.2021.101664]

[68]   M.K. Azameti, and A.W.M. Imoro, "Nanotechnology: A promising field in enhancing abiotic stress tolerance in plants", *Crop Design,* vol. 2, no. 2, p. 100037, 2023.
[http://dx.doi.org/10.1016/j.cropd.2023.100037]

[69]   M. Lechenet, F. Dessaint, G. Py, D. Makowski, and N. Munier-Jolain, "Reducing pesticide use while preserving crop productivity and profitability on arable farms", *Nat. Plants,* vol. 3, no. 3, p. 17008, 2017.
[http://dx.doi.org/10.1038/nplants.2017.8] [PMID: 28248316]

[70]   S.A. Irfan, R. Razali, K. KuShaari, N. Mansor, B. Azeem, and A.N. Ford Versypt, "A review of mathematical modeling and simulation of controlled-release fertilizers", *J. Control. Release,* vol. 271, pp. 45-54, 2018.
[http://dx.doi.org/10.1016/j.jconrel.2017.12.017] [PMID: 29274697]

[71]   M. Kah, and T. Hofmann, "Nanopesticide research: Current trends and future priorities", *Environ. Int.,* vol. 63, pp. 224-235, 2014.
[http://dx.doi.org/10.1016/j.envint.2013.11.015] [PMID: 24333990]

[72]   R.S. Kookana, A.B.A. Boxall, P.T. Reeves, R. Ashauer, S. Beulke, Q. Chaudhry, G. Cornelis, T.F.

Fernandes, J. Gan, M. Kah, I. Lynch, J. Ranville, C. Sinclair, D. Spurgeon, K. Tiede, and P.J. Van den Brink, "Nanopesticides: guiding principles for regulatory evaluation of environmental risks", *J. Agric. Food Chem.,* vol. 62, no. 19, pp. 4227-4240, 2014.
[http://dx.doi.org/10.1021/jf500232f] [PMID: 24754346]

[73]   R. Prasad, A. Bhattacharyya, and Q.D. Nguyen, "Nanotechnology in sustainable agriculture: recent developments, challenges, and perspectives", *Front. Microbiol.,* vol. 8, p. 1014, 2017.
[http://dx.doi.org/10.3389/fmicb.2017.01014] [PMID: 28676790]

[74]   P. Kanmani, and S.T. Lim, "Synthesis and structural characterization of silver nanoparticles using bacterial exopolysaccharide and its antimicrobial activity against food and multidrug resistant pathogens", *Process Biochem.,* vol. 48, no. 7, pp. 1099-1106, 2013.
[http://dx.doi.org/10.1016/j.procbio.2013.05.011]

[75]   P. Rajiv, S. Rajeshwari, and R. Venckatesh, "Bio-Fabrication of zinc oxide nanoparticles using leaf extract of *Parthenium hysterophorus* L. and its size-dependent antifungal activity against plant fungal pathogens", *Spectrochim. Acta A Mol. Biomol. Spectrosc.,* vol. 112, pp. 384-387, 2013.
[http://dx.doi.org/10.1016/j.saa.2013.04.072] [PMID: 23686093]

[76]   S. Jain, G. Bhanjana, S. Heydarifard, N. Dilbaghi, M.M. Nazhad, V. Kumar, K.H. Kim, and S. Kumar, "Enhanced antibacterial profile of nanoparticle impregnated cellulose foam filter paper for drinking water filtration", *Carbohydr. Polym.,* vol. 202, pp. 219-226, 2018.
[http://dx.doi.org/10.1016/j.carbpol.2018.08.130] [PMID: 30286995]

[77]   A.J. Anderson, J.E. McLean, A.R. Jacobson, and D.W. Britt, "CuO and ZnO nanoparticles modify interkingdom cell signaling processes relevant to crop production", *J. Agric. Food Chem.,* vol. 66, no. 26, pp. 6513-6524, 2018.
[http://dx.doi.org/10.1021/acs.jafc.7b01302] [PMID: 28481096]

[78]   L.A. Avila, R. Chandrasekar, K.E. Wilkinson, J. Balthazor, M. Heerman, J. Bechard, S. Brown, Y. Park, S. Dhar, G.R. Reeck, and J.M. Tomich, "Delivery of lethal dsRNAs in insect diets by branched amphiphilic peptide capsules", *J. Control. Release,* vol. 273, pp. 139-146, 2018.
[http://dx.doi.org/10.1016/j.jconrel.2018.01.010] [PMID: 29407675]

[79]   N. Le Van, C. Ma, J. Shang, Y. Rui, S. Liu, and B. Xing, "Effects of CuO nanoparticles on insecticidal activity and phytotoxicity in conventional and transgenic cotton", *Chemosphere,* vol. 144, pp. 661-670, 2016.
[http://dx.doi.org/10.1016/j.chemosphere.2015.09.028] [PMID: 26408972]

[80]   A. Sidhu, H. Barmota, and A. Bala, "Antifungal evaluation studies of copper sulfide nano-aquaformulations and its impact on seed quality of rice (*Oryzae sativa*)", *Appl. Nanosci.,* vol. 7, no. 8, pp. 681-689, 2017.
[http://dx.doi.org/10.1007/s13204-017-0606-7]

[81]   B.J. Mastin, and J.H. Rodgers Jr, "Toxicity and bioavailability of copper herbicides (Clearigate, Cutrine-Plus, and copper sulfate) to freshwater animals", *Arch. Environ. Contam. Toxicol.,* vol. 39, no. 4, pp. 445-451, 2000.
[http://dx.doi.org/10.1007/s002440010126] [PMID: 11031304]

[82]   P. Kanhed, S. Birla, S. Gaikwad, A. Gade, A.B. Seabra, O. Rubilar, N. Duran, and M. Rai, "*In vitro* antifungal efficacy of copper nanoparticles against selected crop pathogenic fungi", *Mater. Lett.,* vol. 115, pp. 13-17, 2014.
[http://dx.doi.org/10.1016/j.matlet.2013.10.011]

[83]   T. Garde-Cerdán, V. Mancini, M. Carrasco-Quiroz, A. Servili, G. Gutiérrez-Gamboa, R. Foglia, E.P. Pérez-Álvarez, and G. Romanazzi, "Chitosan and Laminarin as Alternatives to Copper for *Plasmopara viticola* control: Effect on grape amino acid", *J. Agric. Food Chem.,* vol. 65, no. 34, pp. 7379-7386, 2017.
[http://dx.doi.org/10.1021/acs.jafc.7b02352] [PMID: 28759217]

[84]   J.H. Graham, E.G. Johnson, M.E. Myers, M. Young, P. Rajasekaran, S. Das, and S. Santra, "Potential

of nano-formulated zinc oxide for control of citrus canker on grapefruit trees", *Plant Dis.,* vol. 100, no. 12, pp. 2442-2447, 2016.
[http://dx.doi.org/10.1094/PDIS-05-16-0598-RE] [PMID: 30686171]

[85]   I.E. Popova, J.S. Dubie, and M.J. Morra, "Optimization of hydrolysis conditions for release of biopesticides from glucosinolates in *Brassica juncea* and *Sinapis alba* seed meal extracts", *Ind. Crops Prod.,* vol. 97, pp. 354-359, 2017.
[http://dx.doi.org/10.1016/j.indcrop.2016.12.041]

[86]   I. Mnif, and D. Ghribi, "Potential of bacterial derived biopesticides in pest management", *Crop Prot.,* vol. 77, pp. 52-64, 2015.
[http://dx.doi.org/10.1016/j.cropro.2015.07.017]

[87]   S. Timmusk, L. Behers, J. Muthoni, A. Muraya, and A.C. Aronsson, "Perspectives and challenges of microbial application for crop improvement", *Front. Plant Sci.,* vol. 8, p. 49, 2017.
[http://dx.doi.org/10.3389/fpls.2017.00049] [PMID: 28232839]

[88]   T.C. Sparks, D.R. Hahn, and N.V. Garizi, "Natural products, their derivatives, mimics and synthetic equivalents: Role in agrochemical discovery", *Pest Manag. Sci.,* vol. 73, no. 4, pp. 700-715, 2017.
[http://dx.doi.org/10.1002/ps.4458] [PMID: 27739147]

[89]   J.N. Seiber, J. Coats, S.O. Duke, and A.D. Gross, "Biopesticides: State of the art and future opportunities", *J. Agric. Food Chem.,* vol. 62, no. 48, pp. 11613-11619, 2014.
[http://dx.doi.org/10.1021/jf504252n] [PMID: 25406111]

[90]   Y. Huang, L. Ma, D.H. Fang, J.Q. Xi, M.L. Zhu, M.H. Mo, K.Q. Zhang, and Y.P. Ji, "Isolation and characterisation of rhizosphere bacteria active against *Meloidogyne incognita*, *Phytophthora nicotianae* and the root knot-black shank complex in tobacco", *Pest Manag. Sci.,* vol. 71, no. 3, pp. 415-422, 2015.
[http://dx.doi.org/10.1002/ps.3820] [PMID: 24799254]

[91]   S. Kumar, M. Nehra, N. Dilbaghi, G. Marrazza, A.A. Hassan, and K.H. Kim, "Nano-based smart pesticide formulations: Emerging opportunities for agriculture", *J. Control. Release,* vol. 294, pp. 131-153, 2019.
[http://dx.doi.org/10.1016/j.jconrel.2018.12.012] [PMID: 30552953]

[92]   S.A. Al-Sahli, F. Al-Otibi, R.I. Alharbi, M. Amina, and N.M. Al Musayeib, "Silver nanoparticles improve the fungicidal properties of *Rhazya stricta decne* aqueous extract against plant pathogens", *Sci. Rep.,* vol. 14, no. 1, p. 1297, 2024.
[http://dx.doi.org/10.1038/s41598-024-51855-5] [PMID: 38221517]

[93]   P. Mathur, and S. Roy, "Nanosilica facilitates silica uptake, growth and stress tolerance in plants", *Plant Physiol. Biochem.,* vol. 157, pp. 114-127, 2020.
[http://dx.doi.org/10.1016/j.plaphy.2020.10.011] [PMID: 33099119]

CHAPTER 5

Harnessing Smart Technology for Optimized Livestock Farming: A Comprehensive Overview

Jaspal Kaur Saini[1,*] and **Sanjay Madan**[2]

[1] *Department of Information Technology, Dr. B.R. Ambedkar NIT, Jalandhar, India*

[2] *Applied Artificial Intelligence & Analytics Division, C-DAC, Mohali, India*

Abstract: This chapter provides a detailed overview of smart technologies used in livestock farming, including automation, robotics, data analytics, Internet of Things devices (IoT), and sensor technologies. It begins by defining and summarizing the smart technologies and highlighting their importance in modern livestock management to improve productivity, health management, animal welfare, and efficiency. The objectives and parameters of the chapter are outlined, with a focus on investigating various technological remedies and their consequences for livestock management. The IoT devices and sensor technology section provides readers with an overview of the concepts behind the use of IoT devices and sensor technology, as well as examples of their various applications in environmental and animal health monitoring, livestock management, and operations. The use of automation and robotics in livestock farming is examined, with an overview of their role in agriculture and specific applications in animal handling, feeding, milking, and waste management. In a nutshell, this chapter covers the opportunities and challenges of smart farming along with case studies.

Keywords: Sensor technology, Animal handling, Automation and robotics, IoT devices, Livestock management, Livestock health monitoring, Smart technology.

INTRODUCTION

Livestock farming can be described as one of the many essential parts of agricultural development and also contributes to the world's food system. It encompasses the breeding and management of domesticated animals, such as cattle, sheep, goats, and other birds and livestock, all to produce various resources, including meat, milk, wool, and eggs. The importance of livestock farming is felt not only in terms of meeting the nutritional requirements, but it also contributes to the wealth creation of a vast number of people across the globe, with special emphasis on rural areas.

---

[*] **Corresponding author Jaspal Kaur Saini:** Department of Information Technology, Dr. B.R. Ambedkar NIT, Jalandhar, India; E-mails: sainijk@nitj.ac.in, sainijassi87@gmail.com

In recent decades, changes have occurred, and trends and patterns have evolved, characterized by the development of breeding, improvement in zootechnics and veterinary medicine, leading to growth marked by high productivity and efficiency. The modern trend in livestock husbandry is to enhance production efficiency while ensuring the humane treatment of animals used for production.

The livestock sector has also undergone significant changes in its adoption of technology. Some of these innovations include the incorporation of automatic feeding, health devices, ordering systems, and analytics, all of which have transformed the sector, making it more productive and effective. Such technological development has not only enabled livestock management to be more effective but has also improved the quality of the products consumed.

LITERATURE REVIEW

This section summarizes the structured review of livestock management, technologies, and tools, as well as sensor technologies and wearable devices used for monitoring, health management, and operations in livestock farming.

In precision Livestock farming, the management of livestock is a significant concern, and the involvement of multiple available technologies can somewhat reduce the human effort required to manage basic tasks. It also involves multiple tools and technologies, such as surveillance cameras [1], wireless communication devices, microphones, and other sensors [2], to collect various types of data in real-time from each animal for a decision support system [3, 4]. The grazing pattern and behavior of livestock are monitored through localization technology, which tracks the movement of cattle on the farm and their grazing patterns, aiding in pasture management [5].

Several studies have focused on the behavioral patterns of livestock [6 - 9]. The RGB cameras are used for the automated detection and measurement of feed intake in individual bovines on the livestock farm [10]. It helps farmers effectively manage expenses and feed requirements using advanced algorithms.

Rodenburg *et al.* [11] proposed an algorithm based on point cloud data and depth images for teat detection and localization. The research is also published for other vision-based technologies, including stereovision techniques and thermal imaging [12], as well as the Haar Cascade classifier using data from structured light depth imaging [13]. The research challenge is to design a standard milking cluster device suitable for all bovines, as there is variability in the shape of the udder and stage of lactation. Table **1** shows the technological advancements and research in the field of automated livestock management. The review primarily focuses on precision livestock farming, wearable technologies, and IoT devices.

Table 1. Research and technological overview in livestock management.

Citation	Application Area	Tools & Technologies Used	Objective of the Research
[5]	Behavioral Monitoring	Localization Sensors	Track the location and grazing patterns of livestock for effective pasture management.
[6]	Behavioral Monitoring	IoT sensors with a localization sensor (GPS)	Behavioral study of discrimination between various types of feeding systems for the classification of behavioral patterns in grazing of animals.
[7]	Behavioral Monitoring	IoT sensors in a neck collar	Behavioral analysis of feeding, rest, and detection of estrus events with rumination rate.
[8]	Health monitoring	Noise sensor	Cough sound analysis for the detection of respiratory diseases in bovines.
[9]	Animal Behavior Analysis	Camera and microphone sensors	Sound signal analysis and correlation of the behavior and sound.
[12 - 14]	Automated System	Thermal and depth Image Analysis using multiple techniques	Teat detection and localization for the automated milking system or robotic system in livestock farms.
[15]	Health monitoring	Image Analysis	Automated detection of lameness of the bovines in dairy farms.

SIGNIFICANCE OF LIVESTOCK FARMING

Livestock farming is important for several reasons, which are as follows:

- Food Production: It helps ensure food security as it is a significant source of protein, vitamins, and minerals through meat, dairy, and eggs.
- Economic Impact: Livestock makes a positive contribution to the rural economy through job creation in farming, processing, and distribution, as well as providing income for several families.
- Cultural Heritage: Several communities have traditions associated with the rearing of livestock that have become integral to their diets, practices, and social organization.
- Soil Health: Properly controlled grazing may benefit soil quality and structure, encourage biodiversity, and improve ecological functions.
- Waste Management: By-products of crop farming can be utilized by livestock, and these wastes can be put to good use, such as manure for fertilizers.
- Climate Considerations: Although livestock systems are a source of greenhouse gas emissions, integrated and sustainable livestock systems, such as rotation grazing and feeding programs, can mitigate their impact.

- Diversity of Products: Livestock farming not only involves the production of food but also includes the production of other products, such as leather, wool, and others.

In conclusion, livestock farming is important in food systems, economies, and cultural practices, and it presents both prospects and constraints for sustainability.

TECHNOLOGIES FOR LIVESTOCK FARMING

Various technologies are used in the rearing of livestock with the objectives of increasing efficiency, production, and the well-being of animals. Here are some key technologies used in the industry:

- IoT Devices: Various devices can be attached to animals to help track and monitor their condition, activities, and other factors, such as environmental conditions, that affect them. Previous studies discussed various measures that utilize IoT devices for several purposes, including smart agriculture and healthcare services [15, 16].
- Precision Agriculture Tools: Health status check-ups on pastures and the land through aerial inspection and imagery by drones and satellites, together with the analysis of the grazing patterns.
- Automated Feeding Systems: Automated feeding systems that can release the right portion of feed at the appropriate time, thus feeding the fish efficiently and minimizing wastage.
- Health Monitoring Systems: RFID tags and biometric sensors that monitor symptoms of diseases and behavior that can signal that an individual is unwell.
- Blockchain Technology: This enables the consumer to know where their meat and dairy products were sourced, leading to better traceability and increased transparency.
- Genetic Improvement Tools: Biotechnology-based methods in breeding that make the livestock breeds better in terms of production and disease resilience.
- Data Analytics Platforms: A software that collects data from different sources, especially on breeding, feeding, and management aspects of a farm, and provides analysis for the decision maker. Previously, authors presented various tools for crawling data and the application of LSTM-based deep learning neural networks to forecast the behavior of radical activities [17, 18]. Similarly, the same scale of data crawling tools and techniques can be utilized for monitoring and crawling data in livestock farming. Fig. (1) depicts smart technologies for livestock management.
- Environmental Control Systems: Provisions of controlled environment in barns, including temperature, humidity, and ventilation to facilitate the comfort of animals.

- Mobile Apps: The smart applications that enable farmers to monitor their business, monitor animal health, and communications with suppliers or veterinarians.
- Robotics: robotic systems for milking and cleaning animals, as well as various other systems for continuous observation and controlling animal health, which help save labor costs and increase productivity.
- Artificial Intelligence: Applied in use in statistics and data analysis for decision-making and operations management, and control from patterns determined.

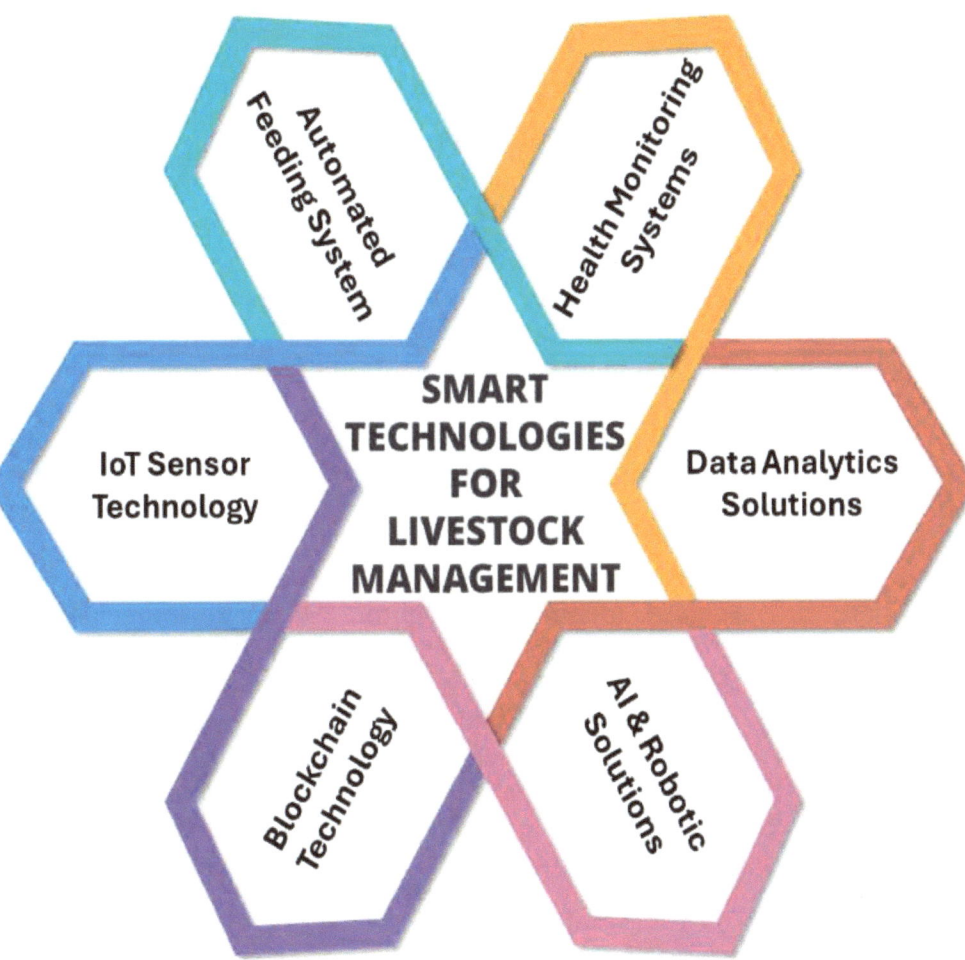

Fig. (1). Smart technologies for precision livestock management.

ROLE OF IOT AND MACHINE LEARNING IN LIVESTOCK FARMING

IoT and Livestock Farming

The advent of IoT (Internet of Things) devices in livestock farming is unprecedented in terms of efficiency, productivity, and even animal welfare. Here are some key IoT applications and devices used in this sector:

- Wearable Sensors: Livestock collars, tags, and other fittings housing sensors that help monitor health and behavior, providing ancillary information on active days, health status, and feeding periods.
- Smart Feeders: These devices have been developed to simplify the process of setting and programming feeding intervals for animals, conducting head counts for feed consumption, and adjusting the amount of feed according to the specific characteristics of each animal.
- Environmental Monitoring: Monitoring instruments are used to assess environmental parameters, including temperature, moisture, and air quality, in barns and pounds to ensure livestock are kept in quite desirable environments.
- GPS Tracking: Livestock GPS tracking devices enable farmers to easily locate and manage free-range animals, as well as monitor their grazing patterns to prevent animal loss.
- Health Monitoring Systems: The IoT devices can be used to monitor an animal's behavior and identify any changes, which could be indications of illness or stress in the animal. Thus, considerable resources are spent on caring for the animal with such IoT applications.
- Automatic Watering Systems: Smart waterers are also installed within the operation to measure the amount of water animals consume and ensure there is clean water available to the livestock at all times.
- Data Analytics Platforms: In modern times, animal health and productivity of livestock, as well as farm management and operations, have improved after centralizing data from various devices, such as information on pregnant cows, in data analytics systems built on the farm to aid decision-making.
- Drones: Aerial observation may help control livestock herding, and drones may also be used to assess pasture conditions.

Machine Learning and Livestock Farming

Machine learning system applications are revolutionary in the area of improving livestock farming, with increased production, enhanced animal welfare, and improved efficiency. Here are some key areas where machine learning is making an impact:

- Health Monitoring: ML algorithms monitor data from wearable sensors to detect early health-related problems, such as signs of diseases or stress, from changes in behavior, temperature, and movements.
- Feed Optimization: The fluid intake and specific diets of cattle, as influenced by age, weight, and growth stages, among others, can be predicted by machine learning algorithms and used to minimize feed wastage when formulating feeds for livestock.
- Predictive Analytics: ML can predict growth rates, reproductive cycles, and the market alongside other factors that can assist the farmer in his/her decisions on breeding and selling of the animals.
- Behavior Analysis: Based on data collected from video monitoring and other sensors, ML can analyze behavioral patterns, which in turn will enhance farmers' understanding of the welfare needs of the animals and the environment.
- Disease Prediction: The information collected can be used to predict the occurrence of diseases in animals, ensuring timely intervention through better biosecurity measures. In another study, authors have predicted the patchy leaves from the sweet lime dataset using a single-shot detector [19]. Such models can also be deployed for disease detection on animals.
- Genetic Improvement: Computer science, in particular, is applied in analyzing various genetic aspects for the selection of breeding stock that possess desirable qualities, thereby improving the genetics of animals in terms of productivity and disease resistance.
- Resource Management: Currently, resource demands, such as water and pasture use, can be effectively and sustainably managed through ML algorithms, thereby reducing costs.
- Market Analysis: The results showed that market data and trends can be utilized through machine learning algorithms to help farmers make adjustments to their production processes for improved and more profitable yields.
- Precision Livestock Farming: By utilizing ML, the firm can support precision farming by promoting customized management approaches through the integration of data gathered from various sources, such as sensors and drones.
- Supply Chain Optimization: The application of ML will help streamline the supply chain and logistics by enabling the prediction of demand for livestock and products, as well as the identification of the most efficient routes for transporting products.

With the implementation of AI-based machine learning, livestock farmers will gain productivity, better health and welfare for their animals, and make more sustainable decisions, ultimately leading to more productive and sustainable livestock farming [20].

Machine Learning Algorithms for Optimised Livestock Farming

Making use of data analytics to promote decision-making and thereby enhancing productivity and efficiency in animal health, ML has become one of the key game-changers in the optimization of livestock farming. Machine learning techniques—such as supervised, unsupervised, and reinforcement learning—are used to analyze the vast amounts of data generated by sensors, cameras, and Internet of Things devices installed in farms. Supervised machine learning has been routinely used, along with historical information, to predict outcomes such as weight gain, milk yield, or the occurrence of a disease. For example, by analyzing feeding patterns, temperature, and activity levels, ML models can predict early signs of an outbreak, ensuring early intervention and a reduction in mortality rates. Unsupervised machine learning methods are used to identify patterns or deviations in behavioral trends.

As a whole, machine learning applications in optimized animal husbandry are classified into three categories: supervised learning, unsupervised learning, and reinforcement learning. It describes a scenario in which the model is trained using labeled data, where each piece of data has an attached outcome. Random forest, Support Vector Machines (SVMs), and Artificial Neural Networks (ANNs) have been widely used for predicting milk yield, as well as for estimating diseases and body weight. For example, an AI mechanism can learn the pair of variables (target and independent variables) from temperature, heart rate, and feeding behavior against the triggering input variable of labor or calving outcome.

RESEARCH CHALLENGES

Livestock farming challenges are as follows:

- Environmental Impact: Livestock Farming is one of the major contributors to global warming, due to the emission of greenhouse gases, deforestation, and land abuse, which raises concerns about climate change and biodiversity loss.
- Resource Management: Water and water feed requirements can sometimes put pressure on resources, especially in drought-prone regions.
- Animal Welfare: There is increasing concern and embarrassment regarding how livestock are treated and raised, which has necessitated positive changes in policies and their enforcement.
- Disease Management: There are many diseases common to cattle and other livestock that can be transmitted from animals to humans.
- Market Fluctuations: Volatility in the prices of feed and even that of farmed livestock, such as pigs, poses a significant challenge to farmers in terms of realizing a steady income as well as controlling expenses.

- Regulatory Pressure: Regulations on emissions, animal welfare, and food safety are becoming increasingly stringent, making farming methods more difficult and expensive.
- Consumer Demand: Changing lifestyles among many people, leading to reduced demand for meat, the adoption of vegetarian diets, or the development of more environmentally responsible food growing methods, can hamper not only livestock farming but also its related industries.
- Labor Shortages: This is common in any region with a high volume of agricultural work scheduled, but there are not enough trained personnel available, which affects farm outputs and management.

CONCLUSION

In this chapter, we covered livestock farming, its importance, and the role of the latest smart technologies in improving livestock farming. There is a rapid rate of adoption and popularity among farmers for automated milking technologies, which helps increase production, reduce labor costs, and effectively manage resources in dairy farms. Automated Milking systems are becoming increasingly popular, and multiple technologies have been used for the detection and localization of teats, which is a motivating example of utilizing technologies. We reviewed the state-of-the-art technologies and techniques to be used for better management, monitoring of livestock, and enhanced productivity. Smart technologies are enabling stock growers and producers to overcome the problems of today's mechanized farming, enhance productivity, sustainability, and the welfare of animals.

REFERENCES

[1]   N. Hostiou, J. Fagon, S. Chauvat, A. Turlot, F. Kling-Eveillard, X. Boivin, and C. Allain, "Impact of precision livestock farming on work and human-animal interactions on dairy farms. A review", *Biotechnol. Agron. Soc. Environ.,* vol. 21, pp. 268-275, 2017.
[http://dx.doi.org/10.25518/1780-4507.13706]

[2]   T.M. Banhazi, L. Babinszky, V. Halas, and M. Tscharke, "Precision livestock farming: Precision feeding technologies and sustainable livestock production", *Int. J. Agric. Biol. Eng.,* vol. 5, pp. 54-61, 2012.

[3]   T.M. Banhazi, H. Lehr, J.L. Black, H. Crabtree, P. Schofield, M. Tscharke, and D. Berckmans, "Precision livestock farming: Scientific concepts and commercial reality", *Proc. XVth Int. Congr. Animal Hygiene: Animal Hygiene and Sustainable Livestock Production (ISAH 2011,* 2011.Vienna, Austria

[4]   G. Terrasson, E. Villeneuve, V. Pilnière, and A. Llaria, "Precision livestock farming: a multidisciplinary paradigm", *Proc. SMART,* pp. 55-59, 2017.

[5]   L. Nóbrega, P. Gonçalves, M. Antunes, and D. Corujo, "Assessing sheep behavior through low-power microcontrollers in smart agriculture scenarios", *Comput. Electron. Agric.,* vol. 173, p. 105444, 2020.
[http://dx.doi.org/10.1016/j.compag.2020.105444]

[6]   R. Dutta, D. Smith, R. Rawnsley, G. Bishop-Hurley, J. Hills, G. Timms, and D. Henry, "Dynamic

cattle behavioural classification using supervised ensemble classifiers", *Comput. Electron. Agric.*, vol. 111, pp. 18-28, 2015.
[http://dx.doi.org/10.1016/j.compag.2014.12.002]

[7]   A.L.H. Andriamandroso, J. Bindelle, B. Mercatoris, and F. Lebeau, "A review on the use of sensors to monitor cattle jaw movements and behavior when grazing", *Biotechnol. Agron. Soc. Environ.*, vol. 20, pp. 273-286, 2016.
[http://dx.doi.org/10.25518/1780-4507.13058]

[8]   L. Carpentier, E. Vranken, D. Berckmans, J. Paeshuyse, and T. Norton, "Development of sound-based poultry health monitoring tool for automated sneeze detection", *Comput. Electron. Agric.*, vol. 162, pp. 573-581, 2019.
[http://dx.doi.org/10.1016/j.compag.2019.05.013]

[9]   G.H. Meen, M.A. Schellekens, M.H.M. Slegers, N.L.G. Leenders, E. van Erp-van der Kooij, and L.P.J.J. Noldus, "Sound analysis in dairy cattle vocalisation as a potential welfare monitor", *Comput. Electron. Agric.*, vol. 118, pp. 111-115, 2015.
[http://dx.doi.org/10.1016/j.compag.2015.08.028]

[10]   T.M. Banhazi, M. Tscharke, W.M. Ferdous, C. Saunders, and S.H. Lee, "Improved image analysis based system to reliably predict the live weight of pigs on farm: preliminary results", *Aust. J. Multi-Discip. Eng.*, vol. 8, no. 2, pp. 107-119, 2011.
[http://dx.doi.org/10.1080/14488388.2011.11464830]

[11]   J. Rodenburg, "Robotic milking: Technology, farm design, and effects on work flow", *J. Dairy Sci.*, vol. 100, no. 9, pp. 7729-7738, 2017.
[http://dx.doi.org/10.3168/jds.2016-11715] [PMID: 28711263]

[12]   A. Ben Azouz, H. Esmonde, B. Corcoran, and E. O'Callaghan, "Development of a teat sensing system for robotic milking by combining thermal imaging and stereovision technique", *Comput. Electron. Agric.*, vol. 110, pp. 162-170, 2015.
[http://dx.doi.org/10.1016/j.compag.2014.11.004]

[13]   A. Rastogi, A. Pal, K.M. Joung, and B.S. Ryuh, "Teat detection mechanism using machine learning based vision for smart Automatic Milking Systems", *Proc. 14th Int. Conf. Ubiquitous Robots Ambient Intell. (URAI*, pp. 947-949, .Jeju, Korea
[http://dx.doi.org/10.1109/URAI.2017.7992872]

[14]   N. O' Mahony, S. Campbell, A. Carvalho, L. Krpalkova, D. Riordan, and J. Walsh, "3D vision for precision dairy farming", *IFAC-PapersOnLine*, vol. 52, no. 30, pp. 312-317, 2019.
[http://dx.doi.org/10.1016/j.ifacol.2019.12.555]

[15]   H. Tian, T. Wang, Y. Liu, X. Qiao, and Y. Li, "Computer vision technology in agricultural automation —A review", *Inf. Process. Agric.*, vol. 7, no. 1, pp. 1-19, 2020.
[http://dx.doi.org/10.1016/j.inpa.2019.09.006]

[16]   D. Thakur, J.K. Saini, and S. Srinivasan, "DeepThink IoT: The strength of deep learning in internet of things", *Artif. Intell. Rev.*, vol. 56, no. 12, pp. 14663-14730, 2023.
[http://dx.doi.org/10.1007/s10462-023-10513-4]

[17]   J.K. Saini, "LSTM based deep learning approach to detect online violent activities over dark web", *Multimedia Tools Appl.*, vol. 83, no. 14, pp. 42379-42390, 2023.
[http://dx.doi.org/10.1007/s11042-023-17222-8]

[18]   J.K. Saini, and D. Bansal, "Computational techniques to counter terrorism: A systematic survey", *Multimedia Tools Appl.*, vol. 83, no. 1, pp. 1189-1214, 2024.
[http://dx.doi.org/10.1007/s11042-023-15545-0]

[19]   D. Thakur, J.K. Saini, and S. Srinivasan, "Fine tuned single shot detector for finding disease patches in leaves", *Proc. Int. Conf. Agric.-Centric Comput,* 2023.Cham
[http://dx.doi.org/10.1007/978-3-031-43605-5_1]

[20]   D. Thakur, and J.K. Saini, "The significance of IoT and deep learning in activity recognition", In: *IoT, Big Data and AI for Improving Quality of Everyday Life: Present and Future Challenges.* Springer Int. Publ.: Cham, 2023, pp. 311-329.
[http://dx.doi.org/10.1007/978-3-031-35783-1_18]

CHAPTER 6

Blockchain and IoT for Smart Agriculture: Enhancing Food Security and Sustainability

Ruchi Mittal[1,*]

[1] *Iconic Data, Tokyo, Japan*

Abstract: The amalgamation of Blockchain and the Internet of Things (IoT) is presently revolutionizing the agriculture domain, proffering unmatched prospects to augment food security, traceability, and sustainable farming methodologies. This chapter explores how various technologies work together to transform agriculture, tackling important issues such as the requirement for precision farming, inefficiencies in the supply chain, and data management. It begins by outlining the core concepts of blockchain technology and emphasizing the importance of maintaining the integrity and transparency of agricultural transactions and data. Next, the chapter examines how Deep Learning processes the data generated by IoT devices, enabling predictive analytics for crop health, yield optimization, and effective resource management. The chapter also discusses how the Internet of Things (IoT) facilitates a data-driven and flexible agricultural ecosystem by enabling real-time monitoring and management of farm environments. This chapter shows how the integration of Blockchain and IoT simplifies agricultural operations, fosters stakeholder trust, supports environmental sustainability, and creates a more robust and effective food supply system through case studies and theoretical debates. The chapter concludes with an outlook on the challenges and potential paths ahead in utilizing these technologies for advanced smart agriculture.

Keywords: Blockchain, Crop health, Data management, Food security, Internet of Things, Precision farming, Predictive analytics, Sustainable farming, Smart agriculture, Supply chain inefficiencies, Yield optimization.

INTRODUCTION

The emergence of Industry 4.0 has led to the development of revolutionary technologies, one of which is the Internet of Things (IoT). The Internet of Things (IoT), especially in its industrialized form known as Industrial IoT (IIoT), is transforming the banking, manufacturing, healthcare, and transportation industries by allowing objects to interact with one another on their own and supporting more

---

[*] **Corresponding author Ruchi Mittal:** Iconic Data, Tokyo, Japan; E-mail: ruchi.mittal138@gmail.com

Shefali Arora Chouhanm Nagendra Pratap Singh, Banalaxmi Brahma & Shashank Gupta (Eds.)

effective decision-making processes [1]. The Industrial Internet of Things (IIoT) offers a new paradigm for industrial operations by bridging established industrial processes with cutting-edge technology, including smart sensors, robotics, machine-to-machine communication, big data analytics, and artificial intelligence.

The supply chain industry represents one of the most significant applications of the Industrial Internet of Things (IIoT) [2]. Supply chains offer significant advantages as they evolve into increasingly automated and sophisticated networks, particularly in the fast-paced modern world, where efficiency and transparency are crucial requirements [3, 4]. Concerns regarding product quality and safety within food supply chains are becoming more widespread among consumers, particularly in light of the growing trend toward organic food. These days, consumers want thorough information on the food they eat, including details about hormone changes, pesticide use, and the product's entire path from farm to table.

Maintaining the documentation of a food item's journey, including its creation, processing, distribution, and consumption, is a critical function of a Food Supply Chain (FSC) [5]. Typically, barcodes or RFID tags are used in FSCs to gather data, with the agricultural, food processing, and distribution sectors being the primary sources of this information. Supply chain authorities are placing a greater emphasis on delivering accurate information to establish credibility and foster confidence, as customer expectations for food quality and transparency continue to rise.

Regulatory agencies have implemented guidelines to improve the transparency and traceability of food supply chains in response to these requests. A significant transition from distributed to centralized systems is now underway, driven by the need for enhanced storage capacity, scalability, and fault tolerance. Designing a food supply chain from a logistical standpoint entails addressing intricate hierarchical placement challenges. Recent research has examined bi-level location and size concerns as well as network designs with many linked levels *via* hubs [6 - 8].

Within this framework, blockchain technology presents itself as a viable means of securely exchanging data across decentralized networks, providing a strong foundation for guaranteeing the transparency and integrity of food supply chains.

Internet of Things (IoT) in Industry 4.0

Industry 4.0 facilitates the integration of all technologies to such an extent that equipment functions independently, and intelligent decision-making also takes place. The Industrial Internet of Things primarily impacts industries such as manufacturing, healthcare, transportation, and finance, as it integrates conventional industrial processes with modern technologies, including smart sensors, robotics, machine-to-machine communication, big data, and artificial intelligence. The IIoT enables the development of integrated and more efficient systems, increasing production efficiency and operational visibility. This trend is most vivid in supply chain management, where IIoT technologies are now being developed to form networks that enhance processes that traditionally required labour and were deemed tedious and impossible to perfect.

Blockchain and Explainable AI in Smart Agriculture

Blockchain enables customers to obtain trustworthy information on the provenance, quality, and safety of food items by preserving unchangeable production process records. Simultaneously, Explainable AI [7] enhances intelligent agriculture decision-making by providing comprehensible insights into AI-driven recommendations, thereby building confidence among farmers and other stakeholders.

Explainable AI and blockchain technology [8, 9] can be leveraged to enhance smart agriculture, highlighting how these innovations have the potential to completely transform the industry by ensuring sustainable practices, traceability, and accountability [10].

In the development of smart agriculture, blockchain technology and Explainable Artificial Intelligence (XAI) are becoming increasingly potent instruments. Blockchain addresses issues with traceability, accountability, and food safety by providing a decentralized, transparent, and safe platform for data recording and sharing throughout the agricultural supply chain [11]. In smart agriculture, the integration of XAI and blockchain not only increases operational effectiveness but also promotes more ecologically friendly and sustainable farming methods [12]. This convergence of technologies is poised to revolutionize the agricultural sector, making it more resilient, transparent, and consumer-focused.

This chapter aims to examine how Industry 4.0 technologies, particularly the Industrial Internet of Things (IIoT), are revolutionizing several sectors, with a special emphasis on the supply chain. The chapter examines how the Internet of Things (IoT) can enhance the openness, efficiency, and decision-making capabilities of food supply chains while meeting the increasing expectations of consumers for product quality and safety.

LITERATURE REVIEW

Smart irrigation systems have the potential to increase agricultural yields and improve water efficiency, according to recent studies. IoT-based irrigation solutions enable farmers to monitor and control water consumption more efficiently, which improves crop quality and quantity, according to the author [13]. Similarly, Khanna and Kaur's study on the use of AI in smart pest management demonstrated that AI-based systems can identify and diagnose pest infestations more precisely, thereby reducing the need for hazardous pesticides [14]. The advantages of smart crop monitoring systems were explored in a study by Lu *et al.* [15], who highlighted the potential of big data analytics and Artificial Intelligence (AI) to analyze agricultural data in real-time and provide valuable insights for enhancing crop management.

Subsequent investigations have demonstrated the benefits of intelligent livestock management in terms of enhancing animal welfare and increasing productivity. IoT-based monitoring devices, according to Lipper *et al.*, enable farmers to keep a closer eye on the health and behaviour of their animals, which boosts output and profits [16]. Shukla *et al.* highlighted the value of blockchain technology in smart supply chain management, emphasizing its potential to enhance traceability and transparency, thereby reducing food waste, improving product quality, and increasing stakeholder confidence [17].

Because blockchain technology enables the efficient tracking of food goods along the supply chain, it has also been recognized for its contribution to enhanced food safety. Blockchain, according to Rahman *et al.*, can increase customer confidence in food items and help stop outbreaks of foodborne disease [18]. Furthermore, writers examined how blockchain technology can enhance payment processing in the agricultural industry, resulting in safer and more efficient transactions among growers, distributors, and other stakeholders [19]. The potential of blockchain technology to improve crop insurance has also been explored [20], as it enables transparent and efficient claims processing, reducing fraud and building trust between farmers and insurance providers.

To enhance decision-making in precision agriculture, several researchers have concentrated on integrating Explainable AI (XAI) by offering clear and comprehensible machine-learning models. According to Ryo, XAI can boost farmers' confidence in AI models used in precision agriculture by helping them comprehend the logic behind them [21]. Additionally, the author discussed how XAI can help estimate agricultural production more accurately by providing more transparent insights into the variables that affect yield and empowering farmers to make more informed management decisions [22].

Spieth has drawn attention to the potential of XAI in the context of pest detection, emphasizing how it might increase the precision and dependability of pest detection models and build higher confidence among farmers and other stakeholders [23]. In a similar vein, Feld Kamp discussed the application of XAI in soil mapping and argued that it can provide more accurate and comprehensive information, which is crucial for effective crop management. Despite extensive research on blockchain and Explainable AI (XAI), a significant knowledge gap remains in understanding how these technologies can be effectively integrated into smart farming to enhance sustainability and optimize agricultural practices [24, 25].

IoT and Blockchain in the Food Industry

Recent developments have proposed solutions combining IoT and BCT to create a more transparent and trustworthy food supply chain. For instance, Lin *et al.* [26] proposed an ecosystem for smart agriculture that leverages BCT and IoT, enabling stakeholders to input data directly *via* smartphones or automatically from IoT devices. This system ensures data integrity and security through blockchain's cryptographic techniques, allowing all stakeholders to access reliable, real-time information about agricultural products.

In terms of payments, the adoption of blockchain technology in agriculture enables secure, transparent, and efficient transactions. For example, BCT can facilitate direct payments between suppliers and retailers, reducing transaction fees and ensuring that farmers receive fair compensation [27]. Furthermore, blockchain-based digital tokens can be used by small farmers to purchase necessary inputs, such as fertilizers, with these transactions being securely recorded and traced on the blockchain [28].

From a management perspective, blockchain offers a solution to the credibility and integration challenges in agricultural traceability systems. Hua *et al.* [29] proposed a distributed peer-to-peer platform that ensures data credibility by making it immutable once it is entered into the system. This platform also facilitates the integration of subsystems from different companies by providing an open data-sharing environment, although privacy concerns remain a challenge.

Blockchain's ability to maintain an unchangeable record of transactions is particularly beneficial for the food industry, where traceability and transparency are paramount. Tian *et al.* [30] discussed a blockchain-based traceability system for the agri-food supply chain in China, highlighting its potential to eliminate counterfeit products from the market. However, the high cost and technological maturity of such systems remain challenges that need to be addressed.

In conclusion, the convergence of IoT and blockchain technologies in the food industry is transforming the way food products are tracked, traded, and managed, leading to enhanced food safety, reduced transaction costs, and improved transparency throughout the supply chain.

LAYERS OF IOT IN THE FOOD INDUSTRY

The IoT architecture for smart farming applications typically consists of five main layers: physical, network, middleware, service, and application.

- **Physical Layer:** The physical layer, also referred to as the perception layer, is responsible for collecting data through various sensors, actuators, Wireless Sensor Networks (WSNs), RFID tags, and other IoT devices. This layer serves as the foundation for smart farming applications by linking physical objects in IoT networks, gathering, monitoring, and processing status information from these objects, and transmitting the processed data to the upper layers. The physical layer also receives control commands from the application layer to perform corresponding actions, such as operating agricultural machinery [31].
- **Network Layer:** The data gathered by the physical layer is sent to the middleware and service tiers by the network layer, which manages connectivity between IoT devices. Additionally, it guarantees that control commands are returned to the physical layer from the application layer. To facilitate smooth connectivity across diverse transmission ranges, this layer incorporates a variety of communication technologies, including Ethernet, mobile networks (2G/3G/4G/5G), ZigBee, LoRa, NB-IoT, Sigfox, Bluetooth, NFC, and Wi-Fi [31].
- **Middleware Layer:** The middleware layer abstracts the complexities of the hardware and software in the IoT system, simplifying the development and deployment of IoT applications and services. This layer serves as an interface between IoT devices and higher layers, facilitating data management, processing, and communication between devices and applications. Middleware platforms, such as cloud-based systems, context-aware frameworks, and service-oriented architectures, are essential in this layer to support various agricultural applications [31].
- **Service Layer:** The service layer provides essential services, such as cloud computing, fog computing, Artificial Intelligence (AI), and big data analytics, which enable the application layer to perform a wide range of agricultural activities. These services support decision-making, automation, and data analysis, enabling farmers to optimize their operations for improved productivity, quality, and profitability. The service layer ensures that the application layer has access to the necessary tools and technologies to execute

smart farming tasks efficiently [31].

- **Application Layer**: In the IoT architecture for smart farming, the application layer is the highest tier and is responsible for utilizing the services provided by the lower tiers to perform specific agricultural tasks. To support coordination and communication among diverse agricultural applications, this layer incorporates several Internet of Things (IoT)-based messaging protocols, including Advanced Message Queuing Protocol (AMQP), Extensible Messaging and Presence Protocol (XMPP), Message Queue Telemetry Transport (MQTT), and Constrained Application Protocol (CoAP). Numerous smart farming operations, including supply chain management, pesticide applications, disease control, smart harvesting, crop monitoring, and smart water management, are made possible by the application layer [31]. Fig. (**1**) depicts the role of IoT in the food supply chain.

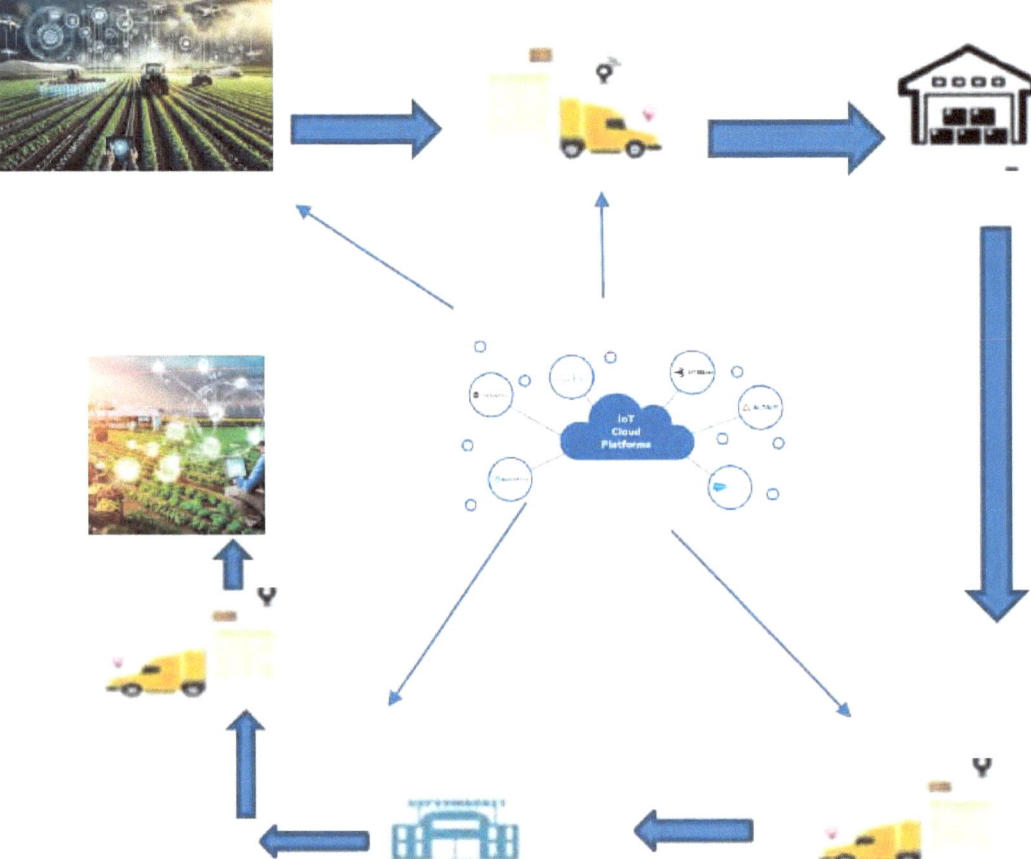

Fig. (1). IoT in food supply chain management.

Real-Life Case Studies in Smart Agriculture

Smart agriculture has been a significant focus of innovation, with numerous real-life implementations demonstrating the potential of IoT and emerging technologies. In this section, we highlight several notable projects that showcase the application of these technologies in the field.

- **Remote Sensing in Precision Agriculture:** Let us consider precision farming as one of the most representative applications of IoT in agriculture, as illustrated by a notable example from Devan *et al.* [32]. UAVs equipped with multispectral sensors were used to monitor the crop and soil conditions. Its use of sensory inputs enabled farmers to optimize irrigation, fertilizer, and pest-control procedures, which helped enhance the yields and rationality of resource utilization for crops.
- **Smart Irrigation Systems:** Smart irrigation systems are another excellent example of the practical application of this approach, particularly in regions where water scarcity poses a significant challenge. For instance, Manisha *et al.* [33] demonstrate how an IoT-based irrigation system can be utilized, incorporating soil moisture sensors and weather information to optimize water resource utilization. This system not only saved up to 30% of the water supply but also improved crop yield through the right moisture status of the soil.
- **Blockchain for Supply Chain Transparency**: The use of blockchain technology has also been implemented in agriculturally enforced supply chains to magnify both transparency and traceability. An example of this is the implementation of a blockchain platform initiated previously [34], which was used to map the tracing of coffee beans from the farm to the consumer. They were also able to provide consumers with information about the origin of the coffee and its quality, which helped them charge premium prices for high-quality products [34].
- **Autonomous Agricultural Robots:** Another study in the field of robotics is a case study that maps the application of autonomous robots for crop monitoring and harvesting, as elaborated by Zhang *et al.* [35]. These robots, utilizing sensors and machine learning as their primary tools, were able to distinguish between ripe fruits and those that needed more time, thereby offering selective harvesting with very high accuracy. This helped reduce labor costs and prevent crop damage.
- **AI-Driven Pest Control:** The application of artificial intelligence in pest detection and control has been well implemented, for instance, by Sharma *et al.* [36], who developed an AI system that operated through real image recognition to detect pest status and timely control the pests, hence avoiding spoilage and cutting down the use of chemical pesticides.

- **Monitoring and management of cattle:** IoT agricultural sensors are utilized for the health of livestock, as well as for the documentation of livestock production, such as crop production. Information concerning the health, welfare, and physical condition of animals is obtained through tracking and monitoring them. Such sensors, for example, can identify animals that are ill, allowing farmers to separate them and prevent the spread of diseases. Crop growers may be able to trim some of the costs associated with having personnel, especially if they use drones to locate animals in real-time. This works similarly to any other IoT product connected to the well-being of pets. For example, SCR from Allflex and Cowlar utilizes smart agricultural sensors or collar tags to collect and report information on the entire herd, including feeding temperature, health, activity, and nutrition data for each cow [37].

- **Drones for agriculture:** The use of agricultural drones for smart farming is perhaps one of the most exciting developments in agriculture. Drones, often referred to as unmanned aerial vehicles, or UAVs, are more capable of gathering agricultural data than satellites and aircraft. In addition to their surveillance capabilities, drones can carry out a wide range of tasks that traditionally required human labor, such as crop planting, pest and disease eradication, agricultural spraying, crop monitoring, and more [37]. Fig. (**2**) depicts the usage of drones in agriculture.

- **Predictive analytics in intelligent agriculture**: Predictive data analytics and precision agriculture go hand in hand. The use of data analytics by farmers helps them make sense of the vast amounts of highly relevant real-time data provided by IoT and smart sensor technologies, enabling them to make critical forecasts about crop harvesting times, disease and pest risks, yield volumes, and other related topics. Farming, which is highly dependent on the weather, can be made more predictable and controlled with the use of data analytics technologies. For instance, farmers can obtain information on crop quality and volume, as well as their susceptibility to adverse weather events such as drought and flooding, using the Crop Performance platform [37].

These case studies highlight the transformative impact of IoT, blockchain, AI, and robotics in smart agriculture, providing a glimpse into the future of farming where technology plays a central role in enhancing efficiency, sustainability, and profitability. Fig. (**3**) depicts the use cases of IoT in smart agriculture.

Fig. (2). .Drones in agriculture.

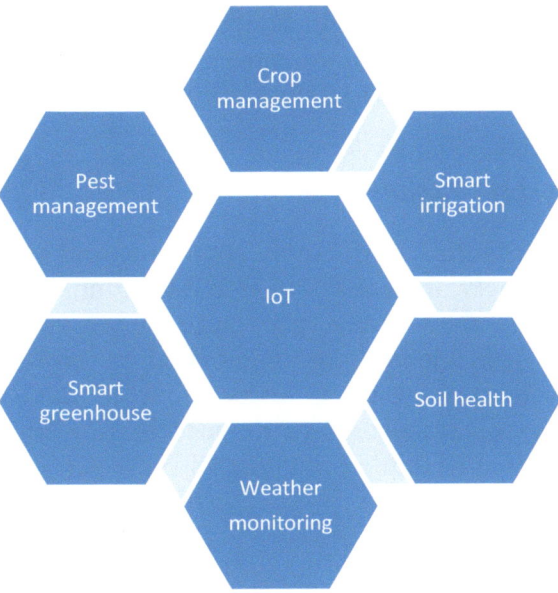

Fig. (3). Use cases of IoT in agriculture.

Challenges in IoT-Based Smart Agriculture

Despite several benefits associated with the application of IoT in smart agriculture, considerable challenges remain that must be addressed to fully realize the technology's potential. These challenges can be broadly classified into the following categories: hardware challenges, interoperability challenges, networking and energy management challenges, educational challenges, cost challenges, and security challenges.

Hardware Challenges

Designing practical and robust IoT devices for agricultural settings remains an arduous task. Most agriculture occurs in environments with dirt, moisture, and sometimes rough weather, and harsh conditions also shorten the performance, specifically in terms of the lifespan of IoT devices [37]. In addition to this, there is also an additional barrier to the large-scale use of agricultural industry IoT devices, which is the requirement for inexpensive power and extended working periods without device maintenance [38].

Interoperability Challenges

The most central of those is the problem of standardization in the development and deployment of IoT in agriculture. Usually, every device or system employs an incompatible communication standard, which in turn sometimes hinders the successful completion of the system; hence, it is not possible to utilize all the devices in one single system. Standardization of these protocols is also crucial for the effective use of IoT devices in agricultural systems, ensuring consistency across various sectors [39].

Networking and Energy Management

In IoT-based smart agriculture, effective networking and energy management are essential. Wide-area networks with dependable connections are essential for farming operations, as they often span large geographic areas. Nonetheless, maintaining reliable network coverage in isolated or rural locations continues to be difficult [40]. Furthermore, there is worry about IoT device energy usage since many agricultural applications require devices to run constantly for extended periods, which can quickly deplete batteries [41].

Educational Challenges

The knowledge and abilities of users are just as important to the effective application of IoT in agriculture as the technology itself. To effectively utilize IoT technology, farmers and agricultural workers require training and education. However, there is often a lack of training programs and educational resources tailored to the needs of farmers, particularly in developing regions [14].

Cost Challenges

Many farmers, particularly smallholders, may find the initial cost of putting up IoT equipment to be exorbitant. Adoption may be seriously hampered by the expenses of acquiring IoT devices, setting up infrastructure, and maintaining the systems [10]. Additionally, farmers may be discouraged from investing in IoT devices because returns on investment are not always instantaneous.

Security Challenges

One of the main issues with IoT-based smart agriculture is security. The danger of cyberattacks, which can jeopardize data integrity and privacy, is increased by the vast number of connected devices [11]. Furthermore, many IoT devices used in agriculture have limited processing power, which makes it challenging to implement robust security measures [12].

CONCLUDING REMARKS

The supply chain tracking of products, trading, and management of food goods have undergone significant transformation with the help of the food industry, IoT technology, and blockchain. This ensures that the data is well collected, transmitted, and processed using a five-layer IoT architecture, from the physical layer to the application layer. This leads to more intelligent and efficient farming business operations. Pest control and supply chain logistics are two areas where blockchain technology enhances the management system of food supply chains, making it more credible and efficient.

Their combination creates the preconditions for a stronger and more customer-oriented agricultural sector, alongside concrete benefits such as enhanced food safety and lower transaction and operational costs. It was found that IoT and blockchain have great potential in smart agriculture, although challenges related to hardware, compatibility, communication, and security persist. This looks quite encouraging for future enhancement. However, to address the current challenges and fully leverage these technologies in the international food industry, further research in this area is necessary.

Therefore, the growing demand for a specific and clear approach to agriculture, which is both environmentally friendly and effective, will likely drive the adoption of blockchain and IoT. Thus, as these technologies advance, the security, strength, and resilience to disruption of the food supply chain will be enhanced, thereby advancing global food security and sustainability. This conclusion highlights the importance of continuing to investigate and implement blockchain and IoT in smart agriculture, with a special focus on problem-solving and opportunities for exploitation.

REFERENCES

[1]   M. Karatas, L. Eriskin, M. Deveci, D. Pamucar, and H. Garg, "Big data for healthcare industry 4.0: applications, challenges and future perspectives", *Expert Syst. Appl.,* vol. 200, p. 116912, 2022.
[http://dx.doi.org/10.1016/j.eswa.2022.116912]

[2]   P. Kumar, R. Kumar, G.P. Gupta, R. Tripathi, A. Jolfaei, and A.K.M. Najmul Islam, "A blockchain-orchestrated deep learning approach for secure data transmission in IoT-enabled healthcare system", *J. Parallel Distrib. Comput.,* vol. 172, pp. 69-83, 2023.
[http://dx.doi.org/10.1016/j.jpdc.2022.10.002]

[3]   M. Karatas, A. Dasci, G.A. Yıldız, and M. Soytaş, "A two-level facility location and sizing problem for maximal coverage", *Comput. Ind. Eng.,* vol. 139, p. 106204, 2020.
[http://dx.doi.org/10.1016/j.cie.2019.106204]

[4]   M. Karatas, and M. Mumtaz, "A multi-objective bi-level location problem for heterogeneous sensor networks with hub-spoke topology", *Comput. Netw.,* vol. 181, p. 107551, 2020.
[http://dx.doi.org/10.1016/j.comnet.2020.107551]

[5]   M. Karatas, B.S. Onggo, and G.A. Yıldız, "Optimising the barrier coverage of a wireless sensor network with hub-and-spoke topology using mathematical and simulation models", *Comput. Oper. Res.,* vol. 106, pp. 36-48, 2019.
[http://dx.doi.org/10.1016/j.cor.2019.02.007]

[6]   W.J. Gordon, C. Catalini, and A.K. Gagneja, "Blockchain technology for healthcare: Facilitating the transition to patient-driven interoperability", *Comput. Struct. Biotechnol. J.,* vol. 16, pp. 224-230, 2018.
[http://dx.doi.org/10.1016/j.csbj.2018.06.003] [PMID: 30069284]

[7]   S. Xuan, L. Zheng, I. Chung, W. Wang, D. Man, X. Du, W. Yang, and M. Guizani, "An incentive mechanism for data sharing based on blockchain with smart contracts", *Comput. Electr. Eng.,* vol. 83, p. 106587, 2020.
[http://dx.doi.org/10.1016/j.compeleceng.2020.106587]

[8]   A. Aljuhani, M.K. Alsmadi, S.A.R. Althunibat, and M.S. Hossain, "Fog intelligence for secure smart villages: Architecture, and future challenges", *IEEE Consum. Electron. Mag.,* vol. 11, no. 3, pp. 81-87, 2022.

[9]   H.Y. Chen, K. Sharma, C. Sharma, and S. Sharma, "Integrating explainable artificial intelligence and blockchain to smart agriculture: Research prospects for decision making and improved security", *Smart Agricultural Technology,* vol. 6, p. 100350, 2023.
[http://dx.doi.org/10.1016/j.atech.2023.100350]

[10] C. Talavera, J. Tobarra, M. Zapata, R. Morales, and F. García, "IoT-based agro-industrial and environmental applications: Overview, challenges and future directions", *Sensors (Basel),* vol. 17, no. 1, p. 155, 2017.
[PMID: 28098825]

[11] R. Muhammad, L. Maglaras, M.A. Ferrag, and Y. He, "IoT-based intrusion detection systems in smart agriculture", *Electronics (Basel),* vol. 9, no. 5, p. 748, 2020.

[12] M.A. Ferrag, L. Shu, and X. Wang, "Security challenges of IoT-based smart agriculture: A comprehensive review", *IEEE Access,* vol. 8, pp. 32056-32081, 2020.
[http://dx.doi.org/10.1109/ACCESS.2020.2973178]

[13] K. Lakhwani, H. Gianey, N. Agarwal, and S. Gupta, "Development of IoT for smart agriculture: A review", In: *Emerging Trends in Expert Applications and Security.* Springer, 2019, pp. 425-432.

[14]   A. Khanna, and S. Kaur, "Evolution of Internet of Things (IoT) and its significant impact in the field of Precision Agriculture", *Comput. Electron. Agric.,* vol. 157, pp. 218-231, 2019.
[http://dx.doi.org/10.1016/j.compag.2018.12.039]

[15]   W. Lu, X. Xu, G. Huang, B. Li, Y. Wu, N. Zhao, and F.R. Yu, "Energy efficiency optimization in SWIPT enabled WSNs for smart agriculture", *IEEE Trans. Industr. Inform.,* vol. 17, no. 6, pp. 4335-4344, 2021.
[http://dx.doi.org/10.1109/TII.2020.2996672]

[16]   L. Lipper, P. Thornton, B.M. Campbell, T. Baedeker, A. Braimoh, M. Bwalya, P. Caron, A. Cattaneo, D. Garrity, K. Henry, R. Hottle, L. Jackson, A. Jarvis, F. Kossam, W. Mann, N. McCarthy, A. Meybeck, H. Neufeldt, T. Remington, P.T. Sen, R. Sessa, R. Shula, A. Tibu, and E.F. Torquebiau, "Climate-smart agriculture for food security", *Nat. Clim. Chang.,* vol. 4, no. 12, pp. 1068-1072, 2014.
[http://dx.doi.org/10.1038/nclimate2437]

[17]   R. Shukla, "Detecting crop health using machine learning techniques in smart agriculture systems", *J. Sci. Ind. Res. (India),* vol. 80, no. 08, pp. 699-706, 2021.

[18]   A. Rahman *et al.,* "Block-sdotcloud: Enhancing security of cloud storage through blockchain-based SDN in IoT networks," in Proc. 2020 2nd Int. Conf. Sustainable Technol. Ind. 4.0 (STI), 2020, pp. 1–6.
[http://dx.doi.org/10.1109/STI50764.2020.9350419]

[19]   C. Fan, S. Ghaemi, H. Khazaei, and P. Musilek, "Performance evaluation of blockchain systems: A systematic survey", *IEEE Access,* vol. 8, pp. 126927-126950, 2020.
[http://dx.doi.org/10.1109/ACCESS.2020.3006078]

[20]   Y. Aoki, K. Otsuki, T. Kaneko, R. Banno, and K. Shudo, "SimBlock: A blockchain network simulator," in IEEE INFOCOM 2019 - IEEE Conference on Computer Communications Workshops (INFOCOM WKSHPS), Paris, France, 2019, pp. 325–329.
[http://dx.doi.org/10.1109/INFCOMW.2019.8845253]

[21]   J. Gerlings, A. Shollo, and I. Constantiou, "Reviewing the need for Explainable Artificial Intelligence (xAI)," arXiv preprint arXiv:2012.01007, 2020. Available: https://arxiv.org/abs/2012.01007.

[22]   M. Ryo, "Explainable artificial intelligence and interpretable machine learning for agricultural data analysis", *Artif. Intell. Agric.,* vol. 6, pp. 257-265, 2022. Available at: https://www.sciencedirect.com/science/article/pii/S2589721722000216

[23]   T. Speith, "A review of taxonomies of Explainable Artificial Intelligence (XAI) methods", *Proc. 2022 ACM Conf. Fairness, Accountability, and Transparency,* pp. 2239-2250, 2022.
[http://dx.doi.org/10.1145/3531146.3534639]

[24]   B. Dutta, A. Krichel, and M-P. Odini, *The challenge of zero-touch and explainable AI.,* J. ICT Stand, pp. 147-158, 2021.
[http://dx.doi.org/10.13052/jicts2245-800X.925]

[25]   P.W. Khan, Y.C. Byun, and N. Park, "IoT-blockchain enabled optimized provenance system for food industry 4.0 using advanced deep learning", *Sensors (Basel),* vol. 20, no. 10, p. 2990, 2020.
[http://dx.doi.org/10.3390/s20102990] [PMID: 32466209]

[26]   Q. Lin, H. Wang, X. Pei, and J. Wang, "Food safety traceability system based on blockchain and EPCIS", *IEEE Access,* vol. 7, pp. 20698-20707, 2019.
[http://dx.doi.org/10.1109/ACCESS.2019.2897792]

[27]   F. Casino, T. Dasaklis, and C. Patsakis, "Enhanced vendor-managed inventory through blockchain," in Proc. 2019 IEEE Smart Energy & Distributed Energy Systems Conference (SEEDA-CECNSM), 2019. doi: 10.1109/SEEDA-CECNSM.2019.8908481.

[28]   J. Hua, X. Wang, M. Kang, and F. Y. Wang, "Blockchain-based provenance for agricultural products: A distributed platform with duplicated and shared bookkeeping," in Proc. 2018 IEEE Intelligent Vehicles Symposium (IV), Changshu, China, 2018, pp. 97–101.

[http://dx.doi.org/10.1109/WETSEB.2019.00012]

[29] S. Gupta, S. Arora, and S. Qamar, "Federated learning in smart farming: applications and challenges", *Convergence of AI, Federated Learning, and Blockchain for Sustainable Development,* pp. 121-146, 2025.
[http://dx.doi.org/10.1007/978-3-031-80949-1_7]

[30] F. Tian, "A supply chain traceability system for food safety based on HACCP, blockchain & Internet of things", *Proc. 2017 IEEE International Conference on System Science and Simulation in Engineering (ICSSSM),* pp. 1-6, 2017.
[http://dx.doi.org/10.1109/ICSSSM.2017.7996119]

[31] N. Feldkamp, "Data farming output analysis using explainable AI", *Proc. 2021 Winter Simulation Conf. (WSC),* pp. 1-12, 2021.
[http://dx.doi.org/10.1109/WSC52266.2021.9715470]

[32] V. Devan, R. Satish, and N. Kumar, "Remote sensing applications in precision agriculture", *IEEE Access,* vol. 7, pp. 816-828, 2021.

[33] M. Manisha, S. Gupta, and A. Kaur, "IoT-based smart irrigation system for water resource optimization", *IEEE Internet Things J.,* vol. 6, no. 4, pp. 5597-5606, 2020.

[34] N. Kshetri, J. Voas, and F. Jain, "Blockchain's roles in meeting key supply chain management objectives", *IEEE IT Professional,* vol. 21, no. 4, pp. 13-19, 2019.

[35] Y. Zhang, L. Wang, and X. Li, "Autonomous robots for smart agriculture: Case studies and challenges", *IEEE Trans. Autom. Sci. Eng.,* vol. 18, no. 2, pp. 479-490, 2021.
[http://dx.doi.org/10.1109/TASE.2016.2523341]

[36] S. Sharma, P. Singh, and M. Kumar, "AI-driven pest control system in agriculture: A real-time approach", *IEEE Trans. Neural Netw. Learn. Syst.,* vol. 32, no. 5, pp. 1990-2000, 2021.

[37] O. Friha, M.A. Ferrag, L. Shu, L. Maglaras, and X. Wang, "Internet of things for the future of smart agriculture: A comprehensive survey of emerging technologies", *IEEE/CAA Journal of Automatica Sinica,* vol. 8, no. 4, pp. 718-752, 2021.
[http://dx.doi.org/10.1109/JAS.2021.1003925]

[38] A. Chlingaryan, S. Sukkarieh, and B. Whelan, "Machine learning approaches for crop yield prediction and nitrogen status estimation in precision agriculture: A review", *Comput. Electron. Agric.,* vol. 151, pp. 61-69, 2018.
[http://dx.doi.org/10.1016/j.compag.2018.05.012]

[39] P. P. Ray, "Internet of things for smart agriculture: Technologies, practices and future direction," Journal of Ambient Intelligence and Smart Environments, vol. 9, pp. 395–420, 2017. [Online]. Available: https://api.semanticscholar.org/CorpusID:31226726

[40] M.S. Farooq, S. Riaz, A. Abid, T. Umer, and Y.B. Zikria, "Role of IoT technology in agriculture: A systematic literature review", *Electronics (Basel),* vol. 9, no. 2, p. 319, 2020.
[http://dx.doi.org/10.3390/electronics9020319]

[41] B.R. Ferrag, M.A. Ferrag, and L. Shu, "Towards security and privacy of IoT-based smart agriculture: Review", *IEEE J. Internet Things,* vol. 8, no. 12, pp. 9053-9076, 2021.

CHAPTER 7

Enhancing the Tomato and Potato Crop Health: A Novel Approach for Ensemble Deep Learning based Disease Classification

Ekamdeep Singh[1,*] and **Tamanna Sood**[1]

¹ Department of Computer Science and Engineering, Punjab Engineering College (Deemed to be) University, Chandigarh-160012, India

Abstract: The primary goal of this chapter is to study the current research in order to detect diseases in tomato and potato crops through the analysis of leaf images. We propose a novel methodology that involves a comprehensive data preprocessing stage, including image resizing and augmentation to enhance the dataset. We study the various pre-trained transfer learning architectures that can be used for classification. In this chapter, we discuss three ensemble models based on the best-performing architectures. Model 1 is a generalized model for both tomato and potato plants, Model 2 is specialized for potato plant diseases, and Model 3 focuses on tomato plant diseases. These ensemble models utilize a weighted average approach to calculate the results. The combination of these models is based on the highest-performing individual base models, ensuring optimal performance. The highest accuracy achieved for potato plant disease identification is 99.06%, while the best accuracy for tomato plant disease identification is 98.12%. The chapter studies and explores the efficacy of ensemble deep learning models in classifying plant diseases with accuracy, offering a robust tool for agricultural disease management.

Keywords: Crop health, Disease detection, Deep learning, Ensemble learning, Transfer learning.

INTRODUCTION

Agriculture has always been a crucial means of livelihood. The Indian economy is heavily dependent on the agricultural industry of the country [1]. It plays a great role in providing employment as well as food security for a large section of people [2]. It is a vital industry for the Indian economy, employing around 58% of

---

* **Corresponding author Ekamdeep Singh:** Department of Computer Science and Engineering, Punjab Engineering College (Deemed to be) University, Chandigarh-160012, India; E-mail: ekamwadhwa20@gmail.com

Shefali Arora Chouhanm Nagendra Pratap Singh, Banalaxmi Brahma & Shashank Gupta (Eds.)

the workforce and adding about 17% to the country's GDP. Tomatoes and potatoes are among the most significant crops globally, providing vital nutrients and serving as the backbone of many farming communities worldwide [3].

However, plant disease has a detrimental impact on these crops, affecting their productivity and quality [4]. Microorganisms, infectious agents such as viruses, fungi and bacteria, and genetic abnormalities are the main contributors to these diseases [5]. Crop diseases cause significant financial losses that impact the entire economy [6]. The variations in the demand and distribution network of agriculture-based consumables affect the overall balance of the economy [7]. Thus, timely identification and diagnosis of crop diseases are essential for optimal production. Traditional methods of classifying plant diseases included the visual examination of plant tissues by skilled professionals, but this approach was inefficient, expensive, and time-consuming [8]. The results of the visual approach were affected by subjectivity and resulted in the inaccuracy of the disease identified [9, 10]. In recent years, advances in computer technology, particularly in Artificial Intelligence (AI) and image processing approaches, have made the identification and diagnosis of crop diseases possible at an early stage. This is an automated procedure that can be used in fields and farms [11].

The various existing studies have proposed different models using machine learning, deep learning, and hybrid methodologies for accurate and efficient crop disease classification. Early machine learning models often relied on handcrafted features and classical algorithms. Deep learning models, particularly CNN's apply automatic feature extraction from raw images and hybrid models use the strengths of both ML and DL techniques. Despite these advancements, several challenges remain. So, there is a need for a novel approach that can further enhance the classification of tomato and potato crops with more accurate results. The present study proposes the weighted average ensemble model by combining the top-performing pre-trained deep learning models that are fine-tuned using the Plant Village dataset. This approach aims to integrate the capabilities of multiple models to increase the accuracy and robustness of disease detection. By integrating these models, the ensemble method can better generalize, addressing the limitations of individual models and improving the results of existing studies.

The remaining sections of the chapter are structured as follows: Section 2 discusses the existing work along with an overview of plant diseases. Section 3 provides detailed insights into the materials and methods employed in the study, including a dataset description, proposed methodology, implementation details and evaluation metrics. In Section 4, the experimentation results are presented. Finally, Section 5 wraps up the chapter by highlighting essential findings, discussing the implications and possible directions for future studies.

BACKGROUND

Overview of Plant Diseases

Plant diseases significantly affect crop health and productivity, which causes agriculture to suffer huge economic losses. These diseases can be broadly divided on the basis of biotic and abiotic causes as shown in Fig. (**1**) below, each of which has a special role in the pathology of plants [12]. To create effective disease management strategies and ensure sustainable farming practices with significant yield, understanding these factors is essential.

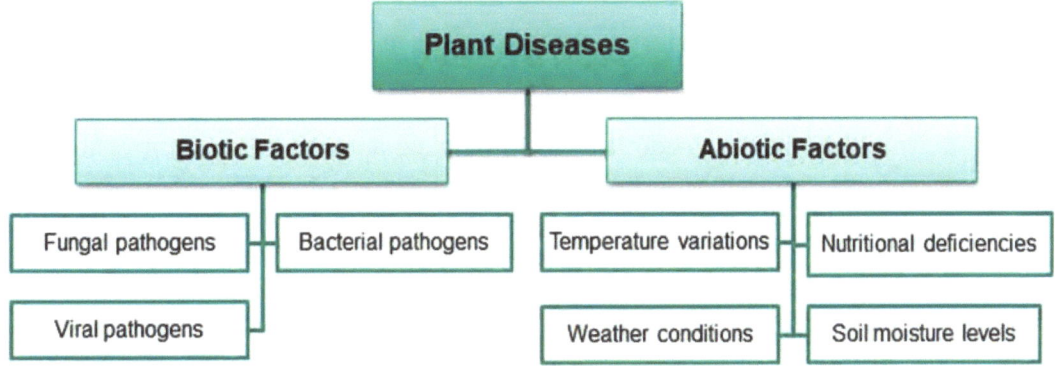

Fig. (1). Causes of plant diseases.

1) Biotic Factors include the living organisms that infect plants and cause the development of diseases. These include:
- **Fungal pathogens:** Fungal infections are characterized by spots, rust, blights, and powdery mildews affecting the stems, leaves and fruits of plants. For example, early blight in potato, and septoria leaf spot in tomato.
- **Bacterial pathogens:** Bacterial infections result in leaf spots, wilts, and soft rots, causing damage to plant tissues. For example, bacterial spots in tomatoes.
- **Viral pathogens:** Viral infections cause symptoms like mottling, stunted growth, leaf curl, and yellowing, and reduce the productivity of plants— for example, the yellow leaf curl virus in tomatoes.

2) Abiotic Factors involve environmental conditions that lead to the development of illnesses in plant species.
- **Temperature variations:** Create physiological stress in plants, can harm their tissues and can inhibit their growth.
- **Nutritional deficiencies:** Lack of vital nutrients can lead to yellowing of leaves, stunted growth and death of plant tissues.
- **Weather conditions:** High humidity can cause fungal growth.
- **Soil moisture levels:** Plant health can be adversely affected by both

excessive and insufficient soil moisture, which increases the plants' susceptibility to disease.

Literature Review

The application of Machine Learning (ML), Deep Learning (DL), and hybrid methodologies has contributed to considerable advances in the identification and categorization of potato and tomato crops. These methods have been applied in several studies to improve the accuracy and effectiveness of disease identification. In the following subsections, we will briefly review the existing research related to potato and tomato disease classification in Sections 2.2.1 and 2.2.2, respectively.

Potential Diseases in Potatoes

Swetha *et al.* (2019) [4] introduced an innovative approach for identifying plant leaf diseases using machine learning classifiers. The method employed a Histogram of Oriented Gradients (HOG) for extracting features related to color, shape, and texture, which were then used to train a Support Vector Machine (SVM), achieving 94% accuracy. Sanjeev *et al.* (2020) [13] designed a system for the early detection of potato leaf diseases, achieving an accuracy of 96.5%. This study utilized a Feed Forward Neural Network (FFNN) trained on a dataset containing 2,152 images of potato leaves. Iqbal *et al.* (2020) [14] proposed a technique for detecting potato diseases by preprocessing PlantVillage dataset images using HSV conversion and thresholding-based segmentation to extract global feature descriptors. A Random Forest (RF) classifier was trained on these features, achieving an accuracy of 97%. Singh *et al.* (2021) [15] used K-means clustering for ROI segmentation and the Grey Level Co-occurrence Matrix (GLCM) for extracting features from potato leaf images. These features were then classified with SVM, achieving 95.99% accuracy for the detection and classification of potato leaf diseases. Kurmi *et al.* (2022) [16] developed a leaf image localization algorithm by combining a bag of visual words, fish vectors, and handcrafted features. These combined features were utilized to train a Logistic Regression (LR) and SVM classifier with an accuracy of 91.9% and 89.6%, respectively. Bhagat *et al.* (2023) [17] employed an efficient feature selection method combining Bag of Words (BoWs) and Speeded-Up Robust Features (SURF) for leaf disease identification using the Plant Village dataset. The selected features were classified using an SVM classifier with an accuracy of 97%.

Sert *et al.* (2021) [18] proposed a deep learning-based methodology for disease detection in potato leaves, leveraging a combined dataset comprising PlantVillage data and manually collected samples. The study used Faster R-CNN with

GoogleNet, achieving an accuracy of 98.06% across five different disease classes. Kothari *et al.* (2022) [19] developed a deep learning-based potato disease detection method. The study developed a novel CNN and compared its performance with that of pretrained CNNs. The novel CNN achieved an accuracy of 97%, while VGG16, ResNet50, and GoogleNet obtained accuracies of 33%, 98%, and 95%, respectively. Mahum *et al.* (2023) [20] proposed a novel Efficient DenseNet model with an accuracy of 97.2% in detecting potato leaf disease in comparison to the 96.03% accuracy of pretrained DenseNet 121. Jha *et al.* (2023) [1] used transfer learning to develop a stacking ensemble model for predicting potato diseases. The ensemble model achieved an improved accuracy of 98.86% in comparison to the individual models, MobileNet, Inception, and ResNet, which had accuracies of 97.2%, 94.2%, and 92.8%, respectively. Nazir *et al.* (2023) [21] presented an optimized and efficient deep learning method for the classification of potato leaf diseases. The proposed EfficientPNet achieved an accuracy of 98.12% on the dataset of 10,800 images. Sofuoglu *et al.* (2024) [12] used Plant Village dataset and introduced a novel CNN for detecting potato plant diseases. This deep learning method produced an impressive accuracy of 98.28%, demonstrating the effectiveness of the CNN architecture in disease classification.

Tiwari *et al.* (2020) [5] utilized the Plant Village dataset and proposed a hybrid approach for potato disease detection. This method extracted the features using VGG19 and then trained multiple classifiers on these features. The highest accuracy of 97.7% was achieved by Logistic Regression, followed by the 93.8% accuracy of SVM and KNN. Sultana *et al.* (2022) [22] proposed a hybrid CNN with SVM comprising pretrained ResNet50, achieving an accuracy of 97.3% and 95.6% on training and testing data, respectively. Ali *et al.* (2023) [23] developed a novel framework based on feature fusion of handcrafted features with deep features extracted by ResNet50. The features were dimensionally reduced using Principal Component Analysis (PCA) and subsequently classified with Linear Discriminant Analysis (LDA), achieving an accuracy of 98.2%. Singh *et al.* (2024) [2] employed a comparative approach for potato leaf disease detection by training deep learning models on two distinct datasets. The study developed a CNN with an accuracy of 94.92% and combined this CNN with KNN to create a hybrid model with an improved accuracy of 96.48%. Table **1** presents a comparison of the accuracy achieved by various existing methods for the classification of potato diseases.

Table 1. Comparison of existing techniques for potato diseases.

Reference	Year	Approach	Methodology	Accuracy
[16]	2022	ML	BoW + FV + HCF + SVM	91.9
[4]	2019	ML	HOG + SVM	94

(Table 1) cont.....

Reference	Year	Approach	Methodology	Accuracy
[22]	2022	Hybrid	ResNet50 + SVM	95.6
[15]	2021	ML	GLCM + SVM	95.99
[2]	2024	Hybrid	CNN + KNN	96.48
[13]	2020	ML	FFNN	96.5
[14]	2020	ML	GFD + RF	97
[19]	2022	DL	Custom CNN	97
[17]	2023	ML	BoWs + SURF + SVM	97
[20]	2023	DL	Efficient DenseNet	97.2
[5]	2020	Hybrid	VGG19 + LR	97.8
[18]	2021	DL	Faster RCNN with GoogleNet	98.09
[21]	2023	DL	Improved EfficientNet V2	98.12
[23]	2023	Hybrid	Feature Fusion + PCA + LDA	98.2
[12]	2024	DL	Custom CNN	98.28

Potential Diseases in Tomatoes

Basavaiah *et al.* (2020) [24] proposed a method for tomato disease classification utilizing multiple feature extraction techniques. Color histograms, Hu moments, and Harlick features were employed to extract color, shape, and texture features, respectively. These multiple features were concatenated to train a Random Forest (RF) model with an accuracy of 94%. Xian *et al.* (2021) [25] used HSV conversion for image preprocessing and Harlick features to develop an extreme machine learning model. The developed model achieved an accuracy of 84.94% for classifying tomato diseases into 10 categories. Mohanty *et al.* (2022) [26] trained an SVM model using features extracted through the Histogram of Oriented Gradients (HOG) technique for tomato plant disease detection, achieving an accuracy of 73%. Lubis *et al.* (2023) [10] developed a tomato disease classification system utilizing the KNN algorithm, which attained an accuracy of 96.58%. The KNN was trained by combining the colour features, Hu-moments features, and Harlick features.

Elhassouny *et al.* (2019) [27] developed a mobile application designed to detect tomato leaf diseases through the use of convolutional neural networks, attaining an accuracy of 90.3%. Liu *et al.* (2020) [28] developed an innovative framework for the early detection of tomato grey leaf spot disease, utilizing the YOLOv3 model with a MobileNetv2 backbone, which achieved an F1 score of 92.72% and an average precision of 90.29%. Lakshmanarao *et al.* (2021) [6] devised a system for predicting and classifying plant disease using deep learning convNets. The developed CNN achieved an accuracy of 95%. Sakkarvarthi *et al.* (2022) [3] developed a novel CNN for tomato crop disease detection with an accuracy of 88.17% compared to pretrained models, ResNet1012, VGG19, and InceptionV3, with accuracies of 69.58%, 70.14%, and 80.24%, respectively. Sreedevi *et al.* (2023) [9] proposed a transfer learning-based weighted ensemble model with an accuracy of 92.78%. For data augmentation, the study used a Generative Adversarial Network (GAN). Najim *et al.* (2024) [11] developed a deep learning-based system for the early detection of tomato leaf disease into 10 disease categories. The developed CNN achieved an accuracy of 96% and f1 score of 92%. Abouelmagd *et al.* (2024) [29] proposed an optimized capsule neural network for classifying tomato plant disease with an accuracy of 96.39% in comparison to the 92.87% accuracy of traditional CNN.

Bhatia *et al.* (2020) [30] introduced a hybrid classifier that combines logistic regression and Support Vector Machine (SVM) to predict powdery mildew disease using the Tomato Powdery Mildew Disease (TPMD) dataset, achieving an accuracy of 92.37%. Gadekallu *et al.* (2021) [7] developed a novel framework for classifying tomato plant diseases using a GPU. The Deep Neural Network (DNN) was trained on the features extracted by the hybrid PCA and whale optimization algorithms with an accuracy of 94%. Al-Gaashani *et al.* (2022) [8] developed a hybrid model by concatenating the features extracted from MobileNetV2 and NasNetMobile. The concatenated features were reduced by PCA and used to train a multinomial logistic regression and a linear SVM with an accuracy of 97% and 95.2% respectively. Hosny *et al.* (2023) [31] trained a softmax classifier on concatenated features of CNN and Local Binary Pattern (LBP). The developed model achieved validation and testing accuracies of 96.6% and 96.5%, respectively. Kaur *et al.* (2024) [32] introduced a hybrid CNN-SVM model for the task of classification of tomato diseases, utilizing multiple datasets. The model achieved an accuracy of 94%, along with precision, recall, and F1 scores of 87.68%, 87.16%, and 87.3%, respectively. A comparison of the accuracy attained by various existing methods for tomato disease classification is provided in Table 2.

Table 2. Comparison of existing techniques for tomato diseases.

Reference	Year	Approach	Methodology	Accuracy
[26]	2022	ML	HOG + SVM	73
[25]	2021	ML	Extreme ML	84.94
[3]	2022	DL	CNN	88.17
[27]	2019	DL	CNN	90.3
[30]	2020	Hybrid	Hybrid SVM-LR	92.37

(Table 2) cont.....

Reference	Year	Approach	Methodology	Accuracy
[28]	2020	DL	YOLOv3 + MobileNetv2	92.72
[9]	2023	DL	Ensemble	92.78
[24]	2020	ML	RF	94
[7]	2021	Hybrid	PCA + WOA + DNN	94
[32]	2024	Hybrid	CNN + SVM	94
[6]	2021	DL	CNN	95
[11]	2024	DL	CNN	96
[29]	2024	DL	Optimized capsule net	96.39
[31]	2023	Hybrid	CNN + LBP + Softmax	96.5
[10]	2023	ML	KNN	96.58
[8]	2022	Hybrid	Deep features + PCA + MLR	97

As shown in Tables **1** and **2**, machine learning and deep learning models have yielded promising results in the detection of potato and tomato diseases. Numerous researchers have used ML techniques like SVM, KNN, and RF, which typically make use of handcrafted features; DL approaches, particularly CNNs, which perform well in automatic feature extraction from raw images; and hybrid models that blend together the ML and DL strengths for enhanced classification and improved performance. The detection of crop diseases is an essential problem that affects agricultural production and crop yield. Several researchers have proposed various models utilizing different methodologies to enhance the accuracy and efficacy of plant disease classification. However, there remains a need for a deep learning-based model that can further improve the process of potato and tomato plant disease recognition, delivering more accurate and precise results.

This study involves the implementation of various pre-trained deep learning architectures and fine-tuning them to specific characteristics of potato and tomato diseases. Additionally, the study has proposed a weighted average ensemble network, combining the three best-performing models, to enhance the results of previous studies by utilizing an open-source Plant Village dataset. Furthermore, a comparative analysis to demonstrate the strengths of our proposed approach with the existing techniques for the same domain is conducted. The proposed framework will assist the farmers in identifying crop diseases at an early stage and, hence, reduce the damage caused.

MATERIAL AND METHODS

Dataset Description

In this chapter, we devise an approach to categorize diseases in the aforementioned crops. The dataset used for this research, sourced from Kaggle, is the Plant Village dataset provided by Emmanuel [33]. This dataset is a comprehensive collection of 54,303 images of both healthy and disease-affected crop leaves, categorized into 38 distinct classes. It encompasses a variety of crops, including tomatoes and potatoes, with images classified under distinct disease categories along with healthy leaves. The high-quality images in the dataset facilitate accurate disease classification, making it an ideal candidate for training deep-learning models.

Key characteristics of the dataset include:

- **Number of Images:** 54,303
- **Number of Classes:** 38 (including different diseases and healthy leaves)
- **Resolution:** High-quality images, typically 256 x 256 pixels
- **Format:** JPEG images

Dataset Composition

The Plant Village dataset includes several classes specifically for tomato and potato crops. Below is the detailed bifurcation of the dataset based on these two crops:

- **Tomato Images:** The dataset includes ten classes for tomatoes, covering a range of diseases and healthy leaves.
- **Potato Images:** The dataset includes three classes for potatoes, focusing on two common diseases and healthy leaves.

Table **3** gives a detailed description of the various classes and the number of images belonging to each class for the tomato and potato disease in the dataset and sample images of each disease class for tomato and potato plant is shown in Figs. (**2** and **3**), respectively. It can be observed from the dataset distribution in Table **3** that the classes are imbalanced.

Table 3. Class-wise description of the dataset.

Plant	Disease	Number of images
Tomato [33]	**Bacterial Spot:** Images of tomato leaves infected with bacterial spots.	2,127
	Early Blight: Images showing early blight disease on tomato leaves.	1,000
	Late Blight: Images depicting late blight disease on tomato leaves.	1,909
	Leaf Mold: Images of tomato leaves with leaf mold.	952
	Septoria Leaf Spot: Images showing septoria leaf spot on tomato leaves.	1,772
	Spider Mites (Two-Spotted Spider Mite): Images of tomato leaves infested with spider mites.	1,671
	Target Spot: Images showing target spot disease on tomato leaves.	1,400
	Yellow Leaf Curl Virus: Images depicting yellow leaf curl virus on tomato leaves.	5,353
	Mosaic Virus: Images of tomato leaves affected by mosaic virus.	373
	Healthy: Images of healthy tomato leaves.	1,591
Potato [33]	**Early Blight:** Images showing early blight disease on potato leaves.	1,000
	Late Blight: Images depicting late blight disease on potato leaves.	1,000
	Healthy: Images of healthy potato leaves.	152

Proposed Methodology

To enhance the health of tomato and potato crops through effective disease classification, we adopted a novel ensemble deep-learning approach. Fig. (**4**) shows the proposed methodology used. The methodology comprises several steps, beginning with data preprocessing and progressing through model training and evaluation. The detailed methodology is outlined below:

Data Pre-processing and Data Augmentation

Given the high quality of images in the dataset, no additional pre-processing techniques were applied beyond image resizing, pixel normalization and image augmentation. All the images of the dataset were resized to fix size of 224 x 224 and pixel values were normalized to a range from 0 to 1, to improve the convergence and efficiency while training the models. In order to remove the class imbalance problem from data and to strengthen the reliability of the models, the training dataset was diversified by applying the data augmentation techniques like random rotations, flips and zooms. Fig. (**5**) shows the augmented data. These augmentations help in simulating real-world variations and improving the model's generalization ability.

Fig. (2). One instance from each class of the dataset for potato (a) Target Spot (b) Tomato Mosaic Virus (c) Yellow Leaf Curl Virus (d) Bacterial Spot (e) Early Blight (f) Healthy (g) Late Blight (h) Leaf Mold (i) Septoria Leaf Spot (j) Spider Mites (Two-Spotted Spider Mite).

Fig. (3). One instance from each class of the dataset for potato (a) Early Blight, (b) Late Blight, (c) Healthy.

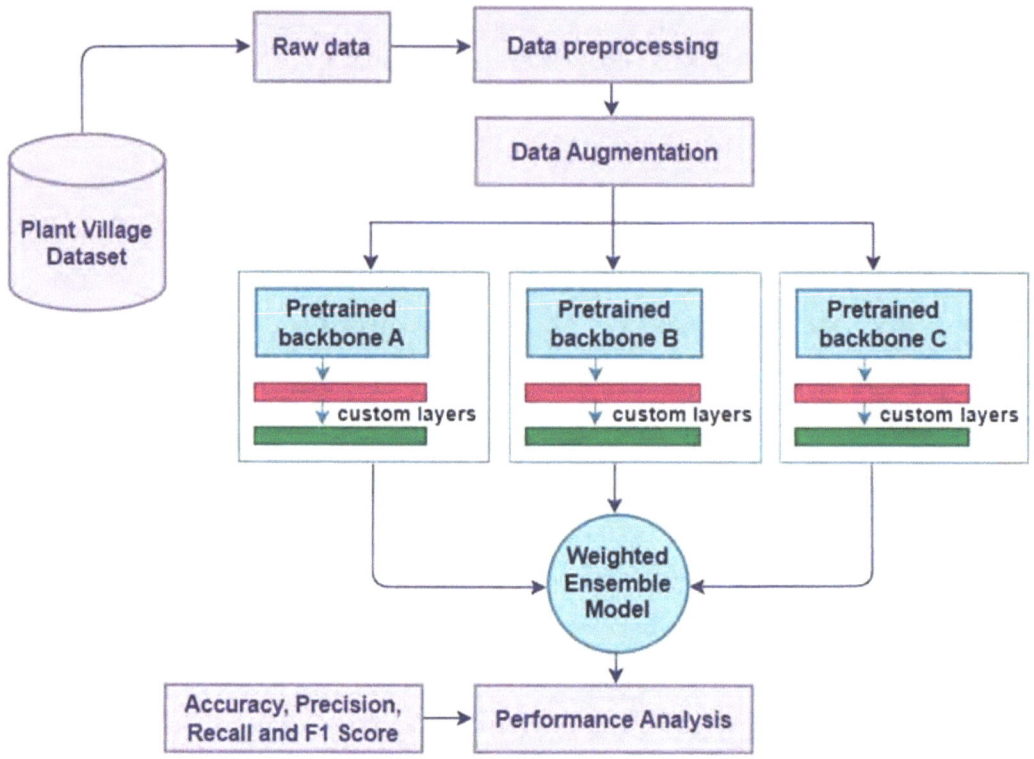

Fig. (4). Proposed methodology.

Fig. (5). Sample augmented images (a) Actual Image (b) Horizontally flipped image (c) Vertically flipped image (d) 90^0 rotated image (e) 180^0 rotated image (f) Zoomed image.

Classification Models

We leveraged several pre-trained Convolutional Neural Network (CNN) architectures to capitalize on their feature extraction capabilities and Table **4** shows the comparison of architecture of used CNN models. The following transfer learning models were employed:

Table 4. Comparison of various CNN architectures.

Model	Image Input Size	Model Depth	Trainable parameters	Size of Model
Xception [34]	299 x 299	71	22,910,480	88MB
VGG16 [35]	224 x 224	16	138,357,544	528MB
ResNet50 [36]	224 x 224	107	25,583,592	98MB
RseNet101V2 [37]	224 x 224	209	44,577,896	171MB
InceptionV3 [38]	299 x 299	48	23,851,784	92MB
InceptionResNetV2 [39]	299 x 299	164	55,873,736	215MB
NASNetMobile [40]	224 x 224	389	5,289,978	23MB
DenseNet121 [41]	224 x 224	121	8,062,504	33MB
MobileNet [42]	224 x 224	88	4,253,864	16MB
ConvNeXtTiny [43]	224 x 224	-	28,589,128	109.42

- **Xception** [34]: Xception, which stands for "Extreme Inception," is a deep convolutional neural network architecture based on depth-wise separable convolutions. It was developed by François Chollet and offers superior performance by using fewer parameters compared to traditional convolutions.
- **VGG16** [35]: VGG16, created by the Visual Geometry Group (VGG) at the University of Oxford, is a deep learning model featuring a total of 16 layers, including 13 convolutional layers and 3 fully connected layers. Its simple yet deep architecture makes it highly effective for tasks involving image classification.
- **ResNet50** [36]: ResNet50, a deep neural network designed by Microsoft Research, consists of 50 layers and utilizes residual connections to improve learning. These connections help mitigate the vanishing gradient issue, allowing for the effective training of very deep networks. Its robust architecture has made it a popular choice for numerous computer vision applications.
- **ResNet101V2** [37]: ResNet101V2 is an improved version of ResNet101, consisting of 101 layers with advanced techniques such as batch normalization after each weight layer. This architecture enhances the original ResNet by providing better convergence and performance.
- **InceptionV3** [38]: InceptionV3 is the third version of Google's Inception

architecture, which uses factorized convolutions and aggressive regularization to achieve higher efficiency and accuracy. It is designed to optimize computational cost while maintaining high performance in image classification.

- **InceptionResNetV2** [39]: InceptionResNetV2 integrates the Inception architecture with residual connections, leveraging the advantages of both techniques. This model aims to provide a balance between depth and computational efficiency, resulting in high accuracy for image recognition tasks.
- **NASNetMobile** [40]: NASNetMobile is a mobile-friendly version of the Neural Architecture Search Network (NASNet), developed by Google. It is optimized for mobile and embedded applications, offering a lightweight yet powerful model for image classification.
- **DenseNet121** [41]: DenseNet121, part of the DenseNet family, consists of 121 layers and dense connections between layers. This connectivity pattern helps to improve gradient flow and feature reuse, resulting in efficient training and strong performance in image classification.
- **MobileNet** [42]: A collection of lightweight convolutional neural networks called MobileNet is created for mobile and embedded vision applications. It is ideal for resource-constrained environments because it reduces the number of parameters and computational cost using depth-wise separable convolutions.
- **ConvNeXtTiny** [43]: ConvNext is a modernized variant of the standard convolutional neural network, designed to match the performance of vision transformers. ConvNeXtTiny is a smaller, more efficient version suitable for applications requiring lower computational overhead while maintaining competitive performance.

Proposed Ensemble Model

The ensemble approach combines predictions from multiple models to enhance overall performance. By utilizing the strengths of diverse architectures, it achieves improved accuracy, robustness, and generalization compared to standalone models. In this study, we propose two ensemble models specifically for potato and tomato disease classification. Ensemble Model-1 addresses the classification of both potato and tomato diseases, while Ensemble Model-2 focuses solely on potato diseases, and Ensemble Model-3 targets tomato diseases. This approach acknowledges that no single model is universally applicable across all datasets; the selection of a model depends on the specific use case and problem context. The ensemble models proposed comprise the following models, as shown in Table **5**.

Table 5. The model architectures used in various ensemble models.

Ensemble Model-1	Ensemble Model-2	Ensemble Model-3
• VGG16 • DenseNet121 • MobileNet	• VGG16 • ResNet101V2 • NASNetMobile	• Xception • InceptionResNetV2 • MobileNet

The ensemble models were constructed using a weighted average approach. The predictions from each of the three models were combined, and weights were assigned based on the validation performance of each model. The weighted average of the predictions was then used to make the final classification decision.

Implementation Details and Evaluation Metrics

This section mentions the implementation details and discusses the various evaluation metrics used to compare the results.

Implementation Details

The framework has been implemented in Python using TensorFlow and Keras libraries within the Jupyter Notebook environment. The implementation was executed on a system equipped with an Intel® Xeon® W-2155 CPU (3.30 GHz processor), 64 GB RAM, a 64-bit operating system, and Windows 11 Pro for Workstations. The dataset was split into 80% for training, 10% for validation, and 10% for testing. The finalized hyperparameters are detailed in Table **6**.

Table 6. Hyperparameters used for model training.

Parameter	Value
Image size	224
Epochs	30
Batch size	32
Optimizer	Adam
Learning Rate	0.0005
Activation Function	ReLU, Softmax
Loss Function	Categorical cross entropy
Early stopping	Patience = 5
Regularization	Regularization parameter(lambda) = 0.01

Evaluation Metrics

The performance of the individual models and the ensemble model was evaluated using the metrics mentioned and explained in Table **7**.

Table 7. Evaluation metrics with formula and description.

Metric	Formula	Description
Accuracy	$\dfrac{TP + TN}{TP + TN + FP + FN}$	Accuracy is defined as the ratio of correctly classified instances, including both true positives and true negatives, to the total number of instances.
Precision	$\dfrac{TP}{TP + FP}$	The proportion of correctly classified positive instances relative to the total number of classified positives.
Recall	$\dfrac{TP}{TP + FN}$	The proportion of correctly classified positive instances relative to the actual number of positives.
F1-Score	$\dfrac{Presision.Recall}{Presision + Recall}$	The single metric that balances both precision and recall by taking their harmonic mean.

RESULTS AND DISCUSSION

This section lists the results obtained and provides a detailed analysis.

RESULTS

The results section provides a comprehensive evaluation of the proficiency of various deep-learning models in classifying diseases in tomato and potato crops. Specifically, we assess the individual models discussed in section 3.2.2 as well as an ensemble model discussed in section 3.2.3 that combines these architectures. Our evaluation is based on four key metrics: accuracy, recall, precision, and F1 score. These measures offer an overall view of each model's performance, capturing different aspects of prediction quality.

In this section, we present and compare the results of these models on the PlantVillage dataset (with respect to tomato and potato diseases), highlighting their ability to accurately identify and classify plant diseases. The accuracy, recall, precision, and F1-score for potato diseases are shown in Table **8**, while the corresponding metrics for tomato leaf diseases are provided in Table **9**.

As we can observe from Tables **7** and **8**, the proposed ensemble models consistently outperform individual models across all metrics. Also, by comparing our results with the existing techniques as mentioned in Table **10**, we can safely say that our model performs better and achieves greater accuracy. The ensemble models achieve a higher F1 score and accuracy for both tomato and potato diseases, demonstrating their robustness and improved generalization. The confusion matrices for ensemble model-2 for potato disease classification and ensemble model-3 for tomato disease classification are shown in Figs. (**6** and **7**), respectively.

Table 8. Performance metrics of models for potato disease.

Potato				
Model	**Accuracy**	**F1 Score**	**Precision**	**Recall**
Xception	96.74%	96.76%	96.79%	96.74%
Vgg16	97.20%	97.14%	97.25%	97.20%
ResNet50	89.30%	89.12%	89.01%	89.30%
ResNet101V2	96.27%	96.30%	96.35%	96.27%
InceptionV3	88.84%	88.71%	88.68%	88.84%
InceptionResNetV2	94.88%	94.87%	95.00%	94.88%
NASNetMobile	95.81%	95.79%	95.84%	95.81%
DenseNet121	98.60%	98.57%	98.61%	98.60%
MobileNet	98.13%	98.16%	98.19%	98.13%
ConvNeXtTiny	91.16%	89.94%	90.78%	91.16%
Ensemble 1	98.60%	98.54%	98.65%	98.60%
Ensemble 2	**99.06%**	**99.04%**	**99.08%**	**99.06%**

Table 9. Performance metrics of models for tomato disease.

Tomato				
Model	**Accuracy**	**F1 Score**	**Precision**	**Recall**
Xception	88.85%	88.82%	88.95%	88.85%
Vgg16	90.48%	90.49%	90.66%	90.48%
ResNet50	77.77%	77.80%	78.63%	77.77%
ResNet101V2	91.04%	91.04%	91.16%	91.04%
InceptionV3	86.59%	86.45%	86.66%	86.59%
InceptionResNetV2	88.22%	88.13%	88.37%	88.22%
NASNetMobile	88.35%	88.38%	88.52%	88.35%
DenseNet121	96.18%	96.17%	96.21%	96.18%
MobileNet	93.92%	93.91%	94.00%	93.92%
Ensemble 1	**98.12%**	**98.12%**	**98.13%**	**98.12%**
Ensemble 3	96.99%	96.98%	97.05%	96.99%

Table 10. Comparison of proposed approach with existing results.

Year	Potato			Tomato		
	Reference	Methodology	Accuracy	Reference	Methodology	Accuracy
2021	[5]	GLCM + SVM	95.99%	[21]	Extreme ML	84.94%
2022	[9]	ResNet50 + SVM	95.60%	[25]	CNN	88.17%
2023	[11]	Efficient DenseNet	97.20%	[28]	Ensemble	92.78%
2024	[16]	CNN	98.28%	[30]	CNN	96%
-	**Proposed Approach**	**Weighted Average Ensemble**	**99.06%**	**Proposed Approach**	**Weighted Average Ensemble**	**98.12%**

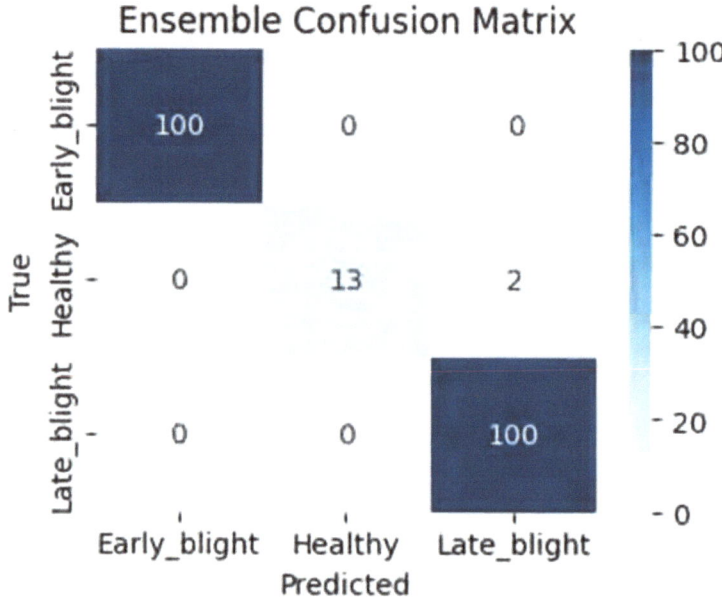

Fig. (6). Confusion matrix of the best ensemble model for potato disease.

DISCUSSION

For the potato disease classification, Ensemble Model-2 performs better than Ensemble Model-1. The ensemble of VGG16, DenseNet121, and MobileNet performs better than the ensemble of VGG16, ResNet101V2, and NASNetMobile due to the complementary strengths of its component models. VGG16 captures fine-grained features with its simple, deep architecture. DenseNet121 improves feature propagation and reuse with dense connections, while MobileNet enhances efficiency with depthwise separable convolutions. This combination results in a balanced, robust model. DenseNet121's efficient feature reuse synergizes well with VGG16 and MobileNet, leading to improved generalization. MobileNet's efficiency helps balance the computational demands of the ensemble, creating a cohesive and resource-effective model. The diverse learning strategies of the (VGG16, DenseNet121, MobileNet) ensemble reduce overfitting and enhance robustness, enabling better generalization across different data types. Empirical results consistently show the superior performance of the (VGG16, DenseNet121, MobileNet) ensemble in accuracy, recall, precision, and F1 score. This performance is because of the effective combination of each model's strengths, efficient learning strategies, and balanced computational requirements, making it a more effective solution for plant disease classification.

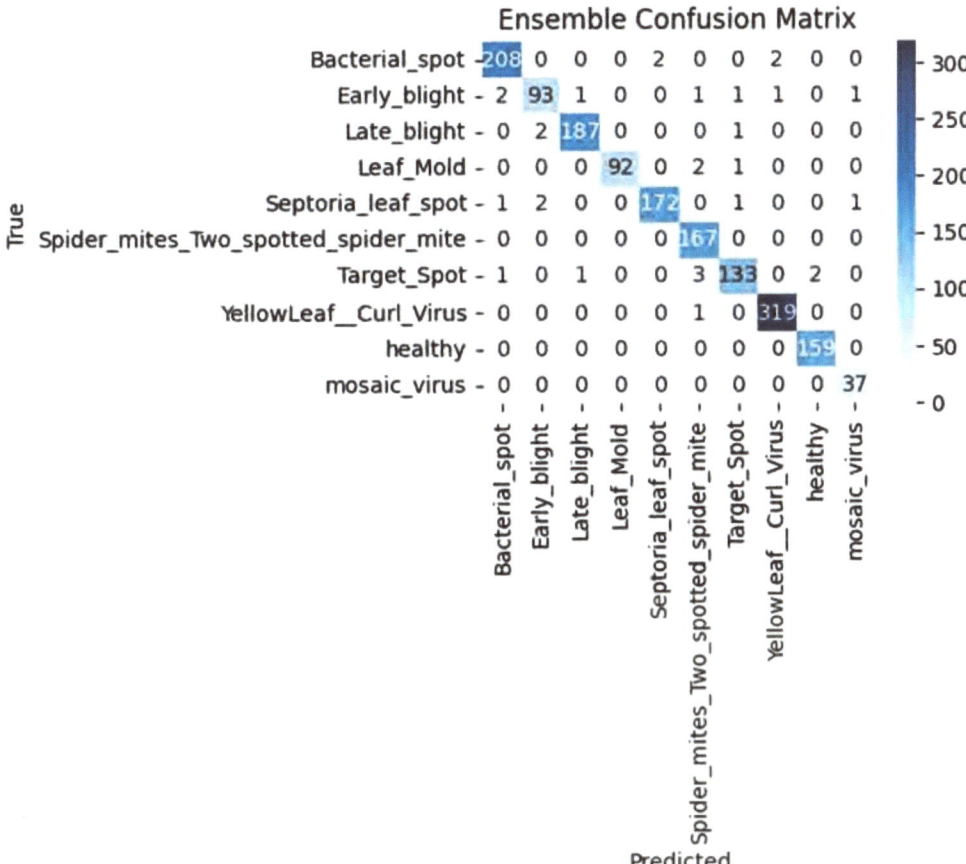

Fig. (7). Confusion matrix of the best ensemble model for tomato disease.

For the tomato disease classification, we can see that Ensemble Model-3 performs better than Ensemble Model-1. The ensemble of Xception, InceptionResNetV2 and MobileNet outperforms the ensemble of VGG16, DenseNet121, and MobileNet due to its advanced architectural innovations and deeper feature extraction capabilities. Xception uses depth-wise separable convolutions to improve efficiency and performance, while InceptionResNetV2 combines Inception modules with residual connections for enhanced feature learning and robustness. MobileNet contributes efficiency and balance to the ensemble. These advanced models detect more complicated patterns and intricacies in the data, resulting in improved outcomes in terms of accuracy, recall, precision, and F1 scores. The superior computational balance, robustness, and generalization capabilities of the (Xception, InceptionResNetV2, MobileNet) ensemble make it more effective in various scenarios compared to the (VGG16, DenseNet121, MobileNet) ensemble.

CONCLUSION

Timely detection and diagnosis of plant diseases in an accurate manner is an important issue that affects food security on a global level. It is challenging to obtain precise and reliable findings using the manual approach of plant disease identification, which takes a lot of time and experience. Deep learning techniques are useful in this situation. In this chapter, we study the various possible diseases in potatoes and tomatoes, and propose a deep learning based weighted ensemble model for accurate and effective classification of plant disease with focus on these crops. The proposed models achieve 99.06% and 98.12% accuracy for potato and tomato plants, respectively, which is a great enhancement over existing methods. The models were trained on an open-source Plant Village dataset available on Kaggle. These models are an important step towards lowering the effort and knowledge needed to detect plant diseases, as well as the effort and time required for manual detection. The outcomes of these models can assist farmers in identifying diseases early, reducing losses in production and increasing food security. These models can be expanded to include other crops as well, offering a more comprehensive solution to the issue of identifying plant disease. Moreover, these have the potential to completely revolutionize the way plant diseases are identified, improving their accessibility, accuracy, and efficiency. To further increase accuracy and disease classification capabilities, future studies will focus on strengthening the ability of deep learning models by integrating data from multiple sources, such as spectroscopic or infrared photography. Future studies could also explore the use of real-time data acquisition systems and mobile applications to improve the practicality and accessibility of disease detection in outdoor settings. To adapt the models to varied plant species and geographical situations, advancements in deep learning could be explored. Collaboration with agricultural experts and stakeholders will be crucial to ensure that these deep learning models satisfy real-world requirements and can be easily applied in a variety of farming settings. Additionally, incorporating other widely used crop datasets, such as those for maize, wheat, and rice, will be considered in future research to broaden the model's applicability across major global crops.

REFERENCES

[1]   P. Jha, D. Dembla, and W. Dubey, "Deep learning models for enhancing potato leaf disease prediction: Implementation of transfer learning based stacking ensemble model", *Multimedia Tools Appl.,* vol. 83, no. 13, pp. 37839-37858, 2023.
[http://dx.doi.org/10.1007/s11042-023-16993-4]

[2]   I. Singh, A. Jaiswal, and N. Sachdeva, "Comparative analysis of deep learning models for potato leaf disease detection", *proceedings of the 14th international conference on cloud computing, data science and engineering, confluence 2024,* Institute of Electrical and Electronics Engineers Inc., pp. 421-425, 2024.
[http://dx.doi.org/10.1109/Confluence60223.2024.10463314]

[3]   G. Sakkarvarthi, G.W. Sathianesan, V.S. Murugan, A.J. Reddy, P. Jayagopal, and M. Elsisi, "Detection and classification of tomato crop disease using convolutional neural network", *Electronics (Basel),* vol. 11, no. 21, p. 3618, 2022.
[http://dx.doi.org/10.3390/electronics11213618]

[4]   V. Swetha, and R. Jayaram, "A novel method for plant leaf malady recognition using machine learning classifiers," 2019 3rd International conference on Electronics, Communication and Aerospace Technology (ICECA), Coimbatore, India, 2019, pp. 1360-1365.
[http://dx.doi.org/10.1109/ICECA.2019.8822094]

[5]   V.D. Tiwari, M. Ashish, N. Gangwar, A. Sharma, S. Patel, and S. Bhardwaj, "Potato leaf diseases detection using deep learning," 2020 4th International Conference on Intelligent Computing and Control Systems (ICICCS), Madurai, India, 2020, pp. 461-466.
[http://dx.doi.org/10.1109/ICICCS48265.2020.9121067]

[6]   A. Lakshmanarao, M. R. Babu, and T. S. R. Kiran, "Plant disease prediction and classification using deep learning ConvNets," in 2021 International Conference on Artificial Intelligence and Machine Vision (AIMV), Gandhinagar, India, 2021, pp. 1–6.
[http://dx.doi.org/10.1109/ICICCS48265.2020.9121067]

[7]   T.R. Gadekallu, D.S. Rajput, M.P.K. Reddy, K. Lakshmanna, S. Bhattacharya, S. Singh, A. Jolfaei, and M. Alazab, "A novel PCA–whale optimization-based deep neural network model for classification of tomato plant diseases using GPU", *J. Real-Time Image Process.,* vol. 18, no. 4, pp. 1383-1396, 2021.
[http://dx.doi.org/10.1007/s11554-020-00987-8]

[8]   M.S.A.M. Al-gaashani, F. Shang, M.S.A. Muthanna, M. Khayyat, and A.A. Abd El-Latif, "Tomato leaf disease classification by exploiting transfer learning and feature concatenation", *IET Image Process.,* vol. 16, no. 3, pp. 913-925, 2022.
[http://dx.doi.org/10.1049/ipr2.12397]

[9]   A. Sreedevi, and C. Manike, "Development of weighted ensemble transfer learning for tomato leaf disease classification solving low resolution problems", *Imaging Sci. J.,* vol. 71, no. 2, pp. 161-187, 2023.
[http://dx.doi.org/10.1080/13682199.2023.2178605]

[10]   B.O. Lubis, D. Oscar, F.W. Fibriany, B. Santoso, Jefi, and A. Rusman, "Classification of tomato leaf disease and combination extraction features using K-NN algorithm", In: *2nd International Conference on Advanced Information Scientific Development (ICAISD) 2021: Innovating Scientific Learning for*

Deep Communication. vol. 2714. AIP Publishing LLC, 2023, p. 1.
[http://dx.doi.org/10.1063/5.0128539]

[11] M.H. Najim, S.K. Abdulateef, and A.H. Alasadi, "Early detection of tomato leaf diseases based on deep learning techniques", *IAES International Journal of Artificial Intelligence (IJ-AI),* vol. 13, no. 1, pp. 509-515, 2024.
[http://dx.doi.org/10.11591/ijai.v13.i1.pp509-515]

[12] C.İ. Sofuoğlu, and D. Birant, "Potato plant leaf disease detection using deep learning method", *Tarim Bilim. Derg.,* vol. 30, no. 1, pp. 153-165, 2023.
[http://dx.doi.org/10.15832/ankutbd.1276722]

[13] K. Sanjeev, N. K. Gupta, W. J. Jeberson, and S. Paswan, "Early Prediction of Potato Leaf Diseases Using ANN Classifier," Oriental journal of computer science and technology, vol. 13, no. 0203, pp. 129–134, Jan. 2021
[http://dx.doi.org/10.13005/ojcst13.0203.11]

[14] M.A. Iqbal, and K.H. Talukder, "Detection of potato disease using image segmentation and machine learning", *2020 International Conference on Wireless Communications Signal Processing and Networking (WiSPNET),* pp. 43-47, 2020.Chennai, India
[http://dx.doi.org/10.1109/WiSPNET48689.2020.9198563]

[15] A. Singh, and H. Kaur, "Potato plant leaves disease detection and classification using machine learning methodologies", *IOP Conference Series: Materials Science and Engineering,* IOP Publishing Ltd, 2021.
[http://dx.doi.org/10.1088/1757-899X/1022/1/012121]

[16] Y. Kurmi, and S. Gangwar, "A leaf image localization based algorithm for different crops disease classification", *Inf. Process. Agric.,* vol. 9, no. 3, pp. 456-474, 2022.
[http://dx.doi.org/10.1016/j.inpa.2021.03.001]

[17] M. Bhagat, and D. Kumar, "Efficient feature selection using BoWs and SURF method for leaf disease identification", *Multimedia Tools Appl.,* vol. 82, no. 18, pp. 28187-28211, 2023.
[http://dx.doi.org/10.1007/s11042-023-14625-5]

[18] E. Sert, "A deep learning based approach for the detection of diseases in pepper and potato leaves", *ANADOLU JOURNAL OF AGRICULTURAL SCIENCES,* no. Jun, pp. 167-178, 2021.
[http://dx.doi.org/10.7161/omuanajas.805152]

[19] D. Kothari, H. Mishra, M. Gharat, V. Pandey, and R. Thakur, "Potato leaf disease detection using deep learning," International Journal of Engineering and Technical Research, vol. 11, 2022.

[20] R. Mahum, H. Munir, Z-U-N. Mughal, M. Awais, F. Sher Khan, M. Saqlain, S. Mahamad, and I. Tlili, "A novel framework for potato leaf disease detection using an efficient deep learning model", *Hum. Ecol. Risk Assess.,* vol. 29, no. 2, pp. 303-326, 2023.
[http://dx.doi.org/10.1080/10807039.2022.2064814]

[21] T. Nazir, M.M. Iqbal, S. Jabbar, A. Hussain, and M. Albathan, "Efficientpnet—an optimized and efficient deep learning approach for classifying disease of potato plant leaves", *Agriculture,* vol. 13, no. 4, p. 841, 2023.
[http://dx.doi.org/10.3390/agriculture13040841]

[22] T. Sultana, and M. Reza, "Identification of potato leaf diseases using hybrid convolution neural network with support vector machine", *International Advanced Computing Conference,* pp. 350-361, 2022.Cham

[23] S. Ali, M. Hassan, J.Y. Kim, M.I. Farid, M. Sanaullah, and H. Mufti, "FF-PCA-LDA: Intelligent feature fusion based pca-lda classification system for plant leaf diseases", *Appl. Sci. (Basel),* vol. 12, no. 7, p. 3514, 2022.
[http://dx.doi.org/10.3390/app12073514]

[24] J. Basavaiah, and A. Arlene Anthony, "Tomato leaf disease classification using multiple feature

extraction techniques", *Wirel. Pers. Commun.,* vol. 115, no. 1, pp. 633-651, 2020.
[http://dx.doi.org/10.1007/s11277-020-07590-x]

[25] T.S. Xian, and R. Ngadiran, "Plant diseases classification using machine learning", In: *Journal of Physics: Conference Series.* IOP Publishing Ltd, 2021.
[http://dx.doi.org/10.1088/1742-6596/1962/1/012024]

[26] R. Mohanty, P. Wankhede, D. Singh, and P. Vakhare, "Tomato plant leaves disease detection using machine learning," in Proc. 2022 IEEE International Conference on Advanced AI and Intelligent Control (ICAAIC), 2022, pp. 544–549.
[http://dx.doi.org/10.1109/ICAAIC53929.2022.9793302]

[27] A. Elhassouny, and F. Smarandache, "Smart mobile application to recognize tomato leaf diseases using Convolutional Neural Networks", *2019 International Conference of Computer Science and Renewable Energies (ICCSRE),* pp. 1-4, 2019.Agadir, Morocco
[http://dx.doi.org/10.1109/ICCSRE.2019.8807737]

[28] J. Liu, and X. Wang, "Early recognition of tomato gray leaf spot disease based on MobileNetv2-YOLOv3 model", *Plant Methods,* vol. 16, no. 1, p. 83, 2020.
[http://dx.doi.org/10.1186/s13007-020-00624-2] [PMID: 32523613]

[29] L.M. Abouelmagd, M.Y. Shams, H.S. Marie, and A.E. Hassanien, "An optimized capsule neural networks for tomato leaf disease classification", *EURASIP J. Image Video Process.,* vol. 2024, no. 1, p. 2, 2024.
[http://dx.doi.org/10.1186/s13640-023-00618-9]

[30] K. He, X. Zhang, S. Ren, and J. Sun, "Identity mappings in deep residual networks," arXiv preprint arXiv:1603.05027, 2016. [Online]. Available: http://arxiv.org/abs/1603.05027.

[31] K.M. Hosny, W.M. El-Hady, F.M. Samy, E. Vrochidou, and G.A. Papakostas, "Multi-class classification of plant leaf diseases using feature fusion of deep convolutional neural network and local binary pattern", *IEEE Access,* vol. 11, pp. 62307-62317, 2023.
[http://dx.doi.org/10.1109/ACCESS.2023.3286730]

[32] A. Kaur, V. Kukreja, N. Thapliyal, M. Aeri, R. Sharma, and S. Hariharan, "Innovative approaches to agricultural sustainability: a hybrid cnn-svm model for tomato disease classification",
[http://dx.doi.org/10.1109/INOCON60754.2024.10511738]

[33] T. O. Emmanuel, 2018, "PlantVillage Dataset," Kaggle. [Online]. Available: https://www.kaggle.com/datasets/emmarex/plantdisease/data

[34] F. Chollet, "Xception: Deep learning with depthwise separable convolutions," Oct. 2016, [Online]. Available: http://arxiv.org/abs/1610.02357

[35] K. Simonyan and A. Zisserman, "Very deep convolutional networks for large-scale image recognition," Sep. 2014, [Online]. Available: http://arxiv.org/abs/1409.1556

[36] K. He, X. Zhang, S. Ren, and J. Sun, "Deep residual learning for image recognition," Dec. 2015, [Online]. Available: http://arxiv.org/abs/1512.03385

[37] K. He, X. Zhang, S. Ren, and J. Sun, "Identity mappings in deep residual networks", http://arxiv.org/abs/1603.05027 Online
[http://dx.doi.org/10.1007/978-3-319-46493-0_38]

[38] C. Szegedy, V. Vanhoucke, S. Ioffe, and J. Shlens, "Rethinking the Inception Architecture for Computer Vision."
[http://dx.doi.org/10.1109/CVPR.2016.308]

[39] C. Szegedy, S. Ioffe, V. Vanhoucke, and A. Alemi, "Inception-v4, inception-resnet and the impact of residual connections on learning."
[http://dx.doi.org/10.1609/aaai.v31i1.11231]

[40] B. Zoph, V. Vasudevan, J. Shlens, and Q.V. Le, "Learning transferable architectures for scalable

image recognition", http://arxiv.org/abs/1707.07012 Online

[41] G. Huang, Z. Liu, L. van der Maaten, and K.Q. Weinberger, "Densely connected convolutional networks", http://arxiv.org/abs/1608.06993 Online

[42] A.G. Howard, "MobileNets: Efficient convolutional neural networks for mobile vision applications", http://arxiv.org/abs/1704.04861 Online

[43] Z. Liu, H. Mao, C-Y. Wu, C. Feichtenhofer, T. Darrell, and S. Xie, "A convnet for the 2020s", http://arxiv.org/abs/2201.03545 Online
[http://dx.doi.org/10.1109/CVPR52688.2022.01167]

CHAPTER 8

The use of Big Data, Deep learning, IoT, and Blockchain in Livestock Management

Indu Sounkhla[1,*] and **Renu Dhir**[1]

[1] *Department of Computer Science and Engineering, Dr. B.R. Ambedkar National Institute of Technology, Jalandhar, Punjab, India*

Abstract: Livestock management is a crucial aspect of agriculture, impacting both the economy and food security worldwide. Traditional methods of monitoring and managing livestock have often been labour-intensive and inefficient. This chapter investigates the transformative impact of Big Data, Deep Learning, Internet of Things (IoT), and Blockchain in the field of livestock management. In recent years, these technologies have revolutionized traditional agricultural practices, providing a holistic approach to ensuring the well-being and productivity of livestock. Big Data analytics play a critical role in collecting and analysing massive datasets from animal-connected sensors and wearables attached to animals, providing farmers with valuable insights into health, behaviour, and environmental conditions. Deep Learning algorithms help automate tasks. such as real-time monitoring, disease detection, and behavioural analysis, leading to proactive interventions for individual animal welfare and the overall health of the flock or herd. The integration of IoT devices creates an interconnected network, enabling the accurate monitoring of animal parameters and environmental factors, thereby optimizing feeding, breeding, and disease control.

Furthermore, blockchain technology ensures transparency and traceability in the livestock supply chain, promoting trust between stakeholders and consumers by recording critical information on the origin, health, and ethical treatment of animals. This chapter presents current research and technological advances, offering a comprehensive exploration of the applications of Big Data, Deep Learning, IoT, and Blockchain in livestock management as mentioned. By examining the synergy between these technologies and their collective impact on livestock welfare, productivity, and sustainability, this work contributes to the growing body of knowledge aimed at advancing modern agricultural practices in the livestock farming sector.

Keywords: Blockchain, Big data analysis, Deep learning, Internet of things, Livestock management.

---

* **Corresponding author Indu Sounkhla:** Department of Computer Science and Engineering, Dr. B.R. Ambedkar National Institute of Technology, Jalandhar, Punjab, India; E-mail: indusounkhla@gmail.com

Shefali Arora Chouhanm Nagendra Pratap Singh, Banalaxmi Brahma & Shashank Gupta (Eds.)

INTRODUCTION

Livestock management is the cornerstone of sustainable agriculture, encompassing diverse practices that optimize the care, productivity, and welfare of domesticated animals. At its core, it involves the art and science of tending to various species, such as cows, goats, sheep, pigs, and poultry, to meet both human needs and animal well-being. From nutrition and healthcare to breeding and marketing, effective livestock management requires a multifaceted approach that balances practical skills, scientific knowledge, and ethical considerations.

Central to livestock management is the commitment to ensuring the health and vitality of animal populations while maximizing their productivity in an environmentally responsible and economically viable manner. Blockchain technology is being implemented in various ways in livestock farming [1]. Through proper nutrition, shelter, healthcare, and breeding practices, livestock managers play a vital role in sustaining the livelihoods of farmers and ranchers, as well as the global food supply chain.

The efficiency, monitoring, and general welfare of animals have been greatly increased with the use of cutting-edge technologies in livestock production. Ji *et al.* [2] investigated how heat stress affected milking and rumination in robotic dairy farms, highlighting the necessity of exact environmental management. Neethirajan and Kemp [3] emphasized how digital cattle husbandry may increase productivity by using automated decision-making and real-time monitoring. Dewangan and Vij [4] presented a self-adaptive edge computing architecture that uses IoT and AI to optimize cattle management in the context of technological developments. According to Kampan *et al.* [5], the use of blockchain technology has also improved the security and traceability of animal products. By establishing a secure cattle stock, Leme *et al.* [6] further emphasized the significance of blockchain.

As we navigate the complexities of modern agriculture, livestock management principles guide us in fostering resilience, efficiency, and sustainability in animal husbandry practices worldwide. Many commercial firms are actively developing and producing robots that can automatically check the atmosphere of cattle farms [7]. In this case, Big Data, Deep Learning, and Blockchain technologies [8, 9] are used to enhance the efficiency of its operations.

Overview of Livestock Management Practices

Livestock management encompasses a rich tapestry of traditional wisdom and modern innovations designed to ensure the health, productivity, and welfare of domesticated animals. Traditional methods, rooted in centuries of agricultural heritage, often emphasize close observation, hands-on techniques, and an intimate understanding of the natural rhythms and needs of livestock species. Practices, such as rotational grazing, where animals are moved regularly between pastures to optimize forage utilization and soil health, have been passed down through generations, promoting sustainable land management and biodiversity conservation.

In contrast, modern livestock management integrates cutting-edge technologies and scientific advancements to enhance efficiency, precision, and scale. Innovations such as precision nutrition, which utilizes data-driven approaches to tailor diets to individual animal requirements, and automated monitoring systems that track animal health metrics in real-time represent just a glimpse of the transformative potential of modern methods. Additionally, genetic selection and breeding programs harness the power of genomics to accelerate livestock development, incorporating traits, such as disease resistance, growth rate, and product quality, thereby driving improvements in overall productivity and profitability.

However, while modern methods offer unprecedented opportunities for optimization and productivity gains, they also raise important considerations around animal welfare, environmental sustainability, and societal values. Traditional wisdom often emphasizes holistic approaches that prioritize the well-being of animals and the health of ecosystems, reminding us of the interconnectedness of all living beings within agricultural systems. As we navigate the complexities of livestock management in the 21st century, there is a growing recognition of the need to integrate the best of both worlds – drawing on the wisdom of the past while embracing the innovations of the future – to forge a path toward a more resilient, equitable, and sustainable agricultural future. Finding a harmonious balance between traditional and modern methods holds the key to unlocking the maximum potential of livestock management in meeting the evolving needs of humanity while safeguarding the planet's health for generations to come. There is a significant impact of heat stress on animal behavior and the efficiency of robotic milking machines.

Modern advances, fueled by cutting-edge technologies and scientific breakthroughs, coexist with traditional methods rooted in millennia of agricultural wisdom to form the dynamic field of livestock management. An emphasis on holistic strategies, such as rotational grazing and selective breeding, is placed on traditional methods rooted in a deep understanding of animal behavior and natural ecosystems, with a focus on maximizing productivity while preserving environmental sustainability and animal welfare. On the other hand, modern techniques utilize instruments such as genetic selection, automated monitoring systems, and precision nutrition to enhance output and profitability by improving efficiency, precision, and scale. The necessity of combining the best features of traditional and modern approaches to livestock management is becoming more apparent as we traverse its complexity in the twenty-first century. This will help create a harmonious balance that increases output, protects cultural heritage, and supports the sustainability of agricultural systems. In addition to assisting livestock farmers with animal production management, the three "F's" (Footprint, Fingerprint, and Forecast) will help create application models integrated for agricultural value, supply, and food chains.

Significance of Integration of Technology in Livestock Management

The integration of technology in livestock management brings forth transformative benefits that enhance productivity, efficiency, and sustainability across the agricultural landscape. By leveraging technologies, such as sensors, data analytics, and automation, livestock managers can monitor and manage animal health, nutrition, and behaviour with unprecedented precision and speed. Real-time data collection enables the early detection of health issues, allowing for prompt intervention and reducing the risk of disease outbreaks. Automated feeding and watering systems ensure that animals receive optimal nutrition, minimizing waste and improving feed efficiency. Additionally, precision technologies facilitate selective breeding programs, accelerating genetic improvements to enhance desirable traits, such as disease resistance, growth rates, and product quality. Overall, technology integration empowers livestock managers to make data-driven decisions, optimize resource utilization, and ultimately increase the profitability and resilience of livestock operations. By harnessing the predictive capabilities of deep learning, livestock farmers can optimize animal welfare, enhance productivity, and mitigate economic losses resulting from disease outbreaks.

Furthermore, the integration of technology in livestock management contributes to broader agricultural sustainability goals by reducing environmental impacts and resource inputs. Precision farming techniques enable more targeted application of inputs such as feed, water, and medications, thereby minimizing waste and pollution. Automated systems can also help optimize grazing patterns and land use, promoting soil health and biodiversity conservation. Moreover, by providing insights into resource usage and animal performance, technology empowers livestock managers to adopt more sustainable practices and mitigate adverse environmental externalities. Ultimately, the integration of technology in livestock management not only enhances economic viability but also fosters a more ecologically sound and socially responsible approach to animal agriculture, aligning with global efforts to build a more sustainable food system for future generations.

Objectives of Chapter

The objectives of the chapter are as follows:

• To provide an overview of livestock management practices and the significance of current technology in livestock management.
• To explore the potential of big data in livestock farming, data collection methods and their utilization to improve livestock farming.
• To explain the ability of Deep Learning models, their application, and their implementation to enhance livestock management.
• To highlight the significance of IoT in livestock with its data collection approach and IoT-enabled solutions.
• To discuss how blockchain technology improves livestock and its application to enhance transparency and trust in the livestock supply chain.
• To enlighten people about integrating big data, deep learning, Blockchain, and IoT in livestock management with its combined application and discuss case studies.
• To disclose the challenges and considerations in livestock farming.
• Lastly, to discuss the conclusion, future directions, and trends of emerging technology and research areas in livestock management

BIG DATA IN LIVESTOCK MANAGEMENT

Big data has transformed livestock management by utilizing advanced analytics and technology to monitor individual animal well-being, predict disease outbreaks, optimize breeding programs, and enhance supply chain efficiency. Farmers can increase productivity, sustainability, and profitability by making informed decisions based on market trends, genetics, animal behavior, and environmental conditions, among other factors, through the use of massive data analysis. This data-driven strategy transforms conventional farming methods into more effective and sustainable operations by enabling targeted interventions, reducing waste, and enhancing overall animal welfare. Furthermore, big data analytics also make Precision Livestock Farming (PLF) possible, which enables farmers to customize management strategies to the unique requirements of each animal [6, 7]. This maximizes resource efficiency and reduces environmental impact. Farmers may increase productivity, enhance animal welfare, and implement sustainable production methods by utilizing these technologies and data-driven approaches. This will ultimately boost the livestock industry's resiliency and profitability.

Understanding Big Data in Agriculture

Understanding the application of big data in agriculture, with a focus on livestock farming, involves recognizing the transformative potential of data analytics in optimizing various aspects of livestock management. This includes gathering, processing, and interpreting enormous volumes of data produced by the cattle industry, utilizing technologies, such as sensors, Internet of Things (IoT) devices, and data analytics platforms. Farmers can increase production, efficiency, and sustainability by making data-driven decisions, evaluating data on animal health, behavior, genetics, environmental factors, and market trends. Animals can undergo individual inspection and treatment during traditional milking. Moreover, comprehending big data in agriculture entails merging information from various sources to gain a thorough understanding of agricultural operations, enabling preemptive actions to address issues, such as disease outbreaks, feed management, and supply chain optimization. Ultimately, gaining a grasp of big data in agriculture, with an emphasis on livestock farming, enables farmers to implement more effective and informed techniques, which enhances animal welfare and boosts the profitability of the livestock industry.

To enhance production processes and systems, big data analytics approaches can also be utilized to aggregate and integrate data across farms. The automation, accessibility, and correctness of the data supplied are what make big data valuable; to ensure data quality, error checking and quality control must be implemented. PLF will need to be applied on farms more frequently, which will require the development of software, database systems, quality control measures, and statistical techniques to compile and display the data and select the most effective data models. Security and privacy are two further significant issues associated with the large amount of data collected on farms. As a result, data collected on agricultural land is currently underutilized because farmers value their privacy.

Big data analytical technology prediction models can be utilized to create digital farming service systems that may improve animal production capacity, productivity, and livestock wellbeing based on data from biological and biometric sensors. For instance, the Moo Care predictive model was created to help dairy producers manage their dairy farming operations by predicting milk production through the integration of big data and Internet of Things (IoT) sensors. Models created from large data sets have been used to identify and forecast chicken diseases. A digital fingerprint that may be used in predictive and adaptive decision-making models combines animals' wearable digital data received from various sensors and cattle husbandry sensing platforms.

Data Collection Techniques in Livestock Farming

In livestock farming, data collection methods include a range of approaches to obtain information about the animal's health, behavior, genetics, and environmental factors. One popular method is using sensor technologies—like accelerometers, GPS trackers, and RFID tags—to connect to individual animals and follow their movements, activity levels, and physiological characteristics in real time. These sensors produce continuous data streams, offering insights into animal behavior patterns, health, and performance indicators.

Farmers can also utilize manual data-gathering techniques, such as visual observations and physical checks, to assess their animals' health and behavior. This may involve conducting routine checks on the animals, maintaining thorough medical records, and documenting observations in either paper or digital form. Additionally, genetic data can be gathered using methods, such as genotyping and DNA sampling, enabling farmers to improve the genetic quality of their herds and make informed breeding decisions. In general, farmers can gather comprehensive datasets that can be examined to optimize livestock management practices and improve farm production and sustainability by integrating sensor technologies with human data collection methods.

Utilizing Big Data Analytics for Improved Livestock Management

The agricultural industry has significant potential to enhance production, efficiency, and sustainability through the application of big data analytics for improved livestock management. Farmers can leverage the vast volumes of data generated by the livestock sector to their advantage by utilizing sophisticated analytics tools and methodologies to gain valuable insights into the environment, genetics, behavior, and health of their animals. Maximizing various areas of livestock management, including health monitoring, feed management, breeding programs, and supply chain logistics, facilitates proactive decision-making and targeted interventions.

Furthermore, as mentioned earlier, big data analytics makes Precision Livestock Farming (PLF) methods easier to implement. Farmers may get real-time data on things like animal behavior, feed intake, and environmental variables by integrating sensor technology, IoT devices, and data analytics systems. This data-driven strategy reduces waste, increases production, and enhances animal welfare while having a smaller negative impact on the environment. It also makes resource allocation more accurate and efficient. All things considered, applying big data analytics to livestock management can transform conventional farming methods and spur long-term innovation in the sector.

Deep Learning Applications in Livestock Management

Deep learning applications have revolutionized livestock management by enabling the precise monitoring and optimization of various animal husbandry practices. Deep learning algorithms can evaluate enormous volumes of data produced by continuously monitoring ambient conditions, health indicators, and animal behavior. These algorithms make use of computer vision and sensor technologies. These tools help forecast disease outbreaks, identify abnormalities in behavior or health, improve breeding operations, and manage feed more efficiently. Deep learning models can also aid in automated decision-making, enhancing overall welfare and productivity in livestock operations by determining optimal feeding schedules or identifying indicators of distress. The usage of AI in livestock farming is demonstrated in Fig. (**1**).

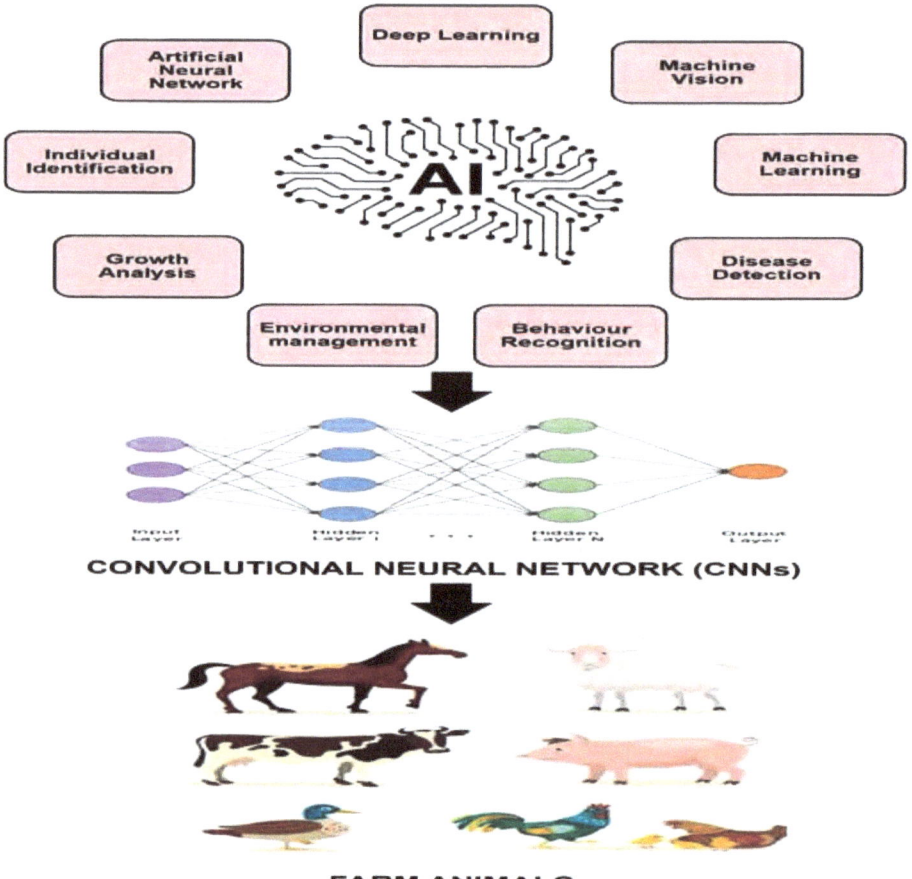

Fig. (1). Usage of AI in livestock farming.

Introduction to Deep Learning (DL) and Neural Networks

DL, a branch of machine learning that draws inspiration from the structure and functionality of the human brain, has become a potent method for addressing intricate challenges in different fields. Deep learning is fundamentally based on neural networks, which are computational models consisting of interconnected nodes, or neurons, arranged in layers. These networks possess the ability to acquire complex patterns and representations from extensive amounts of input, rendering them highly efficient in tasks, such as recognizing images and voice, processing spoken language, and even making independent decisions. Neural networks utilize a technique called backpropagation to modify their internal parameters iteratively during training. This process aims to reduce the discrepancy between expected and actual results, leading to gradual improvement in their performance.

Neural networks are composed of an input layer, which receives data, one or multiple hidden layers that extract progressively more complex characteristics from the input data, and an output layer that generates the final predictions or classifications. Every individual neuron inside the network performs a mathematical operation on its inputs and then applies an activation function to the outcome. This activation function introduces non-linearities, allowing the network to represent and understand intricate relationships within the data effectively. Deep learning has made significant progress due to the abundance of large datasets and the availability of powerful computers. This has led to significant advancements in healthcare, autonomous vehicles, and personalized recommendations. As a result, our approach to solving complex problems in the modern era has undergone a fundamental transformation.

Deep Learning Models for Predictive Analysis in Livestock Health

Deep learning models are already recognized as highly effective tools for predictive analysis in animal health. They can examine large datasets and detect subtle patterns that may indicate health issues or disease outbreaks. Convolutional Neural Networks (CNNs) excel at interpreting visual data—such as X-rays, ultrasound images, or drone-captured images of livestock—to automatically identify abnormalities or signs of illness. Recurrent Neural Networks (RNNs) and their variants, such as Long Short-Term Memory (LSTM) networks, are particularly proficient at analyzing time-series data.

Several advanced CNN architectures, including DCN R-CNN, Grid R-CNN, Cascade R-CNN, Faster R-CNN, Guided Anchoring, the original SSD, and YOLO-v3, have demonstrated strong performance in object detection and image analysis tasks. These models are especially useful for monitoring physiological signals, such as heart rate, temperature, or movement patterns, over time. They can capture intricate temporal relationships and identify deviations from normal behavior, enabling timely interventions and proactive measures to mitigate health risks.

Furthermore, combining deep learning models with sensor technologies and Internet of Things (IoT) devices enables the continuous real-time monitoring of cattle health data. By utilizing data collected from wearable sensors, RFID tags, or environmental sensors placed in barns or pastures, these models can offer uninterrupted analysis of animal welfare, identify irregularities, and predict probable health problems. Furthermore, the advanced predictive capabilities of deep learning models enable proactive management techniques, such as refining feeding schedules, adjusting environmental conditions, or implementing targeted vaccination programs based on anticipated disease risks.

Implementation of Deep Learning in Livestock Behavior Monitoring

An innovative method for enhancing animal comfort and productivity is the application of deep learning in livestock behavior monitoring. Computer vision, a crucial component of deep learning, enables the automatic analysis of video footage or image data to monitor and understand various aspects of animal behavior. Convolutional Neural Networks (CNNs) enable the extraction of significant characteristics from visual data, allowing for the detection of activities such as feeding patterns, social interactions, or signals of distress. Through ongoing surveillance of these actions, deep learning models can identify variations from typical behavior, providing timely indications of potential health issues or environmental pressures.

Moreover, the combination of sensor technologies and deep learning enables the analysis of diverse data types, leading to a comprehensive understanding of animal behavior. Wearable sensors, such as accelerometers and GPS trackers, can record movement patterns and activity levels, while environmental sensors measure parameters like temperature, humidity, and air quality within livestock facilities. Recurrent Neural Networks (RNNs), along with attention mechanisms, can process multiple inputs over time, effectively capturing the complex relationships between animal behavior and environmental conditions.

By integrating data from various sources, deep learning models can offer detailed insights into how external factors influence animal behavior. These insights can support informed management decisions aimed at improving living conditions and reducing stress. The implementation of deep learning in livestock behavior monitoring is illustrated in Fig. (**2**).

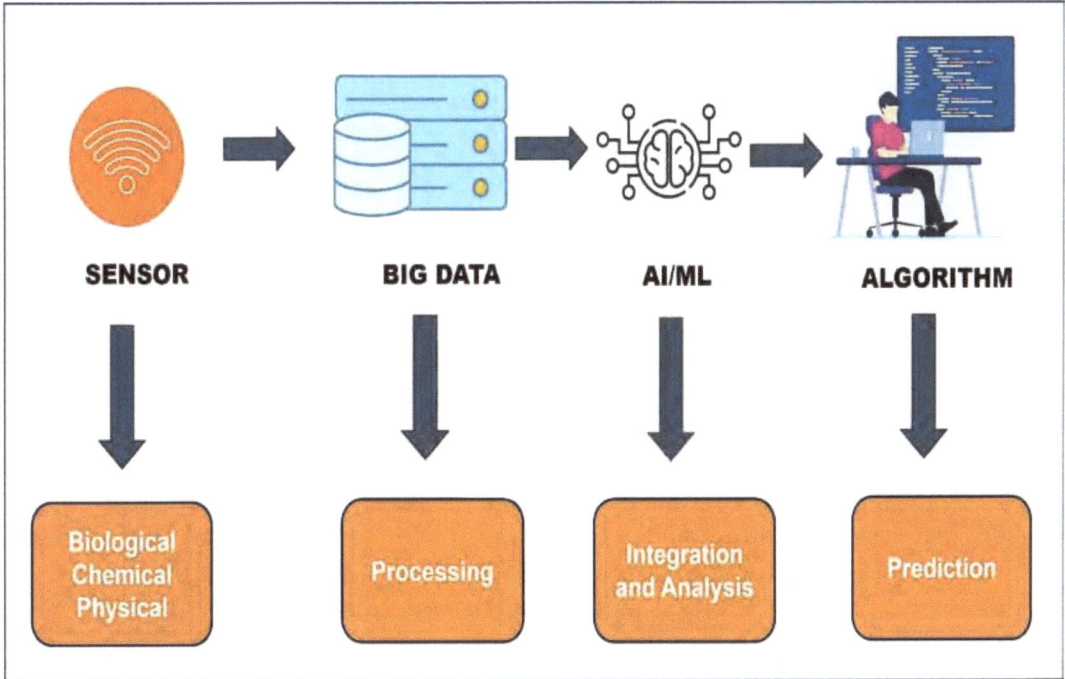

Fig. (2). implementation of deep learning in livestock behaviour monitoring.

Deep learning–based cattle behavior monitoring systems offer numerous advantages to farmers in real-world applications. These systems enable real-time monitoring, allowing for prompt intervention in response to abnormal behavior or potential health issues. By automating and streamlining data analysis processes that were traditionally time-consuming or reliant on subjective observation, deep learning models save time and resources while improving the accuracy and consistency of behavioral assessments.

Moreover, insights gained through continuous monitoring can inform management strategies aimed at improving animal welfare, optimizing feeding and housing practices, and ultimately enhancing the overall efficiency and sustainability of livestock production systems.

IOT IN LIVESTOCK FARMING

The Internet of Things (IoT) has revolutionized livestock [10] management by integrating advanced technologies to improve productivity, efficiency, and animal welfare. Through IoT, farmers can employ various sensors and devices to monitor the health, location, and environment of their livestock in real-time. For instance, wearable devices on animals can track crucial factors such as heart rate, body temperature, and activity levels [11], alerting farmers to potential health issues before they become serious. Environmental sensors placed in barns or pastures can monitor temperature, humidity, and air quality, ensuring optimal living conditions and preventing stress or disease outbreaks.

This data is collected and analyzed through centralized platforms, providing actionable insights that help farmers make informed decisions about feeding, breeding, and overall herd management. Moreover, IoT technology facilitates better resource management and operational efficiency. Smart feeding systems can automatically dispense the exact amount of feed required for each individual animal, thereby reducing waste and ensuring balanced nutrition [12, 13]. GPS-enabled tracking devices enable farmers to monitor the movement and behavior of free-ranging animals, preventing losses and allowing for a quick response to incidents such as theft or predator attacks. These IoT applications enhance livestock productivity and contribute to sustainable farming practices [14 - 16] by optimizing resource utilization and minimizing environmental impact. The convergence of the Internet of Things (IoT) [17], Artificial Intelligence (AI), and Edge Computing has emerged as a powerful solution. Internet of Things (IoT) sensors used in livestock facilities enable the collection of various types of data, including animal behavior, temperature, and feed consumption. As IoT advances, its integration into livestock management promises to enhance animal health and productivity further while supporting farming operations' economic viability.

IoT Devices and Sensors for Livestock Monitoring

The utilization of IoT devices and sensors plays a crucial role in revolutionizing livestock monitoring by offering up-to-the-minute data and valuable insights that improve animal well-being, welfare, and agricultural efficiency. Another possible technological tool for monitoring and maintaining conditions in cattle management is robotics. Wearable sensors, such as smart collars, ear tags, and implantable devices, monitor essential physiological indicators, including heart rate, body temperature, and activity levels. These gadgets facilitate the early identification of health problems, enabling prompt management and minimizing the likelihood of disease epidemics. Additionally, behavior-monitoring sensors can detect changes in feeding, rumination, and movement patterns. This provides valuable information on the welfare of animals, enabling farmers to make informed choices regarding treatment, breeding, and nutrition. As mentioned earlier, environmental sensors installed in barns or pastures observe factors such as temperature, humidity, and air quality to maintain ideal living circumstances and minimize health issues caused by stress. The implementation of IoT in livestock is explained in Fig. (**3**).

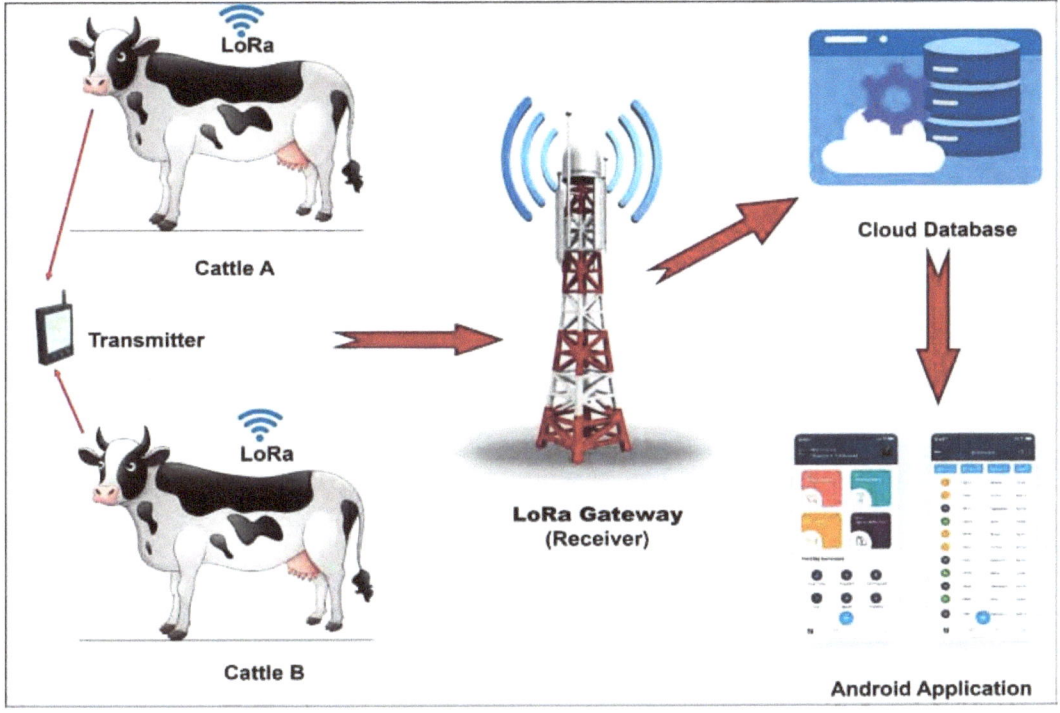

Fig. (3). Implementation of IoT in livestock.

Advanced Internet of Things (IoT) applications also utilize Radio Frequency Identification (RFID) and Global Positioning System (GPS) technologies to monitor and track the whereabouts and mobility of cattle. These systems aid in managing grazing patterns, deter theft, and facilitate the location of animals in the event of an emergency.

Information from these diverse sensors is gathered and examined utilizing centralized platforms, offering farmers detailed control panels and notifications for effective livestock management. The utilization of Deep Learning [18] algorithms helps in the anticipation of probable health concerns and identification of appropriate breeding periods, leading to a substantial enhancement in productivity and a decrease in death rates. The incorporation of Big Data, Deep Learning, IoT [19], and Blockchain technologies in livestock management results in a comprehensive and efficient system that improves production, animal welfare, and transparency in the supply chain. Blockchain technology guarantees the security [20, 21] and transparency of all data transfers, creating an unalterable record of every activity inside the livestock ecosystem. Through the utilization of Internet of Things (IoT) devices and sensors, farmers can attain enhanced production, improved animal welfare, and more environmentally friendly farming methods, ultimately resulting in greater profitability and enhanced operational efficiency. In conclusion, environmental sensors can be deployed in barns or pastures to monitor critical factors such as temperature [22, 23], humidity, and air quality, providing valuable data that supports sustainable farming practices.

Real-time Data Collection and Analysis of Environmental Conditions and Animal Health

Internet of Things (IoT) devices provide farmers with a comprehensive and dynamic view of their livestock operations. Farmers can mitigate stress-induced health issues by maintaining ideal living circumstances and improving the general well-being of animals.

The data collected from these Internet of Things (IoT) devices is relayed instantaneously to centralized platforms, which undergo comprehensive analysis. Sophisticated algorithms analyze this data, producing practical insights and notifications that assist farmers in making prompt and well-informed choices. For instance, if environmental sensors detect an increase in humidity that may result in heat stress, farmers can modify ventilation systems promptly. Likewise, deviations in animal health data might trigger quick veterinarian interventions, enhancing the chances of recovery and reducing losses. This holistic approach not only improves the well-being and efficiency of the cattle but also encourages sustainable agricultural methods by maximizing resource utilization and reducing waste. In general, the utilization of real-time data gathering and analysis revolutionizes livestock management by making it more efficient, proactive, and data-driven.

IoT-Enabled Solutions for Precision Livestock Farming

Internet of Things (IoT) technology significantly enhances the efficiency, productivity, and sustainability of modern farming through precision livestock farming solutions. These systems rely on a network of interconnected devices and sensors that continuously collect data on various aspects of animal health and environmental conditions. Wearable sensors attached to livestock can track vital indicators such as heart rate, body temperature, and activity levels, enabling the early detection of health issues and reducing the risk of disease outbreaks.In parallel, environmental sensors monitor key factors like temperature, humidity, and air quality to help maintain optimal living conditions for the animals. The collected data is processed using advanced algorithms and presented to farmers through intuitive dashboards, allowing them to make informed, data-driven decisions. This not only improves animal welfare but also enhances overall farm efficiency and operational performance.

In addition, precision livestock farming with IoT incorporates automated systems for feeding, milking, and breeding management that are customized to meet the individual requirements of each animal. Intelligent feeding systems distribute the precise quantity of food needed by each animal, considering their health information and nutritional requirements. This improves the animals' development rates. GPS-enabled tracking systems enable farmers to monitor livestock's movement and grazing patterns, thereby reducing losses and assuring the efficient utilization of pastures. Furthermore, these Internet of Things (IoT) solutions anticipate equipment maintenance needs and identify mechanical problems in a timely manner, thereby minimizing periods of inactivity and reducing operational expenses. By utilizing Internet of Things (IoT)- enabled precision farming technologies, farmers can achieve enhanced efficiency, improved animal health, and increased sustainability, ultimately leading to higher profitability and more resilient farming operations.

BLOCKCHAIN TECHNOLOGY IN LIVESTOCK MANAGEMENT

Blockchain technology offers a transformative solution for livestock management by providing a secure, transparent, and immutable system for recording data across the supply chain [24]. Through blockchain, it becomes possible to monitor and verify critical information about livestock, such as origin, health records, breeding history, and ownership, in real-time. This ensures data integrity and reliability, reduces the risk of fraud, enhances traceability, and builds trust among all stakeholders, including farmers, veterinarians, processors, retailers, and consumers.

By leveraging blockchain, all participants in the livestock sector can access accurate, up-to-date information, leading to better-informed decisions, improved productivity, and stronger standards of animal welfare and food safety.

Introduction to Blockchain and its Features

Blockchain is a decentralized digital public ledger system that enables the secure, transparent, and immutable recording of transactions across a network of computers. Originally created as the foundational technology for Bitcoin [25], blockchain has subsequently expanded its capabilities to facilitate several uses beyond digital currencies. Blockchain functions by utilizing a decentralized network of nodes, each storing a complete version of the full ledger. Transactions are organized into blocks, which are subsequently connected in chronological order using cryptographic methods, creating an unchangeable chain. This decentralized approach eliminates the need for a central authority, thereby reducing the likelihood of fraudulent activities and ensuring the integrity of data.

A fundamental characteristic of blockchain is its robust security. Every block in the chain includes a cryptographic hash of the preceding block, a timestamp, and transaction data. The hashing method guarantees that modifying a block would necessitate altering all following blocks, a task that is computationally impractical. In addition, blockchain networks commonly include consensus procedures, such as Proof of Work (PoW) or Proof of Stake (PoS), to verify transactions and uphold the integrity of the ledger. These techniques require nodes to reach a consensus on the legitimacy of transactions before they are included in the blockchain, thereby enhancing the level of security and reliability.

Transparency and traceability are important attributes of blockchain. Due to the ledger's public accessibility and the chronological and immutable recording of all transactions, stakeholders can trace the complete history of every transaction back to its point of inception. This level of transparency promotes confidence among participants, as all acts are clearly visible and can be verified. Additionally, blockchain technology can generate smart contracts, which can execute themselves based on the terms written directly into the code. This enables the automated and dependable fulfillment of contractual obligations without the need for intermediaries. Implementing this can optimize workflows, reduce expenses, and enhance effectiveness across various sectors, including finance, supply chain management, healthcare, and others. The blockchain flow in livestock management is clearly illustrated in Fig. (**4**).

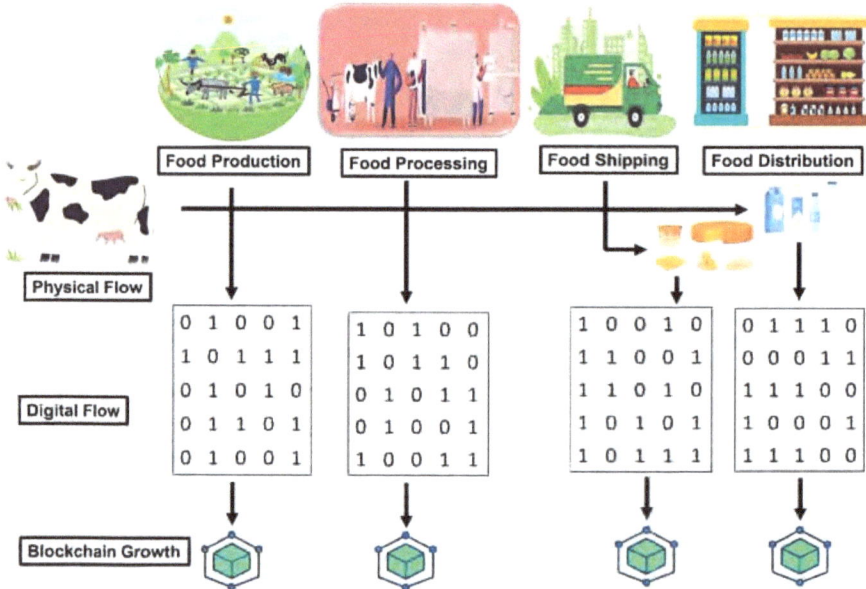

Fig. (4). Blockchain in livestock management.

Application of Blockchain in Livestock Traceability

Every step in the process, including breeding, immunization, movement, and slaughter, is recorded on the blockchain from the moment of birth until the product reaches the consumer's table. This all-encompassing and unalterable document guarantees that all parties involved, including farmers, veterinarians, processors, and retailers, may obtain trustworthy data instantly. Through the use of distinct identifiers, such as RFID tags [12] or QR codes, connected to blockchain records, it becomes straightforward to track the complete history of an animal. This process ensures the authenticity of the animal and minimizes the likelihood of deceit or incorrect labeling. The implementation of blockchain technology significantly enhances the ability to track and trace livestock [16] by providing a secure, transparent, and immutable system for documenting each phase of an animal's life cycle.

The improved capacity to track and trace cattle offers numerous advantages to the livestock industry. Consumers can gain enhanced assurance regarding the safety and quality of meat products by verifying the provenance and health records of the livestock. Regulatory organizations and industry participants benefit from this by making compliance with food safety standards easier and enhancing their ability to respond promptly to disease outbreaks or product recalls. In addition, blockchain technology enhances transparency, which cultivates trust across the supply chain, encouraging the adoption of sustainable and ethical farming methods. Blockchain technology simplifies operations and improves the integrity and effectiveness of livestock management systems.

Enhancing Transparency and Trust in Livestock Supply Chains with Blockchain

As described, blockchain technology significantly enhances transparency and trust within cattle supply chains by creating a secure and immutable ledger that records all transactions and events, from farm to table. This system ensures that all stakeholders have access to accurate and up-to-date information about the origin, health, and medical history of livestock.

By preserving data integrity and enabling complete traceability of each animal's lifecycle, blockchain eliminates the risk of data manipulation. This fosters accountability across the supply chain and reinforces confidence in the integrity of meat production. Consumers gain assurance regarding the safety, quality, and ethical sourcing of meat products, while producers and regulators benefit from streamlined compliance, improved traceability, and enhanced crisis management capabilities. Ultimately, the adoption of blockchain technology promotes more ethical, sustainable, and efficient practices throughout the livestock industry.

Integration of Big Data, Deep Learning, IoT, and Blockchain in Livestock Management

The interplay among Big Data, Deep Learning, IoT, and Blockchain [24] forms a strong foundation for transforming cattle management. Internet of Things (IoT) devices gather up-to-the-minute information on the well-being, actions, and surroundings of animals. This data is subsequently saved and analysed using a robust Big Data system [25]. Big Data offers operational efficiencies and good chances for advancement. Deep learning algorithms process this vast volume of data to provide practical insights, such as the early identification of diseases, more effective feeding schedules, and improved breeding techniques. Blockchain enhances these technologies by guaranteeing the integrity and security of the gathered data, establishing an unalterable and easily visible record of all transactions and activities inside the livestock management ecosystem [26]. This fosters confidence among stakeholders and enables accurate traceability of livestock products from farm to market. Blockchain technology provides two distinct alternatives in terms of accessibility: public and private blockchains. The primary distinction between them is whether or not to allow users to join the chain without authorization. Additionally, the use of Radio Frequency Identification (RFID) [6] and Global Positioning System (GPS) technologies helps to monitor and track the whereabouts and mobility of cattle.

This integrated method offers substantial advantages, including enhanced animal well-being through ongoing monitoring and predictive analytics, increased efficiency through optimal resource allocation, and improved visibility throughout the supply chain. Nevertheless, it is imperative to tackle obstacles, such as data integration, the requirement for technical proficiency, substantial initial expenses, and guaranteeing data confidentiality and protection. In summary, utilizing these sophisticated technologies in livestock management can result in more sustainable, efficient, and reliable farming methods, ultimately benefiting both producers and consumers.

Case Studies Demonstrating the Integration of Advanced Technologies in Livestock Management

Case Study 1: The Netherlands' Intelligent Dairy Farming

A prominent dairy farm in the Netherlands [15] has successfully integrated multiple advanced technologies to optimize livestock management. Continuous monitoring of cow health and activity levels was achieved by attaching IoT sensors to the animals. The collected data was processed using Big Data analytics to identify patterns and detect abnormalities, such as early signs of disease or changes in behavior. Deep learning algorithms further analyzed the data to generate predictive insights, enabling farmers to make informed decisions about feeding schedules, breeding, and veterinary care.

In addition, blockchain technology was implemented to create a secure and transparent ledger of each cow's health records and milk production data, ensuring that all information remained tamper-proof and easily accessible. This integrated system resulted in increased milk production, improved animal health management, and enhanced traceability, ultimately boosting consumer confidence and strengthening the farm's market competitiveness.

Case Study 2: Australia's Integrated Livestock Management

An Australian livestock company implemented a comprehensive management system that integrates IoT, Big Data, Deep Learning, and Blockchain technologies to optimize its beef production processes. IoT sensors monitored cattle movement, grazing patterns, and environmental conditions across extensive pastures. The vast amount of data collected was analyzed using Big Data platforms to identify patterns and improve the allocation of resources, such as water and feed distribution.

Blockchain technology was employed to ensure transparency and security throughout the supply chain by meticulously recording each transaction and livestock movement from the farm to the market. This integrated approach led to greater resource efficiency, enhanced animal welfare, and improved traceability. Consequently, the firm was able to comply with stringent export standards and strengthen its reputation in the global market [27].

CHALLENGES AND CONSIDERATIONS IN LIVESTOCK FARMING

Livestock production faces numerous obstacles that affect its sustainability and profitability. A significant concern is the environmental impact, encompassing the release of greenhouse gases, deforestation, and the overexploitation of water resources. Livestock, especially ruminants such as cattle, emit methane, a powerful greenhouse gas, as a by-product of their digesting process. This phenomenon exacerbates climate change, necessitating the implementation of more environmentally friendly and sustainable farming methods. Furthermore, deforestation for creating grazing pasture and the extensive use of water for both animal hydration and agricultural irrigation exacerbate environmental deterioration, underscoring the need for farmers to adopt techniques that minimize their ecological impact.

Animal welfare is a crucial factor to consider in livestock management. To ensure the health and well-being of animals, it is essential to provide them with suitable diets, appropriate living conditions, and access to veterinary care. Insufficient care, overcrowding, and inadequate sanitation can result in the occurrence of disease outbreaks. These outbreaks not only cause harm to the animals but also present substantial dangers to human health due to the transmission of zoonotic illnesses. Rising customer demand for animal products that are produced and raised humanely has prompted farmers to enhance their welfare standards due to ethical considerations regarding animal treatment.

Additionally, economic concerns present significant obstacles. Farmers often face challenges in financial planning due to the unpredictable fluctuations in market pricing for livestock products. The increasing expenses associated with feed, veterinary care, and equipment place additional pressure on business margins. Moreover, the competitiveness of cattle goods in the international market can be influenced by global trade rules and tariffs. Farmers must navigate these economic uncertainties while striving to maintain sustainable and compassionate practices. For this reason, farmers must have access to technology, education, and financial resources to effectively address these difficulties and secure the long-term sustainability of their enterprises.

CONCLUSION AND FUTURE DIRECTIONS

In summary, livestock husbandry is currently at a critical juncture, as it faces substantial economic, ethical, and environmental challenges. To mitigate the environmental consequences of livestock husbandry, it is essential to implement innovative strategies that promote sustainable land and water use, as well as reduce greenhouse gas emissions. Advancements in feed technology, including methane-reducing additives and the implementation of regenerative agricultural practices, can be instrumental in reducing the sector's ecological impact. Additionally, improving animal welfare standards is essential not only to meet ethical responsibilities but also to satisfy the growing consumer demand for responsibly sourced animal products. The integration of data-driven technologies presents promising opportunities to transform livestock husbandry in the future. Precision agriculture, leveraging data analytics and sensor technologies, can boost productivity, improve animal health, and optimize resource use. Advances in genetics, including selective breeding and potentially gene editing, may lead to more resilient and efficient livestock.

To ensure the successful adoption of these innovations, comprehensive education and training programs must accompany technological advancements, enabling farmers to effectively implement new practices. Furthermore, the transition toward more sustainable and ethical livestock production can be accelerated through financial incentives and supportive policies from governments and international organizations. The future of livestock farming depends on the collaboration among producers, scientists, policymakers, and consumers. By adopting a holistic approach that balances productivity, sustainability, and animal welfare, the livestock industry can adapt to the evolving needs of society and the environment. Current challenges can be overcome by embracing innovation, strengthening education, and establishing enabling policies, ultimately preparing the livestock sector for a sustainable and resilient future.

REFERENCES

[1]   R. Thakur, M. Baghel, S. Bhoj, S. Jamwal, G.A. Chandratre, M. Vishaal, P.C. Badgujar, H.O. Pandey, and A. Tarafdar, "Digitalization of livestock farms through blockchain, big data, artificial intelligence, and Internet of Things", In: *Engineering Applications in Livestock Production.* Academic Press, 2024, pp. 179-206.
[http://dx.doi.org/10.1016/B978-0-323-98385-3.00012-8]

[2]   B. Ji, T. Banhazi, A. Ghahramani, L. Bowtell, C. Wang, and B. Li, "Modelling of heat stress in a robotic dairy farm. Part 3: Rumination and milking performance", *Biosyst. Eng.,* vol. 199, pp. 58-72, 2020.
[http://dx.doi.org/10.1016/j.biosystemseng.2020.02.006]

[3]   S. Neethirajan, and B. Kemp, "Digital livestock farming", *Sens. Biosensing Res.,* vol. 32, no. 100408, 2021.

[4]   O. Dewangan and P. Vij, "Self-adaptive edge computing architecture for livestock management: Leveraging iot, ai, and a dynamic software ecosystem," in BIO Web of Conferences, vol. 82, p. 05010, EDP Sciences, 2024.
[http://dx.doi.org/10.1051/bioconf/20248205010]

[5]   K. Kampan, T.W. Tsusaka, and A.K. Anal, "Adoption of blockchain technology for enhanced traceability of livestock-based products", *Sustainability (Basel),* vol. 14, no. 20, p. 13148, 2022.
[http://dx.doi.org/10.3390/su142013148]

[6]   L. Leme, A. Medeiros, G. Srivastava, and J. Crichigno, "Secure cattle stock infrastructure for the Internet of Things using blockchain," in 2020 43rd International Conference on Telecommunications and Signal Processing (TSP), 2020, pp. 337–341.
[http://dx.doi.org/10.1109/TSP49548.2020.9163494]

[7]   J. Astill, R.A. Dara, E.D.G. Fraser, B. Roberts, and S. Sharif, "Smart poultry management: Smart sensors, big data, and the internet of things", *Comput. Electron. Agric.,* vol. 170, no. 105291, p. 105291, 2020.
[http://dx.doi.org/10.1016/j.compag.2020.105291]

[8]   C.G. Schuetz, S. Schausberger, and M. Schrefl, "Building an active semantic data warehouse for precision dairy farming", *J. Organ. Comput. Electron. Commerce,* vol. 28, no. 2, pp. 122-141, 2018.
[http://dx.doi.org/10.1080/10919392.2018.1444344]

[9]   J. Golosova and A. Romanovs, "The advantages and disadvantages of the blockchain technology," in 2018 IEEE 6th Workshop on Advances in Information, Electronic and Electrical Engineering (AIEEE), 2018, pp. 1–6.
[http://dx.doi.org/10.1109/AIEEE.2018.8592253]

[10]   T. Ahamed, Ed., *IoT and AI in Agriculture: Self-sufficiency in Food Production to Achieve Society 5.0 and SDG's Globally.* Springer Nature, 2023.
[http://dx.doi.org/10.1007/978-981-19-8113-5]

[11]   A.L. Duguma, and X. Bai, "Contribution of Internet of Things (IoT) in improving agricultural systems", *Int. J. Environ. Sci. Technol.,* vol. 21, no. 2, pp. 2195-2208, 2024.

[http://dx.doi.org/10.1007/s13762-023-05162-7]

[12]   M. Irfan, K. Muhammad, N. Naifar, M.A. Khan, Ed., *Applications of Blockchain Technology and Artificial Intelligence: Lead-ins in Banking, Finance, and Capital Market.* Springer Nature, 2024.

[13]   K. Kaushik, *Next-Generation Cybersecurity: AI, ML, and Blockchain.* Springer Nature, 2024.
[http://dx.doi.org/10.1007/978-981-97-1249-6]

[14]   S. Talukder, D. Qiu, P.C. Thomson, L. Cheng, and B.R. Cullen, *Impact of heat stress on dairy cow rumination, milking frequency, milk yield and quality in a pasture-based automatic milking system*, 2023.
[http://dx.doi.org/10.1071/AN22334]

[15]   M.A. Crowe, M. Hostens, and G. Opsomer, "Reproductive management in dairy cows - the future", *Ir. Vet. J.,* vol. 71, no. 1, pp. 1-13, 2018.
[http://dx.doi.org/10.1186/s13620-017-0112-y] [PMID: 29321918]

[16]   P. Kaur and A. Parashar, "A systematic literature review of blockchain technology for smart villages," Archives of Computational Methods in Engineering, vol. 29, no. 4, pp. 2417–2468, 2022.
[http://dx.doi.org/10.1007/s11831-021-09659-7]

[17]   M.S. Farooq, S. Riaz, A. Abid, K. Abid, and M.A. Naeem, "A survey on the role of IoT in agriculture for the implementation of smart farming", *IEEE Access,* vol. 7, pp. 156237-156271, 2019.
[http://dx.doi.org/10.1109/ACCESS.2019.2949703]

[18]   P.A. Vlaicu, M.A. Gras, A.E. Untea, N.A. Lefter, and M.C. Rotar, "Advancing livestock technology: Intelligent systemization for enhanced productivity, welfare, and sustainability", *AgriEngineering,* vol. 6, no. 2, pp. 1479-1496, 2024.
[http://dx.doi.org/10.3390/agriengineering6020084]

[19]   K.C. Nosina and T.S. Latha, "Introduction to cybersecurity with AI, ML, and blockchain," in *Next-Generation Cybersecurity: AI, ML, and Blockchain*, Springer Nature Singapore, 2024, pp. 1–21.
[http://dx.doi.org/10.1007/978-981-97-1249-6_1]

[20]   I. Sounkhla, E. J. Kaur, and N. Dhillon, "A combined coded scheme for OFDM system for achieving improved received signal," 2020.

[21]   S. Gupta, and D. Yadav, "Lane-finding based on structure analysis of lane and computer vision", *2019 International Conference on Communication and Electronics Systems (ICCES),* pp. 1513-1519, 2019.
[http://dx.doi.org/10.1109/ICCES45898.2019.9002280]

[22]   E. Tullo, A. Finzi, and M. Guarino, "Review: Environmental impact of livestock farming and Precision Livestock Farming as a mitigation strategy", *Sci. Total Environ.,* vol. 650, no. Pt 2, pp. 2751-2760, 2019.
[http://dx.doi.org/10.1016/j.scitotenv.2018.10.018] [PMID: 30373053]

[23]   J.R. Barrett, "Livestock farming: eating up the environment?", *Environ. Health Perspect.,* vol. 109, no. 7, pp. A312-A317, 2001.
[http://dx.doi.org/10.1289/ehp.109-a312] [PMID: 11485884]

[24]   M. Alshehri, "Blockchain-assisted internet of things framework in smart livestock farming," Internet of Things, vol. 22, 100739, 2023.
[http://dx.doi.org/10.1016/j.iot.2023.100739]

[25]   M. Torky, and A.E. Hassanein, "Integrating blockchain and the internet of things in precision agriculture: Analysis, opportunities, and challenges", *Comput. Electron. Agric.,* vol. 178, no. 105476, p. 105476, 2020.
[http://dx.doi.org/10.1016/j.compag.2020.105476]

[26]   A.S. Patel, M.N. Brahmbhatt, A.R. Bariya, J.B. Nayak, and V.K. Singh, "Blockchain technology in food safety and traceability concern to livestock products", *Heliyon,* vol. 9, no. 6, p. e16526, 2023.
[http://dx.doi.org/10.1016/j.heliyon.2023.e16526] [PMID: 37265625]

[27]   L.W. Bell, and A.D. Moore, "Integrated crop–livestock systems in Australian agriculture: Trends, drivers and implications", In: *Agricultural Systems, pp.* NULL–NULL.
[http://dx.doi.org/10.1016/j.agsy.2012.04.003]

CHAPTER 9

Next-Gen Precision Agriculture: Integrating AI, IoT, and D2D Communications

Bharti Sandhu[1,*] and **Prashant Kumar**[1]

[1] *Dr. B.R. Ambedkar National Institute of Technology, Jalandhar, Punjab, India*

Abstract: This chapter explores the synergistic integration of Artificial Intelligence (AI), the Internet of Things (IoT), and Device-to-Device (D2D) communications within the context of precision agriculture, a pivotal innovation aimed at enhancing farming efficiency and real-time decision-making. As global demands for food increase and the need for sustainable agricultural practices becomes more urgent, the convergence of these technologies offers a transformative solution. AI's capability for sophisticated analytics allows for predictive insights and enhanced decision-making. Concurrently, IoT devices facilitate comprehensive real-time data collection across various agricultural environments, and D2D communications ensure robust, immediate data exchange, which is crucial for operational efficiency and prompt responses in agricultural settings. The chapter outlines the applications, benefits, and challenges associated with implementing these technologies in agriculture. It discusses how AI-driven systems enhance crop monitoring and soil management, how IoT networks facilitate extensive data acquisition, and how D2D communications improve connectivity and system reliability. Furthermore, it addresses the integration challenges such as interoperability, security, and privacy, and proposes a framework for overcoming these barriers through standardization and best practices. Future directions, such as the implications of 5G technology and advanced AI models on agriculture, are also explored to highlight ongoing research and emerging opportunities. This comprehensive analysis not only underscores the significant enhancements that AI, IoT, and D2D technologies bring to precision agriculture but also emphasizes the necessity for continued innovation and interdisciplinary collaboration to realize their potential in modern farming practices.

Keywords: Artificial intelligence, Agricultural technology integration, Device-to-device communication, Internet of Things (IoT), Precision agriculture.

* **Corresponding author Bharti Sandhu:** Dr. B.R. Ambedkar National Institute of Technology, Jalandhar, Punjab, India; E-mail: Bhartis.cs.22@nitj.ac.in

Shefali Arora Chouhanm Nagendra Pratap Singh, Banalaxmi Brahma & Shashank Gupta (Eds.)

INTRODUCTION

In the face of an ever-expanding global population and the consequent rising demand for food, modern agriculture stands at a critical juncture. The necessity to enhance yield and efficiency while minimizing environmental impacts presents a formidable challenge that traditional farming methods alone are ill-equipped to tackle. Enter the transformative trio of technologies: Artificial Intelligence (AI), the Internet of Things (IoT), and Device-to-Device (D2D) communications. Together, these innovations promise to revolutionize agricultural practices by ushering in an era of precision agriculture that is both sustainable and highly productive [1].

Artificial Intelligence (AI) serves as the brain of this technological triad, offering unparalleled data analysis capabilities that enable predictive insights and decision-making processes far beyond human speed and accuracy [2]. By integrating AI, the agricultural sector can leverage machine learning models to predict crop yields, optimize resource allocation, and manage risks more effectively [3].

The Internet of Things (IoT) acts as the nervous system, providing a network of sensors and devices that continuously collect and transmit data from the field. This real-time data collection enables immediate and precise responses to varying crop needs, soil conditions, and environmental factors [4]. IoT technologies enable remote monitoring and management of agricultural environments, ensuring optimal conditions for plant growth and reducing the need for manual labor [5].

Device-to-Device (D2D) communication serves as the primary link within this ecosystem, enabling direct interactions between devices on the farm. This capability enhances operational efficiency by reducing reliance on centralized networks, which can be prone to delays and failures [6]. D2D communication facilitates the deployment of autonomous agricultural machinery, including drones and robots, thereby further automating farming practices and reducing human workload [7].

The convergence of AI, IoT, and D2D technologies not only elevates the capabilities of each technology but also harmonizes their functionalities to create a cohesive, integrated system. This synergy optimizes agricultural processes, from seeding to harvesting, and ensures that every resource is utilized to its maximum potential. The resulting precision agriculture system can significantly increase crop yields, decrease waste, and minimize the environmental footprint of farming activities.

This chapter aims to explore the integration of these cutting-edge technologies within the realm of precision agriculture. It will discuss their individual and collective contributions to farming efficiency, delve into the challenges they face, and provide insights into future directions for this exciting field. By harnessing the power of AI, IoT, and D2D, the agricultural sector can not only meet the increasing food demands of a growing population but also ensure that farming remains sustainable for future generations. (Fig. **1**) illustrates the architecture of the AI, IoT, and D2D framework used in agriculture.

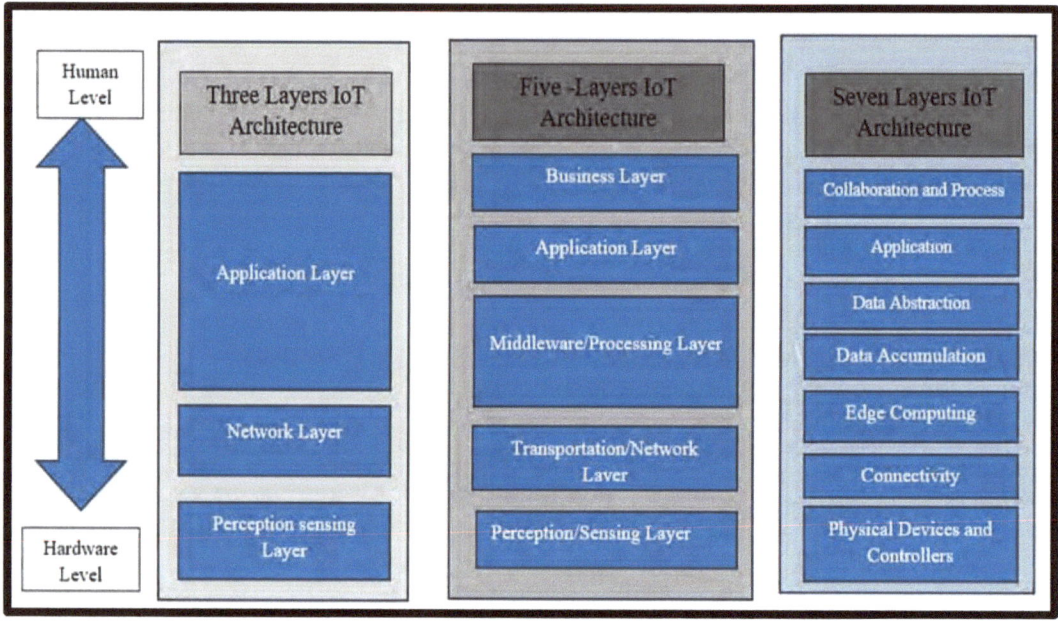

Fig. (1). Conceptual framework of AI, IoT, and D2D in agriculture.

Visual representation of the data flows and interactions between AI, IoT, and D2D devices in an agricultural setting [4].

TECHNOLOGICAL BACKGROUND

As the global agricultural sector faces the dual challenges of increasing productivity and reducing environmental impact, the strategic integration of Artificial Intelligence (AI), the Internet of Things (IoT), and Device-to-Device (D2D) communications emerges as a critical solution. This section provides a foundational understanding of these technologies, their specific applications in agriculture, and how their interplay fosters enhanced efficiency and precision in farming operations.

Overview of AI, IoT, and D2D Technologies

Integrating AI, IoT, and D2D technologies reshapes agriculture into a more data-driven and responsive industry. Each technology brings unique capabilities that, when combined, offer comprehensive solutions to complex agricultural challenges.

Artificial Intelligence in Agriculture

AI in agriculture leverages machine learning, computer vision, and predictive analytics to enhance decision-making and operational efficiency. Its applications include:

Predictive Analytics: AI models predict crop yields and pest invasions by analyzing data from various sources, enabling proactive management.

Image Recognition: Used to detect plant diseases and pests at an early stage, AI-driven image recognition helps in applying targeted treatment, thus minimizing resource use and maximizing crop health.

Automation: AI algorithms control agricultural drones and autonomous tractors for planting, spraying, and harvesting, thereby optimizing these processes for improved resource utilization and reduced waste. Fig. (**2**) shows how AI processes input from IoT devices and provides actionable outputs to both farmers and automated systems. (Fig. **2**) depicts the flow of AI modelling in smart agriculture.

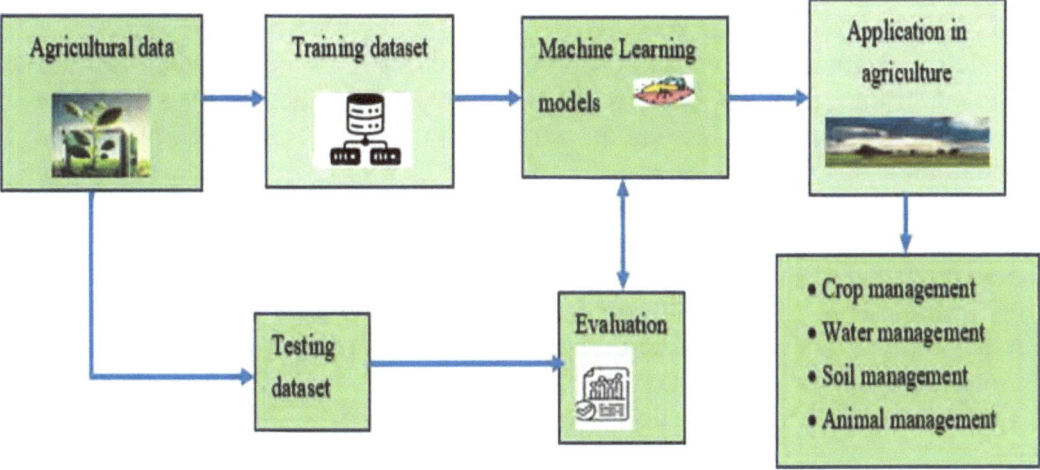

Fig. (2). AI application flow in agriculture [8].

Internet of Things (IoT) in Agriculture

IoT technology in agriculture leverages a comprehensive network of sensors, devices, and equipment interconnected online to facilitate the real-time collection, exchange, and analysis of data [9]. This technology revolutionizes traditional farming methods, optimizing resource use and enhancing crop management through precise and timely interventions [10]. Here are expanded applications and new additions to consider:

- *Precision Livestock Farming:* IoT devices can monitor livestock health and behavior, providing insights into feeding patterns, physical well-being, and reproduction cycles. This data helps farmers make informed decisions about nutrition, medical treatment, and breeding practices [11].
- *Greenhouse Automation Systems:* Within controlled environments, IoT sensors and automated systems manage temperature, humidity, light levels, and CO_2 concentrations to optimize plant growth conditions. This reduces human error and ensures optimal growing environments throughout the year [12].
- *Disease and Pest Detection:* IoT devices with image recognition technology can scan crops for signs of disease or pest infestation. These systems can alert farmers early, allowing for swift action to prevent spread, thereby minimizing crop damage and potential yield loss [13].
- *Supply Chain and Inventory Management:* IoT devices track the storage conditions of produce and automate inventory processes. Sensors monitor temperature and humidity during storage and transport to ensure product quality, reduce waste, and improve supply chain efficiency [14].
- *Yield Prediction and Land Management:* Advanced analytics on data from IoT devices can accurately predict crop yields, enabling farmers to plan for storage, sale, and future planting seasons. Furthermore, IoT applications can assist in soil analysis and land management, ensuring that land is used optimally for sustainable farming practices [15].
- *Energy Management:* IoT systems monitor and manage energy usage in various agricultural operations, particularly in powering irrigation systems and greenhouse environments. This not only conserves energy but also reduces operational costs [16]. As illustrated in Fig. (**3**), the diverse applications of IoT in agriculture encompass a wide range of functionalities, from sensor-based soil monitoring to automated irrigation systems, each designed to enhance operational efficiency and decision-making on farms.

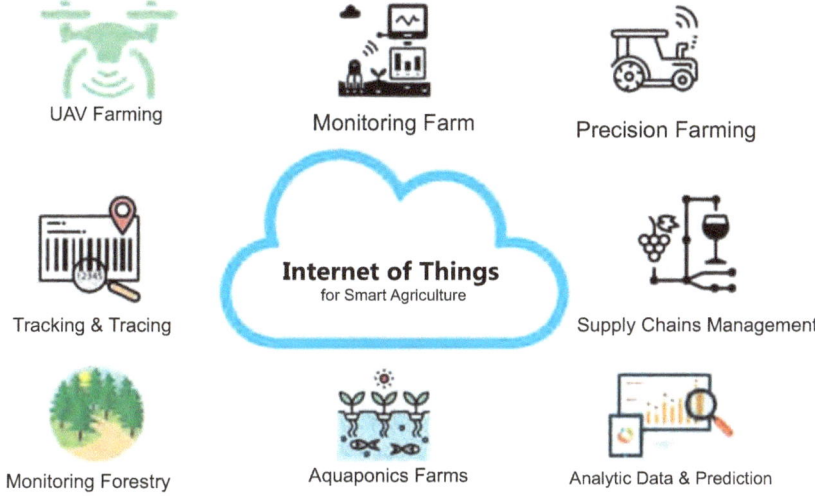

Fig. (3). An illustration of IoT applications in agriculture [17].

(Fig. **3**) depicts the applications of IoT in agriculture.

The vast array of sensor technologies deployed in modern agriculture is pivotal for enhancing various farming operations, from precision irrigation to crop monitoring. The detailed table provided (see Table **1**: Types of sensors and their applications in agriculture) categorizes the main types of sensors—such as moisture, temperature, GPS, and image sensors—and outlines their specific applications within the agricultural sector. This table not only highlights the functional benefits of each sensor type but also provides real-world examples of their deployment in the field, demonstrating how they contribute to increased efficiency and improved decision-making in farming practices. This comprehensive overview helps stakeholders select the most suitable technology for their specific agricultural needs. Table **1** lists the various types of sensors in agriculture.

Table 1. Types of sensors and their applications in agriculture.

Sensor Type	Description	Applications in Agriculture
Mechanical Sensors	Utilize probes and tensiometers to measure soil compaction and mechanical resistance. Detect the force used by roots in water absorption.	- Monitoring soil compaction - Assessing root-zone water absorption

Sensor Type	Description	Applications in Agriculture
Optical Sensors	Use light to measure soil properties. Employ photodiodes and photodetectors to determine clay, organic matter, and moisture content of the soil.	- Soil composition analysis - Moisture and organic matter monitoring
Airflow Sensors	Measure soil air permeability and compaction, and assess soil type and structure.	- Soil health assessment -Evaluating soil aeration and drainage
Location Sensors	Utilize GPS satellites to determine the precise latitude, longitude, and altitude.	- Precision farming - Crop mapping - Field navigation
Electro-chemical Sensors	Use ion-selective electrodes and field-effect transistors to detect soil levels of nitrogen, phosphorus, and potassium.	- Soil fertility analysis -Nutrient management
Dielectric Soil Moisture Sensors	Use electrodes to measure the dielectric constant of soil, which correlates to moisture content.	- Irrigation management -Drought stress monitoring

Device-to-Device (D2D) Communication Basics

D2D communication serves as a cornerstone for optimizing local network performance in precision agriculture by facilitating direct data exchanges between devices without reliance on a centralized network infrastructure [18]. Here are more detailed points and expanded applications of D2D communication:

- Network Resilience and Redundancy: D2D communication can create mesh networks among devices, which increases the resilience of the agricultural monitoring systems against single points of failure. If one device fails or goes offline, data can reroute through other devices, ensuring continuous system operation.
- Bandwidth Optimization: By communicating directly, devices can manage and optimize their bandwidth usage more effectively, prioritizing data transmission based on urgency and relevance. This is particularly useful for large-scale farms where data from numerous sources need to be processed and analyzed quickly.
- Energy Efficiency: D2D communications can reduce energy consumption by minimizing the distance data must travel, and by using protocols designed for low power consumption. This is crucial for battery-operated devices in the field, such as sensors and mobile monitoring units [19].
- Enhanced Data Security: By keeping data exchanges local, D2D communications can enhance the security of sensitive information, reducing exposure to external networks where data might be intercepted or tampered

with.

- Scalability in Device Networks: D2D allows for scalable communication systems that can easily be expanded with additional devices without significant overhead or complexity in network management.
- Support for Autonomous Agricultural Vehicles: D2D communication is instrumental in the coordination and management of autonomous vehicles, such as drones and unmanned tractors. These vehicles rely on D2D to communicate their positions, operational status, and to synchronize activities without human intervention.
- Device-to-Device (D2D) communication significantly enhances the efficiency and responsiveness of agricultural operations. This technology allows devices within close physical proximity to communicate directly without relying on centralized network infrastructures, leading to faster data transmission and reduced latency. The benefits of D2D communication in agriculture include improved coordination among autonomous farming equipment, real-time data sharing, and increased reliability of network communications, especially in remote areas where connectivity is limited. By facilitating direct interactions between devices, D2D communication enables more agile responses to changing conditions and supports advanced agricultural practices such as precision farming and automated machinery operations. These capabilities are crucial for optimizing resource use, minimizing environmental impact, and improving crop yield and quality.

Table **2** outlines the specific benefits and applications of D2D communication in agriculture:

Table 2. Benefits and application of D2D communication in agriculture.

Benefit	Application	Description
Improved Data Transmission	Real-time monitoring	Enables immediate data exchange between sensors and equipment, allowing for instant monitoring and adjustment of farming conditions.
Reduced Latency	Autonomous equipment coordination	Enhances the efficiency of autonomous tractors, drones, and other machinery, ensuring they operate harmoniously and respond quickly to commands.
Enhanced Network Reliability	Remote area connectivity	Provides robust communication options in areas with poor cellular coverage, ensuring the continuous operation of IoT devices.
Increased Scalability	Scalable network expansions	Facilitates the easy addition of new devices to the network without requiring extensive infrastructure modifications.
Direct Device Interactions	Pest and disease management	Allows sensors detecting pest or disease outbreaks to directly communicate with spraying equipment to address issues promptly.

(Table 2) cont.....

Benefit	Application	Description
Energy Efficiency	Energy management in field operations	Reduces the energy consumption of devices by using local communication, which requires less power than transmitting data over long distances.

Interplay Between AI, IoT, and D2D

The convergence of AI, IoT, and D2D creates a robust framework for precision agriculture, driving significant advancements in farm management and operational efficiency.

The integration of Artificial Intelligence (AI), the Internet of Things (IoT), and Device-to-Device (D2D) communications in agriculture represents a transformative approach that leverages the unique strengths of each technology to enhance farming operations. AI provides advanced analytics and predictive capabilities, IoT contributes vast real-time data collection, and D2D offers enhanced connectivity and immediate data exchange. Together, these technologies create a powerful synergy that enhances decision-making, improves resource management, and increases overall productivity and sustainability in the agricultural sector. The following table, Table **3**: Benefits of AI, IoT, and D2D integration in agriculture, encapsulates the individual and combined impacts of these technologies, illustrating how they collaboratively contribute to modernizing agricultural practices and driving efficiency and growth within the sector. The integration of AI, IoT, and D2D in agriculture is not just an enhancement but a necessary evolution to meet future food production needs sustainably and efficiently. The subsequent sections will delve deeper into specific applications, challenges, and future directions of these integrated systems [15]. Table **3** lists the benefits of AI and IoT in agriculture.

Table 3. Benefits of AI, IoT, and D2D integration in agriculture [17].

Benefit	AI Contributions	IoT Contributions	D2D Contributions	Combined Impact
Enhanced Decision-Making	Utilizes predictive analytics to forecast crop yields.	Provides real-time data from field sensors.	Facilitates immediate device-t--device data exchange.	Enables a seamless flow of information that supports rapid, informed decisions based on comprehensive data analysis.

(Table 3) cont.....

Benefit	AI Contributions	IoT Contributions	D2D Contributions	Combined Impact
Precision Farming	Analyzes extensive data to optimize planting and harvesting.	Monitors environmental conditions and crop health.	Improves coordination among automated farming equipment.	Ensures optimal planting, fertilization, and harvesting by precisely adjusting operations as conditions change.
Resource Management	Optimizes input usage (water, nutrients) based on predictions.	Tracks resource distribution and utilization efficiently.	Enhances local network data sharing to manage resources wisely.	Reduces waste and increases efficiency in resource utilization, resulting in cost savings and environmental benefits.
Improved Productivity	Automates complex processes and reduces human error.	Facilitates continuous monitoring and control systems.	Ensures robust connectivity even in remote areas.	Increases crop yield and quality through better monitoring, automation, and precise control.
Sustainability	Supports sustainable practices through enhanced analytics.	Enables the monitoring of environmental impact.	Supports energy-efficient operations in the field.	Contributes to eco-friendly farming by minimizing the carbon footprint and optimizing input use.
Scalability and Flexibility	Adapts algorithms based on data inputs and learning.	Easily integrates with existing farm equipment and systems.	Allows for network flexibility and expansion without infrastructure overhauls.	Facilitates the scaling of technology implementation across various sizes and types of agricultural operations.

CURRENT APPLICATIONS AND CASE STUDIES

The transformative impact of AI, IoT, and D2D communications in agriculture is evident through their applications in monitoring systems, data collection networks, and enhanced connectivity solutions. This section examines specific instances where these technologies converge to optimize agricultural practices, illustrating their effectiveness through case studies and outlining their roles in facilitating real-time decision-making.

AI-Driven Monitoring Systems

The integration of AI into agricultural monitoring systems has revolutionized the way farmers assess crop health and soil conditions. By leveraging machine learning algorithms and data analytics, AI provides detailed insights that lead to more informed decision-making [20].

- *Crop Health Monitoring:* AI algorithms analyze images from drones and ground sensors to detect signs of disease, nutrient deficiencies, or water stress. These systems can pinpoint affected areas, allowing for targeted treatment that conserves resources and minimizes crop damage [21].
- *Soil Condition Analysis:* AI models process data from various sensors to assess soil moisture, pH levels, and nutrient content. This information helps in customizing irrigation and fertilization plans to match the precise needs of different crop zones.
- *Growth Trend Analysis:* AI can analyze time-series data from crop monitoring to identify growth trends and deviations, providing valuable insights for informed decision-making. By comparing current crop data against historical performance, AI algorithms can alert farmers about abnormal growth patterns, enabling early intervention to rectify potential issues.
- *Water Usage Optimization:* AI models not only assess soil moisture levels but can also predict future water needs based on weather forecasts and historical crop water usage data. This predictive capability enables more efficient water management, ensuring that crops receive optimal irrigation to maximize growth and minimize water wastage.
- *Nutrient Management:* Beyond simple content assessment, AI can recommend specific fertilization regimes by analyzing soil nutrient data in conjunction with plant uptake patterns. This targeted fertilization approach not only improves crop yield and quality but also minimizes the environmental impact of excess fertilizer runoff.
- *Disease Prediction and Management:* Leveraging predictive analytics and AI systems, disease forecasts can be made based on current crop health data, historical disease outbreaks, and environmental conditions. Early warnings can prompt preemptive actions, such as adjusting humidity levels or applying fungicides, to prevent widespread crop damage.
- *Integrated Pest Management:* AI-driven systems analyze images and sensor data to identify pest presence and predict infestation risks. by understanding pest life cycles and the environmental factors that influence pest populations, ai can recommend optimal times for pest control measures, thereby reducing reliance on routine pesticide applications. (Fig. **4**) depicts the generalized architecture of the Internet of Things in agriculture.

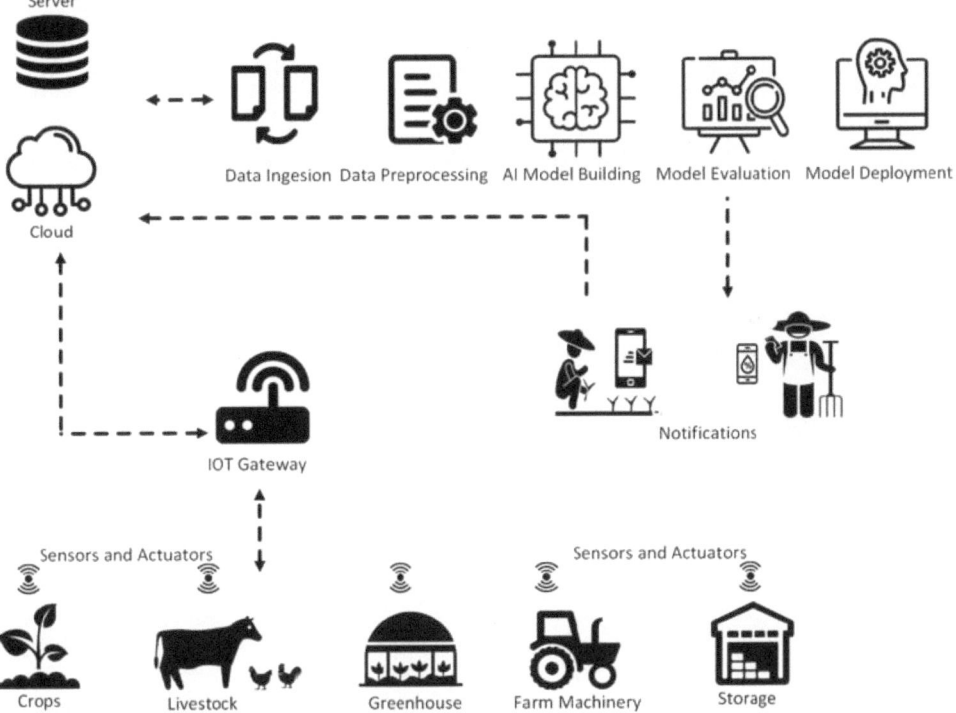

Fig. (4). Generalized architecture internet of things.

(Fig. **4**), "Generalized Internet of Things [17]—Artificial Intelligence/Machine Learning workflow for agricultural solutions," illustrates the flow of data from sensors to AI systems and back to the farm management dashboard, highlighting the AI's role in processing and decision-making.

IOT NETWORKS FOR REAL-TIME DATA COLLECTION

IoT networks play an integral role in modern agriculture, leveraging a comprehensive array of interconnected devices to enhance the monitoring, analysis, and management of farm operations. These networks facilitate a level of precision and responsiveness that is essential for modern precision farming practices.

Sensor Networks

IoT sensor networks, strategically distributed across agricultural lands, provide continuous monitoring of a wide range of environmental and plant conditions [22]. Here are additional points and types of data collected:

- *Soil Conductivity:* Sensors can measure soil salinity, a crucial factor in assessing soil health and suitability for crop production. High salinity can inhibit the absorption of water and nutrients by plants.
- *Atmospheric CO_2 Levels:* Monitoring CO_2 levels can help assess plant growth and photosynthesis rates, providing insights into crop health and potential yield.
- *Solar Radiation:* Sensors that measure the amount and intensity of sunlight can help optimize plant growth and predict weather conditions affecting crop production.

These sensor networks are not only pivotal for gathering data but also for implementing adaptive management strategies that respond dynamically to changing field conditions, thus enhancing both productivity and sustainability.

Data Acquisition and Management

The efficiency of IoT in agriculture depends significantly on the robustness of data acquisition systems and the sophistication of data management practices. Here are further details and functionalities:

- Edge Computing: To reduce latency and bandwidth use, edge computing can be implemented to process data directly at the site of data collection before sending it to the cloud. This is particularly useful for time-sensitive decisions in agriculture.
- Data Integration: IoT systems often integrate data from various sources, including weather stations, satellite images, and on-ground sensors, to create a comprehensive view of agricultural conditions. This integration supports more accurate and holistic decision-making.
- Predictive Analytics: Advanced data analytics are used to predict future conditions and potential issues, such as pest outbreaks or crop diseases, allowing preemptive measures to be taken.

(Fig. **5**), IoT data flow and management in agriculture: This figure illustrates the flow of data from IoT sensors through edge devices to cloud storage.

D2D Communication for Enhanced Connectivity

D2D communication is pivotal in enhancing the robustness and responsiveness of IoT and AI applications in agriculture by enabling devices to connect directly.

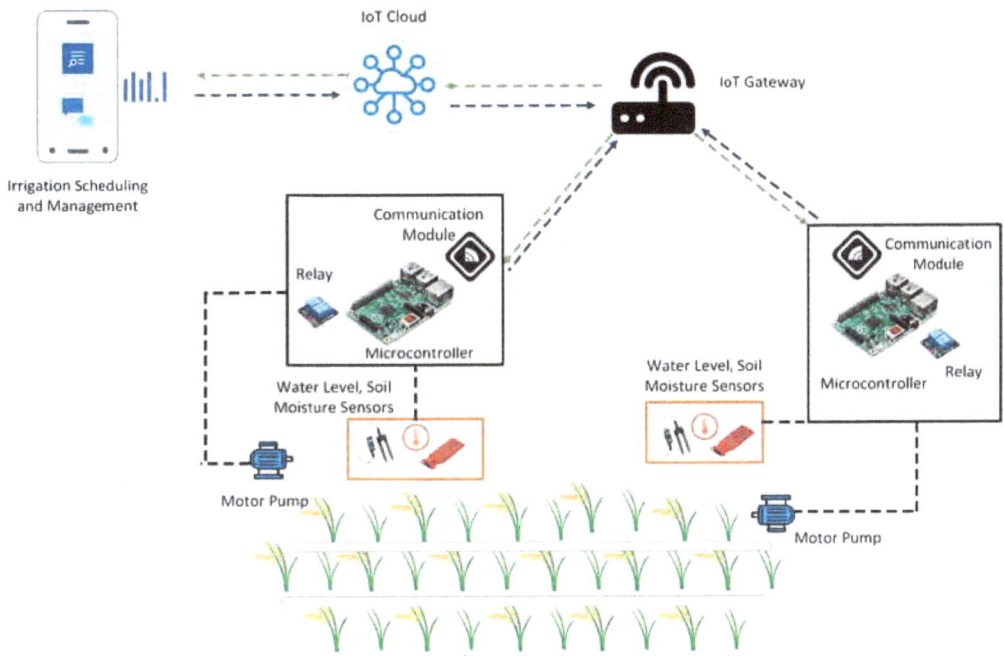

Fig. (5). Automated irrigation systems using the internet of things [17].

Case Studies: Successful Applications

- *Precision Irrigation Systems:* In California's vineyards, D2D communication protocols play a crucial role. Soil moisture sensors communicate directly with irrigation valves using D2D protocols, enabling real-time adjustments that precisely tailor water application to the soil's moisture content. This direct communication ensures that water is not wasted and that vines receive optimal irrigation, thereby improving yield and quality while conserving water.

- *Autonomous Farm Equipment Coordination:* On large-scale crop farms, D2D communications facilitate the seamless coordination of autonomous farm equipment. For instance, autonomous tractors and drones equipped with D2D capabilities can synchronize their operations by sharing real-time data about field conditions without requiring central server mediation. This synchronization helps prevent operational overlaps, optimizes field coverage, and enhances the timeliness of farming interventions, such as planting, spraying, or harvesting.

- *Smart Harvesting Systems:* In orchards in Washington State, D2D communications have played a pivotal role in deploying smart harvesting systems. These systems enable real-time coordination between ground sensors that assess fruit ripeness and autonomous picking machines. As a result, fruits are harvested at their peak quality, reducing waste and increasing market value.

- *Livestock Management Systems:* On dairy farms in the Netherlands, D2D communications enable wearable sensors on livestock to send health and movement data directly to automated milking and feeding machines. This direct line of communication ensures that individual animal needs are met promptly, optimizing feeding schedules and improving milk production efficiency.
- *D2D-Enhanced Pest Management System:* This case study details how a grape farm utilized D2D communications to enhance its pest management system. Soil and canopy sensors detect early signs of infestation and communicate directly with drone sprayers to target affected areas. This targeted approach enables a rapid response to pest outbreaks, thereby minimizing crop damage and pesticide use. The system's efficiency has not only reduced costs but also supported more sustainable farming practices.

ENHANCING REAL-TIME RESPONSE AND DECISION-MAKING

D2D's capability to facilitate immediate device-to-device communication without the need for central network intervention significantly reduces latency. This is crucial for applications where time-sensitive data is involved, such as:

Emergency Responses to Weather Events: Immediate data sharing between devices enables the rapid deployment of countermeasures against sudden weather changes.

Real-Time Disease Management: Quick dissemination of information regarding disease detection to mobile devices and automated systems facilitates instant action, potentially saving vast expanses of crops from infestation.

These applications and case studies demonstrate the significant benefits that AI, IoT, and D2D technologies bring to the agricultural sector, highlighting their potential to enhance efficiency and inform real-time decision-making. The next sections will delve into the integration challenges and advanced solutions that further refine these technologies for agricultural optimization.

INTEGRATION CHALLENGES AND SOLUTIONS

The integration of AI, IoT, and D2D communications into agricultural practices, while promising, introduces a set of technological and operational challenges that must be addressed to realize their potential. These challenges can impede the adoption and effectiveness of these technologies in real-world agricultural settings.

Interoperability and Compatibility Issues

One of the primary challenges in deploying AI, IoT, and D2D solutions in agriculture is ensuring interoperability among diverse systems and devices [23]. The agricultural technology landscape features a wide range of equipment and systems from different manufacturers, each with its proprietary technology:

Standardization: A lack of uniform standards complicates the integration of new technologies with existing agricultural equipment. Without standard protocols, the ability to communicate and operate seamlessly across various devices and platforms is limited.

Legacy Systems Integration: Many farms operate with legacy systems that are not initially designed to communicate with modern IoT devices or utilize AI-driven insights. Upgrading these systems to support new technologies often requires significant investment and a technical overhaul.

Software and Hardware Compatibility: Ensuring that software solutions are compatible with a variety of hardware setups and that they can effectively communicate can be challenging. The diverse range of agricultural environments further complicates this, as hardware must be robust enough to handle various climatic and topographical conditions.

Security and Privacy Concerns

As agricultural systems become increasingly interconnected, they also become more susceptible to cyber threats. The security and privacy of data in IoT and D2D networks are of paramount importance, particularly when sensitive farming data is involved [24]:

Data Breaches: With the increasing collection and sharing of data, agricultural operations face significant exposure to data breaches. These breaches could compromise sensitive operational data, impacting farm operations and competitive positioning.

Unauthorized Access: The open nature of some IoT and D2D networks can make them susceptible to unauthorized access. Ensuring that only authorized personnel can access and manipulate the systems is crucial for maintaining both operational integrity and data privacy.

Network Security: Protecting the network infrastructure from external attacks and ensuring the integrity of data in transit requires robust encryption and secure communication protocols. This is particularly challenging in rural areas where the IT infrastructure may not be as advanced.

Resource Constraints

Implementing sophisticated technologies like AI, IoT, and D2D communications often demands significant resources in terms of capital investment, technical expertise, and ongoing maintenance [25]:

High Initial Costs: The cost of purchasing and installing IoT sensors, upgrading existing systems, and training staff can be significantly high for smaller operations.

Technical Skill Shortage: There is often a shortage of necessary technical skills among agricultural workers to deploy and manage advanced technologies effectively. This gap can limit the adoption and proper utilization of AI, IoT, and D2D systems.

Maintenance and Support: Continuous maintenance and technical support are required to ensure the smooth operation of integrated systems. This ongoing requirement can strain the resources of farming operations, especially those with limited budgets.

Proposed Architectural Solutions

To address the technological and operational challenges presented by integrating AI, IoT, and D2D communications in agriculture, it is essential to develop and implement robust architectural solutions. These solutions aim to enhance system compatibility, ensure data security, and improve resource management, making the adoption of advanced technologies feasible and effective for modern agricultural practices.

Framework for Integration

A well-defined architectural framework is crucial for the seamless integration of AI, IoT, and D2D technologies. This framework should be designed to support interoperability, scalability, and security across diverse agricultural environments [26]:

- *Unified Communication Protocols:* Developing standardized communication protocols that enable different devices and systems to interact seamlessly is fundamental. This involves adopting universal data formats and transmission standards that ensure devices from various manufacturers can communicate effectively with one another.
- *Modular System Design:* Implementing a modular design allows for the flexible integration of various technological components. This approach enables farms to

upgrade their systems incrementally, adding or modifying modules as needed without overhauling the entire system.

- *Edge Computing Capabilities:* Incorporating edge computing into the IoT network architecture can significantly reduce latency and bandwidth demands. By processing data locally at the edge of the network, immediate responses to data inputs are facilitated, enhancing real-time decision-making capabilities in agricultural operations.

Standardization and Best Practices

To overcome interoperability challenges and enhance system functionality, the adoption of industry-wide standards and best practices is vital:

- *Security Standards:* Implementing robust security protocols is critical to safeguard agricultural data. This includes the use of end-to-end encryption for data transmission, secure authentication mechanisms for device access, and regular security audits to identify and address vulnerabilities.
- *Best Practice Guidelines:* Establishing a set of best practices for the deployment and maintenance of AI, IoT, and D2D systems in agriculture can guide farmers and technology providers. These guidelines should cover aspects such as optimal sensor placement, data privacy policies, and strategies for energy-efficient system design.
- *Regulatory Compliance:* Ensuring that all technological implementations comply with local and international regulations governing data protection, device usage, and environmental impact is crucial. Compliance helps in building trust and ensures that agricultural operations are not only efficient but also legally sound.

FUTURE DIRECTIONS AND EMERGING TECHNOLOGIES

As the agricultural sector continues to evolve, emerging technologies are poised to further revolutionize farming practices. The advent of 5G networks and advancements in AI techniques are particularly significant, promising to enhance the capabilities of AI, IoT, and D2D communications in agriculture. This section explores these technologies, their potential impact on precision agriculture, and how they can lead to more efficient, sustainable, and data-driven farming methods.

The Role of 5G and Beyond in Agriculture

The deployment of 5G technology is set to significantly boost the efficiency and effectiveness of AI, IoT, and D2D implementations in agriculture by providing ultra-reliable, low-latency communications and massive machine-type communications. 5G will facilitate faster, more reliable data transmission, enhancing the real-time capabilities necessary for precision farming [27].

- *Enhanced Data Transmission:* 5G's high-speed connectivity improves the volume and velocity of data transfer between IoT devices and central servers, enabling more granular, real-time monitoring and control.
- *Reduced Latency:* Crucial for autonomous systems, the ultra-low latency of 5G networks enhances the responsiveness of AI-driven machinery and D2D communications, allowing for instantaneous adjustments to farming operations based on real-time data.
- *Increased Connectivity:* With its ability to connect more devices per square kilometer, 5G expands the potential scale of IoT deployments in agriculture, supporting more comprehensive data collection and device interaction over larger areas.

Advanced AI Techniques for Predictive Analytics

Advancements in AI, particularly through machine learning and deep learning, are driving significant improvements in predictive analytics within agriculture, making forecasts more accurate and enhancing farming practices.

Machine Learning Models

Machine learning models in agriculture analyze historical data and identify patterns to predict future outcomes, such as yield predictions, pest infestations, and optimal planting times [28].

Regression Models: Used for predicting quantitative outcomes such as yield based on various input features like weather conditions and soil quality.

Classification Models: Help in identifying crop diseases or pest presence, classifying images or sensor data into categories based on trained datasets.

Time Series Forecasting: Utilize time series data to forecast weather patterns and their impact on crop cycles, enabling farmers to plan more effectively.

Anomaly Detection Models: Identify unusual patterns in crop growth or soil conditions that may indicate the presence of pests, diseases, or irrigation issues.

Reinforcement Learning: Deployed for adaptive decision systems in precision farming, learning and optimizing strategies based on operational feedback.

Deep Learning Applications in Precision Agriculture

Deep learning extends the capabilities of traditional machine learning by enabling the processing and learning from vast amounts of unstructured data, such as images from drones or satellite photos [29].

- *Image Processing:* Deep learning models process images to detect anomalies in crops, identify weed species, and assess crop health more accurately than ever before.
- *Natural Language Processing (NLP):* Used to interpret and analyze farmer reports and agricultural literature to extract insights and enhance decision-making processes.
- *Semantic Segmentation:* Deep learning models perform pixel-wise classification on images to understand and segment different parts of a field, allowing precise action such as targeted pesticide application.
- *Generative Adversarial Networks (GANs):* These generate synthetic agricultural data for training models where data may be scarce, such as simulating plant diseases for better model training.
- *Transfer Learning:* Apply pre-trained models to new, smaller datasets, often in specific agricultural contexts, thereby speeding up the deployment of robust models without requiring extensive computation.

CONCLUSION AND FUTURE WORK

The integration of Artificial Intelligence (AI), the Internet of Things (IoT), and Device-to-Device (D2D) communications within precision agriculture is a transformative movement toward more sustainable, efficient, and productive farming practices. This synergy enhances real-time decision-making, optimizes resource utilization, and improves overall crop management through the application of precision techniques. The use of AI enables sophisticated analytics and predictive insights, IoT devices facilitate the collection of exhaustive real-time data, and D2D communications ensure robust and immediate data exchange across various agricultural tools. These integrated technologies not only promise to increase the yield and profitability of farms but also aim to reduce the ecological footprint of agricultural practices, addressing both economic and environmental sustainability goals.

Future research should focus on overcoming the challenges of interoperability and security that currently impede the seamless integration of these technologies. Exploring advanced cryptographic methods to protect data exchanged between IoT devices and developing universal standards for device communication could address these issues. Additionally, with the rapid advancement of 5G technology, further studies are needed to fully understand its capabilities in supporting AI and IoT frameworks in agriculture. This includes testing 5G's potential to handle the increased data loads and its reliability in rural farm settings. Ultimately, continued innovation, supported by interdisciplinary research and robust policy frameworks, will be crucial in realizing the full potential of AI, IoT, and D2D technologies in revolutionizing global agricultural practices.

REFERENCES

[1]   W. K. Alazzai, B. Sh. Z. Abood, H. M. Al-Jawahry, and M. K. Obaid, "Precision farming: The power of AI and IoT technologies," E3S Web of Conferences, vol. 491, p. 04006, Feb. 2024 [http://dx.doi.org/10.1051/e3sconf/202449104006]

[2]   R. Sharma, "Artificial intelligence in agriculture: A review", *5th International Conference on Intelligent Computing and Control Systems (ICICCS),* pp. 937-942, 2021. [http://dx.doi.org/10.1109/ICICCS51141.2021.9432187]

[3]   M. Javaid, A. Haleem, I.H. Khan, and R. Suman, "Understanding the potential applications of artificial intelligence in agriculture sector", *Advanced Agrochem,* vol. 2, no. 1, pp. 15-30, 2023. [http://dx.doi.org/10.1016/j.aac.2022.10.001]

[4]   K. Saranya, P. Uva Dharini, P. Uva Darshni, and S. Monisha, "IoT based pest controlling system for smart agriculture", *2019 International Conference on Communication and Electronics Systems (ICCES),* IEEE, pp. 1548-1552, 2019. [http://dx.doi.org/10.1109/ICCES45898.2019.9002046]

[5]   A. Rehman, T. Saba, M. Kashif, S.M. Fati, S.A. Bahaj, and H. Chaudhry, "A revisit of internet of things technologies for monitoring and control strategies in smart agriculture", *Agronomy (Basel),* vol. 12, no. 1, p. 127, 2022. [http://dx.doi.org/10.3390/agronomy12010127]

[6]   P. Pawar, and A. Trivedi, "Device-to-device communication based iot system: Benefits and challenges", *IETE Tech. Rev.,* vol. 36, no. 4, pp. 362-374, 2019. [http://dx.doi.org/10.1080/02564602.2018.1476191]

[7]   M.S.M. Gismalla, A.I. Azmi, M.R.B. Salim, M.F.L. Abdullah, F. Iqbal, W.A. Mabrouk, M.B. Othman, A.Y.I. Ashyap, and A.S.M. Supa'at, "Survey on Device to Device (D2D) communication for 5gb/6g networks: Concept, applications, challenges, and future directions", *IEEE Access,* vol. 10, pp. 30792-30821, 2022. [http://dx.doi.org/10.1109/ACCESS.2022.3160215]

[8]   A. Subeesh, and C.R. Mehta, "Automation and digitization of agriculture using artificial intelligence and internet of things", *Artificial Intelligence in Agriculture,* vol. 5, pp. 278-291, 2021. [http://dx.doi.org/10.1016/j.aiia.2021.11.004]

[9]   M.S. Farooq, S. Riaz, A. Abid, K. Abid, and M.A. Naeem, "A survey on the role of iot in agriculture for the implementation of smart farming", *IEEE Access,* vol. 7, pp. 156237-156271, 2019. [http://dx.doi.org/10.1109/ACCESS.2019.2949703]

[10]   E.E.K. Senoo, E. Akansah, I. Mendonça, and M. Aritsugi, "Monitoring and control framework for IoT, implemented for smart agriculture", *Sensors (Basel),* vol. 23, no. 5, p. 2714, 2023. [http://dx.doi.org/10.3390/s23052714] [PMID: 36904920]

[11]   K. Potter, "Technological innovations in precision livestock farming.". Available: https://www.researchgate.net/publication/379644337

[12]   M.F. Siddiqui, "A. ur Rehman Khan, N. Kanwal, H. Mehdi, A. Noor, and M. A. Khan, "Automation and monitoring of greenhouse", *2017 International Conference on Information and Communication Technologies (ICICT),* IEEE, pp. 197-201, 2017.

[http://dx.doi.org/10.1109/ICICT.2017.8320190]

[13]   D.O. Kiobia, C.J. Mwitta, K.G. Fue, J.M. Schmidt, D.G. Riley, and G.C. Rains, "A review of successes and impeding challenges of iot-based insect pest detection systems for estimating agroecosystem health and productivity of cotton", *Sensors (Basel),* vol. 23, no. 8, p. 4127, 2023. [http://dx.doi.org/10.3390/s23084127] [PMID: 37112469]

[14]   S. Taj, A.S. Imran, Z. Kastrati, S.M. Daudpota, R.A. Memon, and J. Ahmed, "IoT-based supply chain management: A systematic literature review", *Internet of Things,* vol. 24, p. 100982, 2023. [http://dx.doi.org/10.1016/j.iot.2023.100982]

[15]   M. Dhanaraju, P. Chenniappan, K. Ramalingam, S. Pazhanivelan, and R. Kaliaperumal, "Smart farming: internet of things (IoT)-based sustainable agriculture", *Agriculture,* vol. 12, no. 10, p. 1745, 2022.
[http://dx.doi.org/10.3390/agriculture12101745]

[16]   J. Xu, B. Gu, and G. Tian, "Review of agricultural IoT technology", *Artificial Intelligence in Agriculture,* vol. 6, pp. 10-22, 2022.
[http://dx.doi.org/10.1016/j.aiia.2022.01.001]

[17]   V.K. Quy, N.V. Hau, D.V. Anh, N.M. Quy, N.T. Ban, S. Lanza, G. Randazzo, and A. Muzirafuti, "IoT-enabled smart agriculture: architecture, applications, and challenges", *Appl. Sci. (Basel),* vol. 12, no. 7, p. 3396, 2022.
[http://dx.doi.org/10.3390/app12073396]

[18]   U.N. Kar, and D.K. Sanyal, "An overview of device-to-device communication in cellular networks", *ICT Express,* vol. 4, no. 4, pp. 203-208, 2018.
[http://dx.doi.org/10.1016/j.icte.2017.08.002]

[19]   M. Li, and H.L. Tsai, "Energy-efficient device discovery mechanism for device-to-device communications in 5G networks", *Energies,* vol. 14, no. 2, p. 270, 2021.
[http://dx.doi.org/10.3390/en14020270]

[20]   N. Basurto, C. Cambra, and A. Herrero, "AI-driven visualizations for performance monitoring and anomaly detection in robots," in 2020 IEEE/ACS 17th International Conference on Computer Systems and Applications (AICCSA), IEEE, Nov. 2020, pp. 1–6.
[http://dx.doi.org/10.1109/AICCSA50499.2020.9316513]

[21]   G. Devi, N. Sowmiya, K. Yasoda, K. Muthulakshmi, and K. Balasubramanian, "Review on application of drones for crop health monitoring and spraying pesticides and fertilizer", J. crit. rev., vol. 7, no. 06, Apr. 2020.
[http://dx.doi.org/10.31838/jcr.07.06.117]

[22]   M. Arooj, M. Asif, and S. Zeeshan, "Modeling smart agriculture using sensorML", *Int. J. Adv. Comput. Sci. Appl.,* vol. 8, no. 5, 2017.
[http://dx.doi.org/10.14569/IJACSA.2017.080562]

[23]   S.S. Albouq, A.A.A. Sen, N. Almashf, M. Yamin, A. Alshanqiti, and N.M. Bahbouh, "A survey of interoperability challenges and solutions for dealing with them in IoT environment", *IEEE Access,* vol. 10, pp. 36416-36428, 2022.
[http://dx.doi.org/10.1109/ACCESS.2022.3162219]

[24]   M. Wang, and Z. Yan, *"Security in D2D communications: A review,"* in *2015 IEEE Trustcom/BigDataSE/ISPA.* IEEE, 2015, pp. 1199-1204.
[http://dx.doi.org/10.1109/Trustcom.2015.505]

[25]   G. Kornaros, "Hardware-assisted machine learning in resource-constrained IoT environments for security: Review and future prospective", *IEEE Access,* vol. 10, pp. 58603-58622, 2022.
[http://dx.doi.org/10.1109/ACCESS.2022.3179047]

[26]   A. A. Issa, S. Majed, S. Abdul Ameer, and H. M. Al-Jawahry, "Farming in the digital age: Smart agriculture with AI and IoT," E3S Web of Conferences, vol. 477, p. 00081, Jan. 2024.

[http://dx.doi.org/10.1051/e3sconf/202447700081]

[27] S. Rathinavel, R. Kavitha, J. Gitanjali, and R. Saiprasanth, "Role of 5G technology in enhancing agricultural mechanization", *IOP Conf. Ser. Earth Environ. Sci.,* vol. 1258, no. 1, p. 012010, 2023. [http://dx.doi.org/10.1088/1755-1315/1258/1/012010]

[28] A. Sharma, A. Jain, P. Gupta, and V. Chowdary, "Machine learning applications for precision agriculture: A comprehensive review", *IEEE Access,* vol. 9, pp. 4843-4873, 2021. [http://dx.doi.org/10.1109/ACCESS.2020.3048415]

[29] I. Mashood Nasir, A. Bibi, J. Hussain Shah, M. Attique Khan, M. Sharif, K. Iqbal, Y. Nam, and S. Kadry, "Deep learning-based classification of fruit diseases: An application for precision agriculture", *Comput. Mater. Continua,* vol. 66, no. 2, pp. 1949-1962, 2021. [http://dx.doi.org/10.32604/cmc.2020.012945]

CHAPTER 10

The Role of Big Data and Deep Learning in Crop Management

Narendra Kumar[1,*], Shefali Arora[1] and Shashank Gupta[1]

[1] *Department of Computer Science and Engineering, Dr. B.R. Ambedkar National Institute of Technology, Jalandhar, Punjab, India*

Abstract: The integration of big data and deep learning technologies has brought about a paradigm shift in crop management practices, offering innovative solutions to address the complex challenges faced by farmers and agricultural experts. This chapter explores the pivotal role of big data in collecting, storing, and analyzing vast amounts of agricultural data from diverse sources, such as satellite imagery, sensors, and drones. It highlights how deep learning algorithms leverage this data to provide real-time insights into crop health, soil conditions, and environmental factors, enabling precision agriculture and predictive analytics. Additionally, this chapter discusses how deep learning models facilitate crop monitoring, disease detection, and yield optimization by analyzing image data and forecasting future outcomes. Furthermore, it examines the implications of these technologies on supply chain management and decision support systems in agriculture. Overall, the study underscores the transformative potential of big data and deep learning in revolutionizing crop management practices, fostering sustainability, and enhancing productivity in the agricultural sector.

Keywords: Big data, Crop management, Crop monitoring, Deep learning, Precision agriculture, Predictive analytics.

INTRODUCTION

Agronomy and plant breeding are costly fields that are essential for providing water and ensuring food safety for the earth's growing population [1]. Agriculture is leveraging advancements in big data analytics, genomics, robotics, remote sensing, satellite imagery, and sensor technology.

Farming is the foundation of human society, supplying essential nutrients, fiber, and fuel for nourishment. Efficient crop management is crucial for meeting the increasing global food demand, ensuring food security, and achieving sustainable

[*] **Corresponding Author: Narendra Kumar:** Department of Computer Science and Engineering, Dr. B.R. Ambedkar National Institute of Technology, Jalandhar, Punjab, India. Email: narendra51968kumar@gmail.com

Shefali Arora Chouhanm Nagendra Pratap Singh, Banalaxmi Brahma & Shashank Gupta (Eds.)

agricultural practices. In recent years, advancements in technology have revolutionized crop management, with big data and deep learning emerging as transformative tools. The term "big data" refers to the vast amount of data collected from numerous sources, characterized by its high volume, diversity, and complexity. As a branch of artificial intelligence, deep learning entails teaching neural networks to identify patterns and draw conclusions from massive amounts of data. Together, these technologies offer unprecedented opportunities to enhance crop management practices by enabling precise, data-driven decisions. This chapter examines the intersection of big data and deep learning in crop management, exploring their roles, applications, and future potential in transforming the agricultural sector.

Agriculture, the primary consumer of water at 85%, often suffers from inefficient usage due to leaky channels, seepage, and evaporation, while inadequate irrigation can stress crops [2]. Soil moisture is influenced by rainfall, soil quality, climate, and vegetation. Efficient water management is essential for water conservation and optimal crop yields. Several factors, including soil salinity and inadequate soil management, impact crop growth. Farmers need advanced information to provide precise irrigation. It is essential to evaluate crop attributes, including moisture levels in the soil at various layers.

Tools and technology for hyperspectral and multispectral analysis have shown promise for enhancing food production and methods by providing producers and crop planners with insights into crop health and development [3]. Agricultural big data technology addresses the issues of the new data era [4]. Farmers can utilize machine learning to address issues related to decision-making, water and soil management, crop management, and animal management. Crop management involves predicting yields, detecting diseases and weeds, assessing crop quality, and identifying species. Livestock management focuses on both animal care and production. Designing agricultural big data systems is challenging due to the need to adjust technology and adapt deep learning approaches as data volumes increase.

Crop protection, crucial for preventing crop yield losses, entails controlling insects, weeds, and plant diseases [5]. The development of resistance to herbicides has made weed control more difficult. New developments, such as the IoT, allow farmers to gather enormous amounts of data from sensors that monitor crops, water, and soil; this increases productivity and reduces dangers from pests and illnesses. Advanced sensing techniques, including RGB, thermal, NIR, hyperspectral, and multispectral imaging, are increasingly deployed in smart farming [6]. Advancements in technology are paving the way for digital agriculture, which will benefit plant breeders and agronomists significantly [7]. Blockchain technology holds promise for enhancing data security and transparency in the agricultural sector [8]. Sensors, mounted on drones or satellites, generate large volumes of diverse data requiring efficient storage and analytics solutions. This phenomenon, known as big data, poses challenges due to its volume, variety, and velocity. To address these challenges, the concept of 'big sensor data' is introduced, highlighting its potential in modern agriculture. Numerous agricultural applications, including crop management, yield prediction, disease identification, and monitoring of soil, water, and land, extensively utilize these techniques. In a single acquisition [9], hyperspectral data collection can detect hundreds of spectral bands that comprise the electromagnetic range of an observation situation. A substantial amount of spectrum and spatial details is contained in the resulting hyperspectral information cube.

Deep learning, a fast-growing area of AI, offers scalable and modular strategies for analyzing big data. The combination of deep learning and big data for crop security, supported by intelligent sensing and instrumentation, is expected to transform agriculture and smart farming systems. By leveraging data-driven methods, farmers can refine their decision-making processes [10], ultimately enhancing crop yields and reducing the impact of weeds, pests, and diseases.

Agricultural remote sensing applications face big data issues due to the increased velocity and volume of data generated by hyperspectral images or videos. Big data, machine learning [11], as well as deep learning, have numerous exciting applications in agriculture when it comes to hyperspectral and multispectral data. In the processing of agricultural data, collective neural networks and scalable parallel discriminant analysis have not yet received enough attention. Validation experiments and data analytics have been conducted using hyperspectral data from the agricultural sector [12].

Deep learning has been effectively used to construct decision support systems across numerous fields. Consequently, there is growing interest in applying it to other critical areas, such as agriculture. Total energy consumption in agriculture includes fertilizers, power, chemicals, human labour, and water. Yield predictions are crucial for ensuring food security, managing crop production, scheduling irrigation, and predicting labor requirements for harvesting and storage. Thus, calculating product yield helps decrease energy use.

Effective crop management involves a comprehensive approach that integrates various components to ensure optimal crop growth, yield, and sustainability. (Fig. **1**) depicts the key components required for crop management.

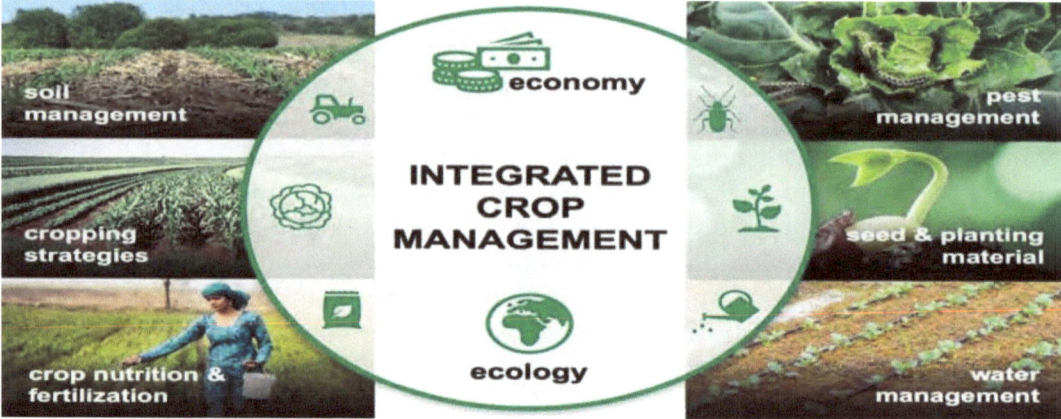

Fig. (1). Key components for crop management.

The following are the key components required for successful crop management:

- Soil Testing and Analysis: Regular soil testing to measure pH, nutrient levels, organic matter, and moisture content. Use of soil analysis data to inform fertilization and amendment practices.
- Soil Fertility: Application of appropriate fertilizers based on soil test results. Using organic materials, like compost, to increase the amount of nutrients and the structure of the soil.
- Soil Conservation: Application of erosion prevention techniques, including contour plowing and cover crops, and terracing. Adoption of no-till or reduced-till farming practices to preserve soil structure and reduce erosion.
- Irrigation Systems: Installation of efficient irrigation systems, such as drip, sprinkler, or centre pivot. Efficient irrigation scheduling involves the use of climate data and moisture levels [13] in the soil sensors.
- Water Conservation: The application of water conservation strategies like composting and the selection of cultivars of crops resilient to dryness. Monitoring and managing water resources to avoid over-irrigation and waterlogging.
- Crop Selection: Selecting plant kinds which are appropriate for the soil and climate in the area, and market demand [14], and choosing disease-resistant and high-yielding varieties to enhance productivity.
- Crop Rotation: The rotation of crops can disrupt the cycles of pests and diseases, enhance soil health, and lower the demand for chemical inputs. Crops with varying root systems and nutritional requirements should be rotated to maintain a balanced soil nutrient profile.
- Integrated Pest Management (IPM): Monitoring pest and disease levels using traps, scouting, and remote sensing technologies, and managing populations of

pests by implementing cultural techniques like combining and changing crops, as well as biological barriers like helpful insects.

- Chemical Control: Judicious use of pesticides and fungicides based on pest and disease thresholds.
- Nutrient Management: Distributing fertilizers in accordance with crop needs for nutrients and the findings of soil tests and using chemicals that have a proper balance and contain the macro- and micronutrients, such as N, P, K, zinc, iron, and Mn, that are necessary.
- Organic Amendments: Incorporating organic materials, such as manure and compost, and green manure to enhance soil fertility and structure, and practicing cover cropping to add organic matter and nutrients to the soil.
- Data Management and Analysis: Gathering information on weather, crop health, insect populations, and soil conditions using detectors, IoT gadgets, drones, and satellite imagery [15], keeping detailed records of planting dates, crop performance, and inputs used, and analyzing collected data to identify trends, diagnose problems, and make informed management decisions. Precision agriculture [16] enables the precise application of inputs, such as nutrients, pesticides, and water, based on current field conditions, maximizing their usage and reducing waste.
- Technology Integration: Implementing precision agriculture techniques to optimize input use and increase efficiency, and using GPS-guided equipment for precise planting, fertilization, and irrigation.
- Weather Forecasting: Using weather forecasting tools and services to plan field activities, such as planting, irrigation, and harvesting, and monitoring real-time weather data to adjust management practices based on current conditions.
- Climate Adaptation: Adopting crop varieties and management practices that are resilient to climate variability and extremes and implementing strategies, such as agroforestry and conservation agriculture, to lessen the effects of global warming.
- Market and Economic Management: Analyzing market trends and prices to make knowledgeable crop selections and sales timing, diversifying crops to reduce market risk and increase income stability, developing detailed budgets and financial plans for crop production, and managing costs and investments to ensure profitability and sustainability.

By integrating these key components, farmers can achieve effective and sustainable crop management, resulting in improved yields, more efficient resource use, and enhanced environmental stewardship. The use of advanced technologies and data-driven decision-making further enhances the ability to manage crops efficiently and respond to challenges in real time.

Big Data in Crop Management

Crop management can be difficult, particularly in semi-arid regions when crops do not receive adequate water from rainfall or natural drainage. Irrigating crops presents numerous difficulties. Excessive watering can cause damage due to waterlogging or root rot, while insufficient watering can lead to drought stress. Instead of determining the exact amount of water required, it is essential to consider various parameters, including soil conditions, plant growth, and climate. Advanced data analysis methods utilize large volumes of information and sensor inputs to examine satellite images across vast areas, providing valuable insights that help farmers make informed decisions about crop management and irrigation. (Fig. **2**) presents the application of big data in crop management.

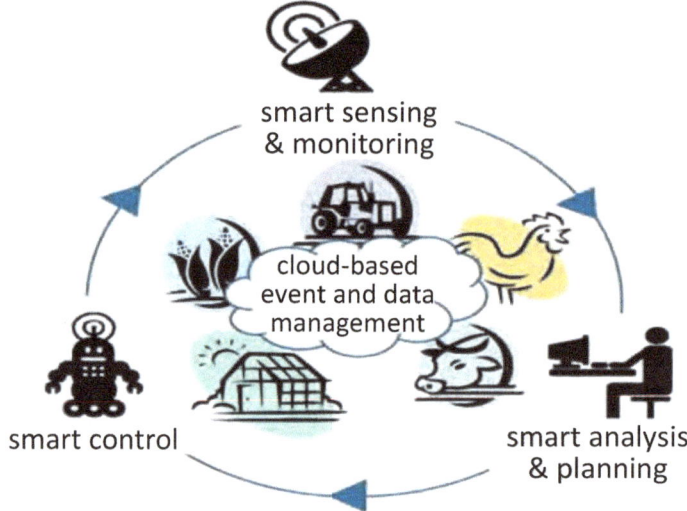

Fig. (2). Big data in crop management. Sources of agricultural big data

The following are the sources of agricultural big data:

- Remote Sensing: Satellites and drones are examples of remote sensing technology that can provide vital information on weather patterns, crop health, and soil conditions. High-resolution images and spectral data enable farmers to monitor crop growth [17], identify stress factors, and make timely interventions.
- Weather Data: Accurate weather data is vital for predicting crop yields and planning agricultural activities [18]. Weather stations, satellite data, and climate models generate extensive datasets that inform decisions on irrigation, pest control, and harvest timing.
- Soil Data: A healthy soil is an essential component of crop yield. Sensors and

soil sampling techniques collect information on levels of nutrients and moisture in the soil, pH, and other parameters [19, 20]. This information guides fertilization, irrigation, and soil management practices.

- Genomic Data: Advancements in genomics have led to the accumulation of vast datasets on plant genetics. Genomic data helps in understanding plant traits, disease resistance, and yield potential, aiding in the development of improved crop varieties.
- Market Data: Market trends and price fluctuations influence farming decisions. Big data analytics [17] on market data helps farmers predict demand, optimize pricing, and plan crop cycles to maximize profitability.

(Fig. **3**) depicts various sources of agricultural big data.

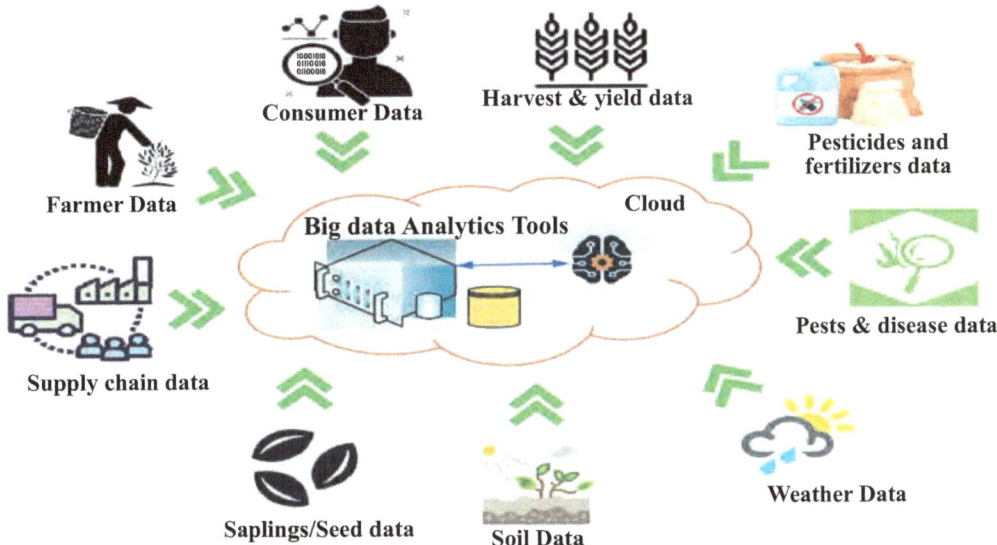

Fig. (3). Sources of agricultural big data.

Data Collection Techniques

The following are a few data collection techniques:

- IoT Devices: A network of interconnected gadgets that gather and transmit information in real-time is referred to as the IoT. In agriculture, IoT devices, such as soil sensors, meteorological stations, and intelligent drainage systems, provide real-time tracking and practical insights.
- Satellites: Satellite images provide a macro-level view of farming areas, enabling thorough tracking and assessment. Satellite data helps assess crop

health, estimate acreage, and detect anomalies.

- Drones: Drones are equipped with sensors and cameras to collect data and high-definition pictures from farming areas. They enable specific actions by providing accurate data on agricultural status, pest problems, and irrigation requirements.
- Sensors: Numerous devices measure data, including temperature, nutrient levels, and water content in the soil, positioned on the Earth's surface. Farmers can make well-informed decisions about watering, fertilizing, and pest management by utilizing current information from these sensors.

Data Integration and Management

The combination of big data and deep learning presents mutually beneficial outcomes, enhancing the comprehensive efficacy and efficiency of agricultural management. Big data provides the extensive datasets needed for training deep learning models, while deep learning algorithms extract actionable insights from these datasets.

- Data Storage Solutions: Effective data storage is essential for managing large datasets. Cloud-based platforms offer scalable storage solutions, ensuring data accessibility and security. Technologies like Hadoop and distributed databases enable the processing and storage of vast amounts of crop information.
- Data Cleaning and Pre-processing: Raw data collected from various sources often contains noise and inconsistencies. Data cleaning and pre-processing involve removing errors, normalizing data, and transforming it into a suitable format for analysis and interpretation.
- Data Analysis Tools: The detection of significant patterns and trends from agricultural data is made possible by sophisticated data analysis tools and methodologies, including machine learning methods [18], statistical models, and visualization tools. These tools support predictive analytics, enabling farmers to anticipate challenges and optimize their crop management practices.
- Frameworks and Platforms for Integration: Several frameworks and platforms facilitate the integration of deep learning and big data in agriculture. Tools like TensorFlow, Keras, and Apache Spark provide robust solutions for data processing, model training, and deployment, enabling seamless integration.
- Safety and Confidentiality of Data: Concerns regarding the safety and confidentiality of data are raised by the gathering and processing of data related to agriculture. To overcome these issues, it is crucial to implement robust data encryption, effective access control, and compliance with relevant data protection laws.
- Cost and Resource Management: Deploying big data and deep learning solutions requires significant investments in infrastructure, technology, and expertise.

Efficient resource management and cost-effective solutions, such as open-source tools and collaborative partnerships, can mitigate these challenges.

Role of Big Data in Crop Management

The big data revolution is transforming crop management by enabling a data-driven approach to farming, which significantly improves efficiency, productivity, and sustainability. By aggregating and analyzing extensive datasets from various sources, including satellite imagery, IoT sensors [11], weather forecasts, and market trends, big data provides farmers with actionable insights. Predictive analytics, powered by big data, helps forecast crop yields, identify early indicators of pest invasions, and detect diseases, enabling timely interventions that reduce crop loss. Soil health monitoring is enhanced through continuous data collection from sensors, ensuring optimal nutrient management and soil conservation. Big data also supports efficient irrigation managing by combining crop moisture levels with meteorological data, leading to precise watering schedules that conserve water and improve crop health. Additionally, market analysis using big data helps farmers choose their crops carefully and plan when to sell them, thus maximizing profitability. Supply chain efficiency is enhanced through data-driven logistics and storage optimization, which reduces food waste and ensures timely delivery.

In general, big data provides farmers with the information and resources they need to make more informed decisions, which ultimately leads to stronger and more environmentally friendly farming methods. (Fig. **4**) depicts the role of big data in crop management.

Role of Deep Learning in Crop Management

Training artificial neural networks to identify patterns and provide predictions using massive datasets is known as deep learning. Deep learning models construct hierarchical characteristics from unprocessed data, in contrast to standard machine learning, which depends on human extraction of features [18]. (Fig. **5**) illustrates the application of deep learning in agriculture.

Deep learning significantly enhances crop management by providing sophisticated tools for analyzing enormous quantities of agricultural data, resulting in additional informed and precise farming practices. By utilizing Convolutional Neural Networks (CNNs) [12] and other deep learning models, farmers can detect diseases and pests at an early stage through image recognition, enabling timely and targeted interventions. These models can also predict crop yields by analyzing historical data and current environmental conditions, aiding in better planning and distribution of resources. Data is processed by a

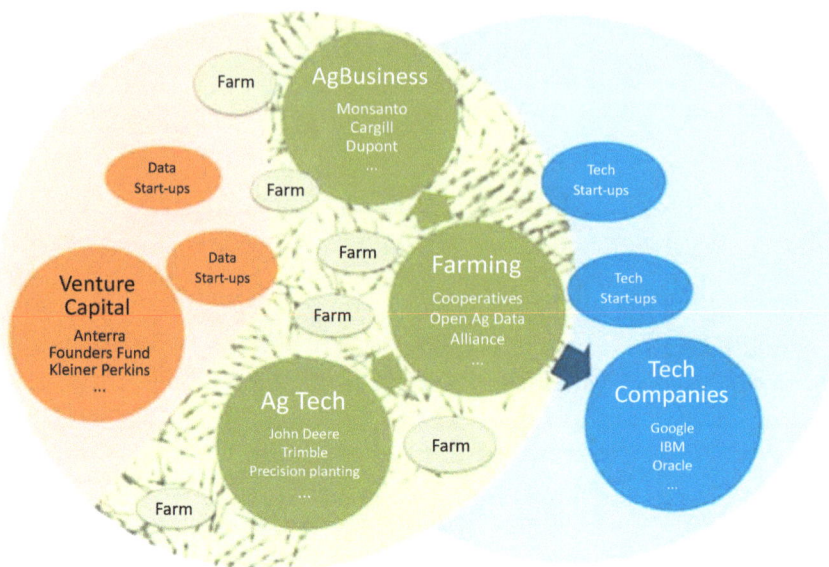

Fig. (4). Role of big data in crop management.

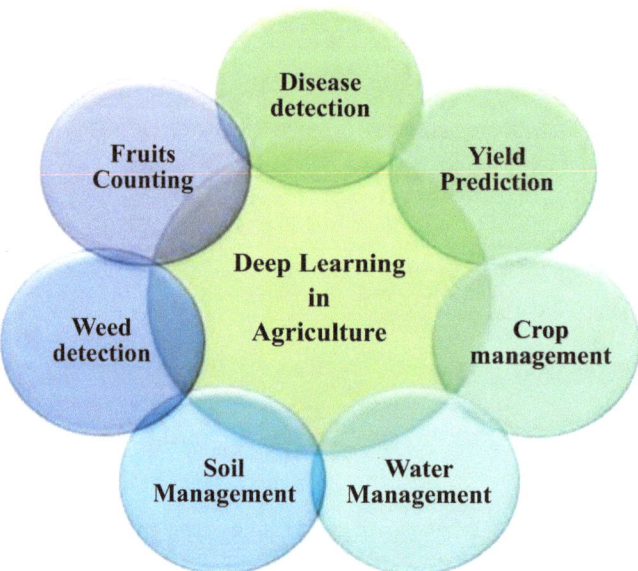

Fig. (5). Deep learning in agriculture.

neural network from soil sensors and satellite imagery to monitor soil health and optimize irrigation schedules, ensuring efficient water use and improved crop productivity. Additionally, deep learning facilitates precision agriculture by creating detailed field maps that highlight variations in soil and crop health, enabling the precise application of inputs, such as pesticides and fertilizers. Deep learning-powered autonomous farming equipment can accurately carry out operations, such as planting, trimming, and harvesting, saving labor expenses and boosting productivity.

Furthermore, deep learning models analyze weather patterns using climate data and assess their impact on crops, helping farmers adapt to changing conditions. Crop management is made more information-driven, effective, and economical by deep learning, enhancing productivity and resilience in agriculture. (Fig. **6**) depicts the role of deep learning in crop management.

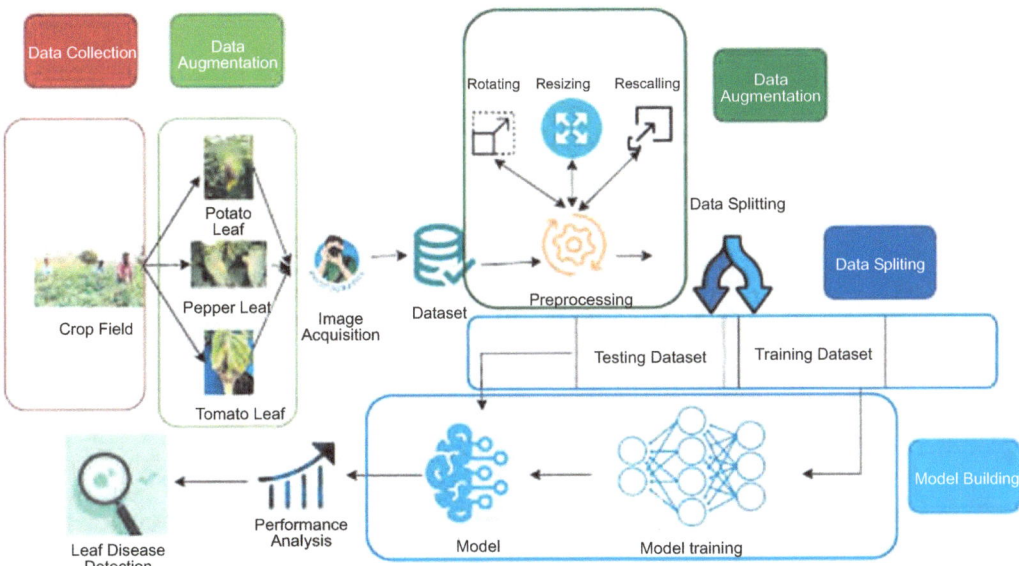

Fig. (6). Role of deep learning in crop management.

Objectives of the Chapter

The main objective of the chapter is to provide a comprehensive understanding of how big data and deep learning technologies are transforming crop management practices. It aims to provide an understanding of the following aspects:

- Fundamental Concepts: Understanding the basic principles of big data and deep learning, and their relevance to modern agricultural practices.
- Data Sources, Collection, and Management: Identifying various sources of agricultural data, including remote sensing, weather data, soil data, genomic data, and market data, as well as the techniques and technologies used for data

collection and learning about the processes involved in storing, cleaning, preprocessing, and analyzing large datasets to ensure data quality and usability.

- Applications of Deep Learning (DL): Exploring the diverse applications of DL in crop management, such as disease and pest detection, yield prediction, soil health monitoring, and climate impact analysis.
- Case Studies and Real-World Examples: Reviewing successful implementations of big data and DL in agriculture to understand practical applications, challenges encountered, and lessons learned.
- Integration Strategies: Examining the benefits and challenges of integrating big data and deep learning to identify frameworks and platforms that facilitate this integration.
- Future Trends and Innovations: Anticipating future developments in technology and data analytics that will further enhance crop management, including emerging technologies, innovations in data analytics, and predictive and prescriptive solutions.
- Policy and Regulatory Considerations: Understanding the importance of supportive policies and regulations in encouraging the acceptance of these technologies while ensuring data privacy, security, and ethical use.

This chapter is meticulously organized into nine sections, each exploring critical aspects of big data and deep learning in crop management. We begin with an introduction that sets the stage for the revolutionary effects of these techniques on agricultural management. Section 2 delves into the foundational concepts, highlighting the integration of big data and DL with traditional farming practices. In Section 3, the focus shifts to sustainability, examining how these technologies contribute to sustainable agricultural practices. Section 4 presents a comprehensive overview of various applications, from crop monitoring and precision farming to irrigation management and harvesting automation. Section 5 addresses the challenges and considerations, such as adoption barriers, technological infrastructure, and climate change adaptation. Section 6 examines post-harvest and sustainability aspects, including innovative practices, supply chain transparency, and case studies that demonstrate successful implementations. Security and vulnerabilities in deploying these technologies are thoroughly examined in Section 7. A real-world case study, "Crop Management Using Big Data [2] in Semi-Arid Environments," is detailed in Section 8. Finally, Section 9 concludes the chapter with a summary and future directions for research and application in this dynamic field.

FOUNDATIONS OF BIG DATA AND DEEP LEARNING IN CROP MANAGEMENT

Foundations of big data and DL in crop management involve leveraging vast datasets and advanced algorithms to enhance agricultural practices. Big data enables the gathering and analysis of diverse data sources, such as weather patterns, soil conditions, and crop health metrics. Deep Learning models, like Convolutional Neural Networks (CNNs) [21 - 24] and Recurrent Neural Networks (RNNs), process this data to predict yields, detect diseases, and optimize resource use. The integration of IoT devices and remote sensing technologies enables real-time data collection and informed decision-making. This combination increases production, long-term viability, and efficacy in contemporary farming. Key foundations of crop management include:

- Ensuring the soil has the proper nutrients, pH levels, and structure to support healthy crop growth through procedures, such as crop rotation.
- Efficient use of water resources through methods such as drip irrigation, rainwater harvesting, and planning irrigation or spraying based on crop needs and weather conditions.
- Choosing appropriate kinds of crops that are suited to local conditions for growth. Crop rotation helps prevent soil erosion and reduces the accumulation of diseases and pests.
- Applying fertilizers and soil amendments based on soil tests and crop requirements to ensure optimal nutrient availability and uptake, enhancing growth and yield.

SUSTAINABILITY WITH BIG DATA AND DEEP LEARNING

Sustainability, big data, and deep learning intersect in various impactful ways:

- Resource Management: Big data analytics enables the maximization of resource usage, such as energy and water, by examining purchasing trends and pinpointing areas for efficiency improvements.
- Environmental Monitoring: Deep Learning models can analyze satellite imagery or sensor data to monitor deforestation, air quality, and other environmental indicators in real-time, aiding in early detection and response to environmental changes.
- Supply Chain Optimization: Big data analytics can track products across supply chains, identifying inefficiencies and opportunities to reduce carbon footprints through optimized logistics and transportation routes.
- Renewable Energy: Deep learning techniques can enhance the efficiency of

sustainable energy sources, such as solar and wind, by predicting energy production and optimizing operations based on weather patterns and energy demand.

- Climate Modeling: Big data enables climate scientists to process enormous volumes of data from numerous sources, improving [13] the accuracy of climate models and aiding in policy-making for mitigating climate change.
- Consumer Behavior Analysis: Big data analytics enables the evaluation of consumer behavior to understand preferences for sustainable products and services, influencing market strategies and promoting eco-friendly choices.

Overall, the integration of big data and DL in sustainability efforts offers promising solutions for addressing global environmental challenges and promoting the adoption of environmentally friendly practices.

APPLICATION OF BIG DATA AND DEEP LEARNING IN CROP MANAGEMENT

Big data and DL applications in crop management are diverse and significantly enhance agricultural efficiency and productivity. Deep learning has revolutionized the way farmers track, evaluate, and improve their farming methods. It has found several applications in crop management. Here are some key applications:

- Precision Agriculture: Precision farming, which utilizes equipment to track and regulate variations in agricultural products, is enabled by big data. Moreover, deep learning processes vast quantities of data by collecting information from various sources, such as satellites, drones, and IoT sensors. This data can be utilized to produce detailed maps of crop fields, highlighting differences in the soil and crop health, which allows for efficient use of water, fertilizers, and pesticides.
- Yield Prediction: Analyzing historical data in conjunction with current weather and soil conditions enables more accurate crop yield predictions. Deep learning models can analyze past yield data in conjunction with current environmental factors, such as weather, soil conditions, and farming practices, to forecast future agricultural production. This helps farmers make informed decisions on both cultivation and harvesting.
- Pest Detection and Management: Big data enables the identification of patterns and the prediction of pest and disease outbreaks. By using data analytics, farmers can implement targeted actions, reducing crop damage and lowering the need for broad pesticide application. Deep learning algorithms can process data from images, sensors, and environmental conditions to identify and predict pest infestations. By recognizing pest patterns and behaviors, these models can help farmers implement targeted pest management strategies.

- Soil Health Monitoring: Current information on soil water content can be obtained from data gathered by soil sensors, as well as nutrient levels and pH levels. To monitor the condition of the soil, deep learning can be employed to decode data from satellite photography and soil monitors. By processing complex data, these models can give information about soil moisture, nutrient levels, and other key parameters. This helps farmers apply the actual quantity of water and fertilizers, promoting soil health and enhancing crop productivity.
- Climate Adaptation: Analyzing climate data helps farmers adjust their practices to changing weather patterns. Deep learning models are able to evaluate climate data to forecast its impact on crop growth and health. By understanding climate trends and anomalies, farmers can select more resilient varieties of crops and adjust planting schedules to mitigate the effects of atmospheric variability.
- Crop Phenotyping: Deep learning can be used for high-throughput phenotyping by analyzing plant traits from images and other data sources. This helps in selecting the best-performing plant varieties for breeding programs, ultimately leading to increased tolerance and crop production.
- Resource Optimization: Big data analytics allows for efficient resource management by making the best utilization of energy, chemical fertilizers, and groundwater. This leads to cost savings and reduces the environmental footprint of agricultural practices.
- Autonomous Farming Equipment: Big data and DL are key technologies in the development of independent cropping apparatus, like drones and robots. These machines are able to carry out responsibilities like planting, harvesting, and monitoring crops with high precision, reducing labor costs and increasing efficiency.
- Supply Chain Efficiency: Big data enhances the efficiency of the crop supply chain by providing insights, using deep learning methods, into logistics, storage conditions, and transportation routes. This helps reduce food waste and ensures that the yield remains in optimal condition upon reaching the market.
- Sustainability and Environmental Impact: By leveraging big data and DL methods, farmers can implement sustainable practices that decrease the climate impact of farming. Data-driven insights play a crucial role in maintaining biodiversity, conserving water, and reducing greenhouse gas emissions. (Fig. 7) illustrates the applications of big data and deep learning in crop management.

In summary, big data applications in crop management enhance precision, efficiency, and sustainability in farming, support farmers to optimize their practices, increase yields, and decrease costs. Deep learning is revolutionizing crop management by offering advanced tools for disease and pest detection, yield prediction, precision agriculture, and other applications. The following are the main benefits of integrating these technologies into crop management [19]:

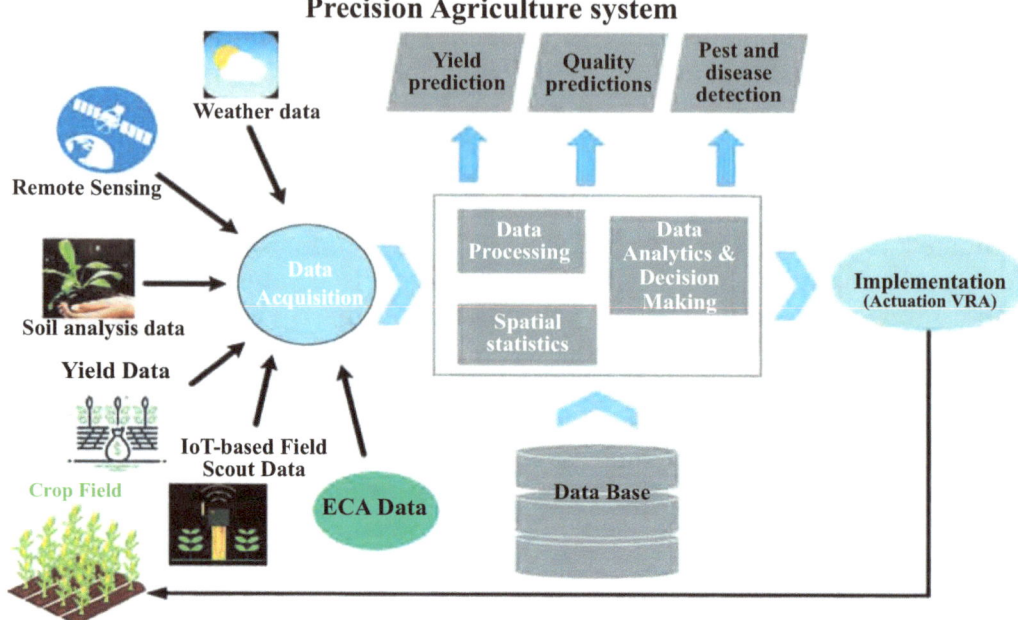

Fig. (7). Applications of big data and deep learning in crop management.

- Big data and deep learning provide actionable insights derived from vast datasets, enabling farmers to make well-informed choices. Examining both current and past data helps in predicting crop performance and identifying the best management practices.
- Deep learning models can evaluate various data inputs (*e.g.*, weather, soil conditions, historical yields) to forecast future crop yields with high accuracy. Accurate yield predictions help farmers plan resource allocation, marketing strategies, and financial management more effectively.
- Predictive analytics can identify potential threats to crop yields, such as adverse weather conditions, pest outbreaks, and diseases. Farmers can minimize potential losses and take preventive action when they receive early warnings.
- Deep learning systems are able to identify early indicators of illnesses and insect infestations by analyzing images and data from sensors. Early recognition minimizes crop losses by enabling prompt treatments that stop the spread of diseases and pests.
- Irrigation timetables [20] can be optimized using big data analytics and deep learning models based on soil moisture levels, weather predictions, and crop water needs. Efficient water use conserves resources and reduces costs, especially in water-scarce regions.
- Data-driven insights guide the use of fertilizers and soil amendments, ensuring

that plants receive the proper nutrients at the right time. This optimized nutrient management enhances soil health and increases crop productivity.

- Sensors and data analytics enable the prediction of soil conditions at the optimal time, providing continuous feedback on soil health. Deep learning models aid in understanding complex soil interactions and the effects of various procedures on maintaining soil health.
- Big data and deep learning can model and estimate the impact of climate change on agricultural production. By applying this knowledge, farmers can adapt their methods to suit the changing environment better and ensure their long-term viability.
- Data analysis using big data reveals patterns in the market, consumer preferences, and cost fluctuations. Farmers can make well-informed decisions about which crops to grow and when to sell them, thereby maximizing their profitability.
- Identifying possible hazards and creating mitigation plans are made easier with the aid of predictive analysis. Managing risks effectively ensures financial stability and reduces the likelihood of significant losses.
- Effective use of water, soil, and other resources through data-driven management conserves natural resources. Furthermore, sustainable practices ensure the long-term viability of farming operations.

Big data integration and deep learning [21, 22] in crop management offer numerous benefits that increase productivity, sustainability, and profitability.

CHALLENGES AND CONSIDERATIONS OF BIG DATA AND DEEP LEARNING IN CROP MANAGEMENT

Big data and deep learning have the potential to revolutionize crop management, but they also present several challenges, such as:

- Data Volume and Variety: Crop management involves a wide range of data sources, such as weather patterns, soil conditions, crop health metrics, and historical yield data. Managing and integrating these diverse datasets on a large scale is a significant challenge.
- Data Quality and Reliability: Ensuring the quality, accuracy, and reliability of data used for training deep learning models is crucial. Inaccurate or biased data can lead to unreliable model predictions and decisions.
- Computational Resources: Deep learning models often require substantial computational resources for training and inference. Deploying these models in real-time or near real-time scenarios on the farm can be challenging due to limitations in computational power and connectivity [23].
- Interpretability of Models: Understanding how deep learning models arrive at

their decisions is crucial in crop management, as these decisions can have a direct impact on yield and profitability. Ensuring that models are interpretable and provide actionable insights is essential for farmer adoption.

- Scalability and Adaptability: Crop management practices vary widely across different regions and farming practices. Developing deep learning models that can scale across diverse agricultural contexts and adapt to local conditions is a significant consideration [24].
- Privacy and Security: Agricultural data, including crop management data, is sensitive and valuable. Ensuring data privacy and security throughout the data lifecycle, from collection and storage to analysis and application, is critical for gaining farmers' trust and regulatory compliance.
- Integration with Existing Systems: Integrating big data and deep learning solutions into existing farm management systems and workflows can be a complex process. Compatibility with existing equipment, software, and data formats is essential for seamless adoption and integration.
- Skill and Knowledge Gaps: Implementing deep learning in crop management requires expertise in both machine learning and agricultural science. Bridging the gap between data scientists and agronomists is crucial for developing effective solutions.
- Cost Effectiveness: Demonstrating the economic benefits and Return On Investment (ROI) of adopting big data and deep learning in crop management is essential for widespread adoption. Cost-effective solutions that enhance productivity, minimize input costs, and optimize resource utilization are key considerations.

Addressing these challenges requires collaboration among researchers, farmers, technology developers, and policymakers to develop robust, scalable, and user-friendly solutions that can effectively leverage big data and deep learning to enhance crop management practices.

POST-HARVEST AND SUSTAINABILITY ASPECTS

Post-harvest management and sustainability are critical aspects of crop management, focusing on optimizing resource use, reducing waste, and enhancing environmental and economic sustainability. The following are key considerations for both:

Post-Harvest Management:

- Handling and Storage: Proper handling techniques and storage conditions are crucial to maintaining crop quality and minimizing losses. This includes controlling temperature, humidity, and ventilation to prevent spoilage.
- Processing and Value Addition: Processing crops into value-added products not

only extends shelf life but also increases market value. This can include drying, milling, canning, or other methods suitable for the crop type.

- Packaging and Transportation: Efficient packaging and transportation methods help reduce physical damage and spoilage during transit, contributing to overall sustainability by minimizing losses.
- Quality Control and Traceability: Implementing quality control measures ensures that only high-quality products reach consumers. Traceability systems can also enhance consumer trust by providing information on the origin and handling of the crop, thereby increasing transparency and confidence.

Sustainability Aspects

- Resource Use Efficiency: Optimizing water, fertilizer, and energy use through precision agriculture techniques reduces environmental impact while improving economic efficiency.
- Biodiversity and Ecosystem Services: Promoting biodiversity on farms through crop rotation, agroforestry, and habitat preservation supports ecosystem health and resilience, benefiting long-term sustainability.
- Waste Reduction and Recycling: Minimizing post-harvest losses through better storage and handling practices reduces waste. Recycling organic waste into compost or bioenergy can further enhance sustainability.
- Social and Economic Sustainability: Ensuring fair labor practices, supporting local communities, and maintaining economic viability for farmers are integral to sustainable crop management.
- Climate Resilience: Adapting crop management practices to changing climatic conditions, such as drought-resistant crop varieties or improved irrigation techniques, enhances resilience and sustainability.

By integrating these aspects into their crop management practices, farmers can enhance productivity and minimize environmental impact.

SECURITY AND VULNERABILITIES IN BIG DATA AND DEEP LEARNING FOR CROP MANAGEMENT

Security and vulnerabilities in big data and DL in agricultural supervision are critical considerations as agriculture increasingly integrates advanced technologies. The following key points should be noted:

- Data Privacy Concerns: Ensuring robust data security measures in big data crop management is crucial to prevent illegal access and misuse of this information.
- Cybersecurity Risks: As more agricultural operations rely on interconnected systems and IoT devices, they become liable to cyber threats like hacking, data

leaks, and ransomware attacks. Securing these networks and devices through encryption, access controls, and regular updates is crucial.

- Integrity of Data: Ensuring the precision and consistency of data used in DL models is vital for effective crop management decisions. Manipulation or corruption of data, intentional or accidental, can lead to erroneous insights and operational failures.
- Model Security: DL models used in crop management, such as for disease detection or yield prediction, can be vulnerable to adversarial attacks. In these attacks, the algorithm is tricked by changing the input data, perhaps resulting in inaccurate forecasts and economic losses for farmers.
- Ethical Considerations: The application of big data and deep learning in agriculture raises moral issues, including data ownership, consent for data use, and equitable access to technology among farmers of varying scales and regions.

Addressing these security and vulnerability challenges requires a holistic approach that combines robust cybersecurity practices, ethical guidelines, regulatory compliance, and continuous monitoring of data integrity and model performance. By doing so, the agricultural sector can harness the full capabilities of big data and DL technologies while mitigating potential risks.

CASE STUDY

Case Study 1: "Crop Management Using Big Data in Semi-Arid Environments" (Sayad *et al.*, 2015 [2])

Objective

The objective of this case study is to demonstrate how big data and remote sensing technologies can optimize crop and water management in semi-arid regions. Specifically, it aims to outline the challenges of traditional irrigation practices, describe the implementation of a web service for real-time data and insights, and showcase its practical application among farmers in Morocco. The study evaluates the impact on water usage, crop yields, and economic benefits, highlights the advantages of precision agriculture, and offers a replicable model for sustainable agricultural water management in similar environments.

Implementation

As an example of this notion, Sayad *et al.* [2] deployed a web service that enables farmers to complete tasks online. Key components of the service include:

Graphic User Interface: The graphical interface enables online crop management and monitoring. This interface allows users to access the framework "mapshup" and perform various operations, such as drawing plots on a map, regulating agriculture, and water supplies. It is divided into two sub-interfaces:

- User Interface: Provides comprehensive control over crop management, including a home section, user access, and map access.
- Mapshup Interface: Plots can be created and managed by consumers on a geographic map. Registered users can store and track crop development, while visitors can create plots without needing to save data.

Results

- Reduced Water Usage: Farmers achieved an average water usage reduction of 25%, attributed to precise irrigation guided by appropriate time data on soil moisture and crop needs. Efficient water distribution minimized losses due to evaporation, percolation, and runoff.
- Improved Crop Yields: Crops experienced reduced water stress, resulting in a 20% increase in yields compared to previous seasons. Enhanced plant health and development were observed, resulting in improved overall productivity.
- Economic Benefits: Lower water consumption led to reduced irrigation costs, saving farmers approximately 30% on water expenses. Increased crop yields resulted in higher revenues, thereby boosting farmers' profitability.
- User Engagement and Satisfaction: Farmers found the web service to be user-friendly and valuable, with over 80% reporting improved decision-making in their irrigation practices. The visualization tools provided clear, actionable insights, allowing farmers to adjust their strategies dynamically.
- Environmental Impact: The optimized water usage contributed to the conservation of local water resources, promoting sustainable agricultural practices. Reduced water wastage and efficient resource management helped in mitigating the environmental impact of irrigation activities.
- Scalability and Replicability: The success of the implementation demonstrated the scalability of the technology, encouraging its adoption in other semi-arid regions facing similar challenges. The model provided a framework for integrating advanced technologies into traditional farming practices, enhancing overall agricultural efficiency.

This case study demonstrates the successful application of a big data and remote sensing-based strategy for crop management in semi-arid regions. By providing farmers with accurate, real-time data and a user-friendly interface for managing their crops, the web service enabled more efficient water use and improved crop yields.

CONCLUSION AND FUTURE WORK

In conclusion, big data and deep learning hold immense potential to revolutionize crop management, offering significant benefits for productivity, sustainability, and global food security. Through continued research, innovation, and collaboration, these technologies can help build a more productive, sustainable, and resilient agricultural future. The integration of big data and deep learning into crop management represents a transformative shift in agriculture, addressing critical challenges, such as climate change, population growth, and resource limitations. By leveraging vast datasets from satellite imagery, IoT sensors, and weather data, farmers can make informed decisions that optimize resource use and enhance productivity. Deep learning algorithms, capable of analyzing complex patterns, provide real-time insights for crop monitoring, yield prediction, pest and disease detection, and soil health assessment. These technologies not only improve efficiency and accuracy but also promote sustainable farming practices.

Future research should focus on developing more sophisticated predictive models that can integrate a wider range of data sources and provide even more accurate forecasts. Enhancing the predictive power of these models will enable farmers to make more informed decisions, ultimately leading to further improvements in productivity and sustainability. Several key areas are instrumental in shaping this future, which are as follows:

- **Integration of Blockchain Technology**: Integrating blockchain with big data and deep learning can create robust systems for tracking and verifying data, ensuring its accuracy, and protecting the privacy of farmers.
- **Enhanced Sensor Technologies**: Advancements in sensor technologies will enable more precise and comprehensive data collection. Research should aim at developing next-generation sensors that can monitor a broader range of parameters with higher accuracy. These sensors will provide more detailed data for analysis, further enhancing the capabilities of deep learning models.
- **Addressing Technical Challenges**: Efforts should be directed towards addressing the technical challenges, which include improving data quality and standardization, developing methods for integrating heterogeneous data sources, and optimizing computational resources to handle the large-scale data processing required.
- **Expanding Accessibility**: To maximize the benefits of big data and deep learning, it is essential to make these technologies accessible to farmers of all scales, including smallholder farmers in developing regions. Future efforts should focus on creating affordable and user-friendly solutions.
- **Educational Initiatives**: Educational initiatives are crucial for equipping

farmers with the knowledge and skills necessary to utilize these technologies effectively. Training programs, workshops, and online resources can help farmers understand the potential of big data and deep learning, enabling them to leverage these tools for improved crop management.

- **Long-Term Sustainability**: Ultimately, the goal is to achieve long-term sustainability in agriculture. Future research and development should focus on creating solutions that not only enhance productivity but also promote environmental stewardship. By prioritizing sustainability, we can ensure that agriculture remains viable for future generations while meeting the needs of the present.

Big data and deep learning hold immense potential to transform crop management, enhancing productivity, sustainability, and profitability. By leveraging vast datasets and advanced algorithms, farmers can make informed, data-driven decisions that optimize resource utilization and enhance crop yields. The integration of big data and deep learning will play a pivotal role in addressing the challenges of modern agriculture and ensuring food security for the future.

REFERENCES

[1]   N. Shakoor, D. Northrup, S. Murray, and T.C. Mockler, "Big data driven agriculture: Big data analytics in plant breeding, genomics, and the use of remote sensing technologies to advance crop productivity", *Plant Phenome J.,* vol. 2, no. 1, pp. 1-8, 2019.
[http://dx.doi.org/10.2135/tppj2018.12.0009]

[2]   Y.O. Sayad, H. Mousannif, and M. Le Page, "Crop management using Big Data", *International Conference on Cloud Technologies and Applications,* pp. 1-6, 2015.

[3]   K.L.M. Ang, and J.K.P. Seng, "Big data and machine learning with hyperspectral information in agriculture", *IEEE Access,* vol. 9, pp. 36699-36718, 2021.
[http://dx.doi.org/10.1109/ACCESS.2021.3051196]

[4]   R.H.L. Ip, L.M. Ang, K.P. Seng, J.C. Broster, and J.E. Pratley, "Big data and machine learning for crop protection", *Comput. Electron. Agric.,* vol. 151, pp. 376-383, 2018.
[http://dx.doi.org/10.1016/j.compag.2018.06.008]

[5]   U. Ahmed, J.C.W. Lin, and G. Srivastava, "Semisupervised federated learning for temporal news hyperpatism detection", *IEEE Trans. Comput. Soc. Syst.,* vol. 10, no. 4, pp. 1758-1769, 2023.
[http://dx.doi.org/10.1109/TCSS.2023.3247602]

[6]   M. Pathan, N. Patel, H. Yagnik, and M. Shah, "Artificial cognition for applications in smart agriculture: A comprehensive review", *Artificial Intelligence in Agriculture,* vol. 4, pp. 81-95, 2020.
[http://dx.doi.org/10.1016/j.aiia.2020.06.001]

[7]   L.P. Awasthi, S. Das, R.F. Lee, and S. Pattanayak, *Plant Pathology.* CRC Press: Boca Raton, FL, USA, 2024.
[http://dx.doi.org/10.1201/9781003326915]

[8]   P. Chawla, A. Kumar, A. Nayyar, M. Naved, Ed., *Blockchain, IoT, and AI technologies for supply chain management.* CRC Press: Boca Raton, FL, USA, 2023.
[http://dx.doi.org/10.1201/9781003264521]

[9]   K.P. Seng, L.M. Ang, L.M. Schmidtke, and S.Y. Rogiers, "Computer vision and machine learning for viticulture technology", *IEEE Access,* vol. 6, pp. 67494-67510, 2018.

[http://dx.doi.org/10.1109/ACCESS.2018.2875862]

[10]   R. Pitakaso, K. Sethanan, K.H. Tan, and A. Kumar, "A decision support system based on an artificial multiple intelligence system for vegetable crop land allocation problem", *Ann. Oper. Res.,* 2023.

[11]   M. Bouni, B. Hssina, K. Douzi, and S. Douzi, "Advancing precision agriculture: Machine learning-based crop recommendation for optimal yield", *International Conference on Information, Communication and Computing Technology,* Springer: Switzerland, pp. 80-93, 2024.Cham

[12]   N.E. Benti, M.D. Chaka, A.G. Semie, B. Warkineh, and T. Soromessa, "Transforming agriculture with machine learning, deep learning, and IoT: Perspectives from Ethiopia—challenges and opportunities", *Discover Agriculture,* vol. 2, no. 1, p. 63, 2024.
[http://dx.doi.org/10.1007/s44279-024-00066-7]

[13]   N. Mahdizadeh Gharakhanlou, and L. Perez, "From data to harvest: Leveraging ensemble machine learning for enhanced crop yield predictions across Canada amidst climate change", *Sci. Total Environ.,* vol. 951, p. 175764, 2024.
[http://dx.doi.org/10.1016/j.scitotenv.2024.175764] [PMID: 39182775]

[14]   D. Garg, and M. Alam, "Smart agriculture: A literature review", *Journal of Management Analytics,* vol. 10, no. 2, pp. 359-415, 2023.
[http://dx.doi.org/10.1080/23270012.2023.2207184]

[15]   E.E. Ammar, S.A. Aziz, X. Zou, S.A. Elmasry, S. Ghosh, B.M. Khalaf, N.A. EL-Shershaby, G.F. Tourky, A. AL-Farga, A.N. Khan, M.M. Abdelhafeez, and F.E. Younis, "An in-depth review on the concept of digital farming", *Environ. Dev. Sustain.,* 2024.
[http://dx.doi.org/10.1007/s10668-024-05161-9]

[16]   G.P.O. Reddy, M.S. Raval, J. Adinarayana, S. Chaudhary, Ed., *Data Science in agriculture and natural resource management.* Springer: Cham, Switzerland, 2022.
[http://dx.doi.org/10.1007/978-981-16-5847-1]

[17]   A. Kamilaris, A. Kartakoullis, and F.X. Prenafeta-Boldú, "A review on the practice of big data analysis in agriculture", *Comput. Electron. Agric.,* vol. 143, pp. 23-37, 2017.
[http://dx.doi.org/10.1016/j.compag.2017.09.037]

[18]   R. Yadav, A.K. Mishra, M.S. Pandey, and B. Pandey, "IoT and machine learning-based monitoring of the growth of crops using blockchain technology", *International Conference on Advanced Network Technologies and Intelligent Computing,* Springer: Cham, Switzerland, pp. 154-176, 2023.
[http://dx.doi.org/10.1109/ICICAT57735.2023.10263755]

[19]   M.S. Suchithra, and M.L. Pai, "Improving the prediction accuracy of soil nutrient classification by optimizing extreme learning machine parameters", *Inf. Process. Agric.,* vol. 7, no. 1, pp. 72-82, 2020.
[http://dx.doi.org/10.1016/j.inpa.2019.05.003]

[20]   Y. Tace, M. Tabaa, S. Elfilali, C. Leghris, H. Bensag, and E. Renault, "Smart irrigation system based on IoT and machine learning", *Energy Rep.,* vol. 8, pp. 1025-1036, 2022.
[http://dx.doi.org/10.1016/j.egyr.2022.07.088]

[21]   C. Zhang, P. Yue, L. Di, and Z. Wu, "Automatic identification of center pivot irrigation systems from landsat images using convolutional neural networks", *Agriculture,* vol. 8, no. 10, p. 147, 2018.
[http://dx.doi.org/10.3390/agriculture8100147]

[22]   A. Subeesh, S. Bhole, K. Singh, N.S. Chandel, Y.A. Rajwade, K.V.R. Rao, S.P. Kumar, and D. Jat, "Deep convolutional neural network models for weed detection in polyhouse grown bell peppers", *Artificial Intelligence in Agriculture,* vol. 6, pp. 47-54, 2022.
[http://dx.doi.org/10.1016/j.aiia.2022.01.002]

[23]   V.C. Patil, K.A. Al-Gaadi, D.P. Biradar, and M. Rangaswamy, "Internet of things (IoT) and cloud computing for agriculture: An overview", In: *Proceedings of Agro-Informatics and Precision Agriculture.* AIPA, 2012, pp. 296-292.

[24]   K. Alibabaei, P.D. Gaspar, and T.M. Lima, "Crop yield estimation using deep learning based on climate big data and irrigation scheduling", *Energies,* vol. 14, no. 11, p. 3004, 2021.
[http://dx.doi.org/10.3390/en14113004]

CHAPTER 11

AI-Driven Cybersecurity in Agriculture: The Future of Farming

Shikha Gupta[1,*], Nishi Gupta[2] and Lakshay Aggarwal[3]

[1] *Department of Information Technology, MAIT, Rohini, New Delhi, India*

[2] *Department of Engineering and Technology, Gurugram University, Haryana, India*

[3] *Department of Computer Science and Engineering, D.A.V. Institute of Engineering and Technology, Jalandhar, India*

Abstract: Digital technologies such as the Internet of Things (IoT), drones, autonomous machinery, and advanced data analytics are quickly revolutionizing the agricultural industry. This digital transformation, known as precision agriculture, has greatly improved productivity, sustainability, and efficiency in farming methods. Nevertheless, the industry is confronted with increasing cybersecurity issues despite these advancements. The growing dependence on interconnected systems has created vulnerabilities that cybercriminals are exploiting more and more, endangering not just individual farms but also the entire food supply chain. This section explores the cybersecurity environment in the agricultural industry, highlighting major risks like phishing, ransomware, data breaches, and industrial espionage. It highlights the importance of strong cybersecurity measures to safeguard the integrity and functionality of contemporary agricultural systems. The chapter emphasizes the crucial importance of Artificial Intelligence (AI) in dealing with these challenges, providing AI-based solutions for identifying threats, automating responses, and safeguarding data. The future success of the agricultural industry's digital transformation relies on protecting its technological infrastructure from cyber threats. This section supports the idea of implementing a holistic cybersecurity plan that includes AI, various security layers, and ongoing education and awareness efforts. Through enhancing its digital progress, the agricultural industry can guarantee continuous expansion, adaptability, and the capacity to fulfill international food requirements in a progressively interconnected globe. The chapter states that the future of agriculture relies not just on technological advancements but also on the industry's dedication to cybersecurity. Ensuring the security of digital agricultural systems is crucial for sustaining global productivity, sustainability, and food security.

* Corresponding author Shikha Gupta: Department of Information Technology, MAIT, Rohini, New Delhi, India; E-mail: shikha.gpt1@gmail.com

Keywords: Agricultural supply chain, Agricultural technology, Artificial Intelligence (AI), Autonomous machinery, Cybersecurity in agriculture, Cyber risk management, Data analytics in farming, Internet of things (IoT), Precision agriculture, Smart farming.

INTRODUCTION

In the current era of technology, cybersecurity has become increasingly important. Every day, a large number of people and organizations are impacted by various cyberattacks, including phishing, DDoS, password, and data breach attacks. Government, consumers, and organizations using computer networks are all at serious risk from cybercriminals. It has always been difficult to put in place efficient procedures and controls to lessen the likelihood of cyberattacks and other crimes. In this aspect, upholding the highest standards necessitates deliberate effort. The only technologies that are useful in preventing cyberattacks are intelligent ones. Both management and individuals must properly control cyberattacks.

All significant stakeholders, including the government, business community, owners of infrastructure, and end users, have a responsibility to ensure cybersecurity. Governments and multinational organizations are important players in cybersecurity. The agricultural sector is dealing with new prospects and problems as it advances through the use of advanced digital and automated technologies. The switch to "precision agriculture" or "smart farming" is completely changing how we cultivate, tend to, and harvest crops. The evolution is being fueled by technologies like the Internet of Things (IoT) [1], drones, autonomous machines, and advanced data analytics, which promise increased sustainability, productivity, and efficiency.

The deployment of these most recent innovations, however, does enhance vulnerabilities to online dangers. Once thought of as low-tech, the agriculture sector is now facing questions regarding data security, privacy, and the integrity of its digital systems. The rising number of cyberattacks in this industry puts individual farms, the broader food supply chain, and even global food security at significant risk.

"Agri-cybersecurity," or cybersecurity in agriculture [2], is a buzzword that's becoming increasingly significant as the agricultural sector incorporates more automated and digital technologies. Known as "smart farming" or "precision agriculture," this technological integration in agriculture utilises drones, Internet of Things (IoT) devices, autonomous machinery, and data analytics to increase productivity and efficiency. However, as a result of the industry's growing connectedness and reliance on digital tools, cyber risks are also becoming more prevalent.

The agricultural sector can continue to benefit from advancements in technology while safeguarding itself from the increasing possibility of cyberattacks by understanding and addressing these concerns. All parties involved have to collaborate to ensure the sustainability and resilience that characterize modern agriculture. Beyond the immediate safety of data and systems, the implications of cybersecurity in agriculture using AI include ensuring food security, maintaining the integrity of supply networks, and bolstering the overall resilience of agricultural operations. As cyber threats [3] become more sophisticated, the agricultural industry must implement strong AI-driven cybersecurity measures to safeguard its assets and ensure global food systems' stability and expansion.

The present study examines the application of AI technology to enhance agricultural productivity while also mitigating cyberattacks. AI applications are transforming agriculture in a variety of ways, including data analytics, predictive modeling, automated machinery, and precision farming. However, these developments also raise the possibility of cyberattacks, which have the potential to jeopardise important data, cause operational disruptions, and endanger food security.

It is essential to understand how AI (Artificial Intelligence) can be used to improve cybersecurity in agriculture using a combination of theoretical insights and real-world case studies. In this crucial area, responsible AI technology deployment also requires legal frameworks and ethical considerations.

By investigating the intersection of artificial intelligence and cybersecurity, interested parties can acquire the skills and knowledge required to manage the complex processes of modern farming. Ultimately, it emphasizes the importance of developing robust agricultural systems that can withstand the evolving cyber threats of the modern era.

(Fig. **1**) presents the architecture of various devices, applications, and layers that are a part of innovative agriculture systems:

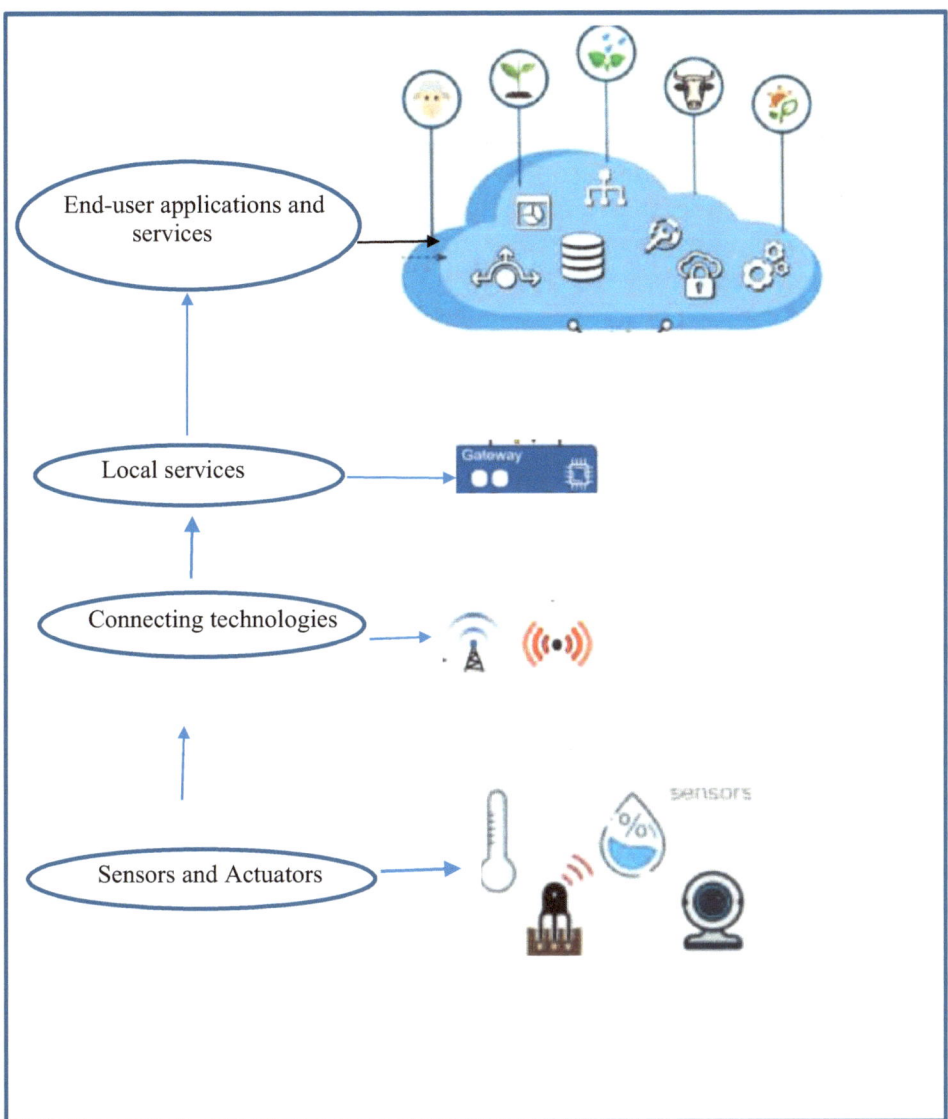

Fig. (1). Components in a smart agriculture system.

THE PRESENT PANORAMA OF AGRICULTURE AND CYBERSECURITY

As the world continues to develop over time and adopt AI (Artificial Intelligence), the agricultural industry is also evolving its infrastructural aspects by integrating various automation tools [4]. Hence, it not only results in enhanced crop yield but also increases the overall farm management. Advanced tools like the Internet of

Things (IoT), drones, autonomous machinery, and advanced data analytics [5] have refined the current scenario as it has increased precision and reduced the dependency on seasonal labor. In the present scenario, one can make informed decisions that would yield better results.

On the contrary, traditional farming relied on manual labor and handheld processes. As a result, the quality of the yield was unpredictable, and it was very costly. Farmers relied on their experience, intuition, and broad generalizations to make decisions about planting, irrigating, and harvesting. This approach often led to inefficiencies, resource wastage, and inconsistent yields. With the introduction of digital technologies, farming has transitioned from these conventional methods to more precise and efficient practices.

IoT (Internet of Things) [6]: Real-time data on crop health, weather patterns, and soil conditions can be obtained from Internet of Things devices, including sensors and smart devices. With the use of this information, farmers may more effectively and efficiently manage waste by precisely adjusting irrigation, fertilization, and pest management.

Drones and Aerial Imaging [7]: Drones equipped with high-resolution cameras and sensors provide aerial perspectives of fields, enabling thorough crop development and health monitoring, including weed identification, water management, and seed emergence assessment. Early diagnosis of problems like nutritional deficits or pest infestations is made easier with the use of this technology.

Autonomous Machinery [8]: By eliminating the need for physical labor and boosting operational efficiency, automated tractors, harvesters, and planting equipment have transformed labor-intensive jobs. These devices are capable of precise operation thanks to GPS (Global Positioning System) and AI algorithms. The agriculture sector may now use robot localization, path planning, and environment observation and mapping by virtue of such types of equipment.

Data Analysis [9]: Farming operations are becoming more data-driven and data-enabled as smart machines and a variety of sensors proliferate on farms. As a result, data analytics has become an essential technique for deriving useful insights from large data to support decision-making in farm management. This entails integrating data analytics into agriculture through the collection, processing, and analysis of the massive amounts of data generated by sensors, drones, IoT devices, and self-governing machinery. Farmers can now access insights that were previously unattainable, enabling them to make more accurate and informed decisions.

The need to address concerns and meet the world's growing food demand is driving the shift to precision agriculture. Farmers can enhance their sustainability and productivity by utilising digital technologies, thereby strengthening the agricultural sector. Precision agriculture has benefits that extend beyond individual farms. These benefits include increased food security, reduced environmental impact, and increased economic viability for farming communities.

Recognising the cybersecurity threats that come with digital transformation in agriculture is essential. Modern farming systems are vulnerable to cyberattacks that can impair data integrity, disrupt operations, and threaten food security because of their interconnectedness. Strong cybersecurity measures must be implemented to protect agricultural technological breakthroughs and guarantee the industry's survival and future growth.

Common Cyber Threats in the Agriculture Sector

While the rapid growth of technology has yielded unparalleled advantages, it has also presented an array of unexpected cybersecurity difficulties. In-depth examination of the cyber threat environment in the digital age is provided by this report, along with useful suggestions for preventative actions. It identifies various cyber threats, such as ransomware, phishing schemes, malware, and insider threats, that are becoming increasingly prevalent in multiple industries, including agriculture [10]. The study examines the cutting-edge strategies employed by cybercriminals, including advanced persistent threats, social engineering, and zero-day exploits. The expanding threats connected to cutting-edge technology like cloud computing, artificial intelligence, and the Internet of Things (IoT) are also covered.

Agriculture is more vulnerable to cyberattacks as it uses more digital tools. To safeguard the industry, it is necessary to address the new vulnerabilities brought about by the reliance on digital tools and networked systems. To effectively protect agricultural operations from cybersecurity threats, it is essential to understand these risks. In order to overcome these risks, the research highlights the significance of a multi-layered security approach. Necessary preventive measures that are included in this strategy include strong network security, secure coding techniques, user awareness training, encryption, access controls, and incident response planning.

Distributed Denial of Service (DDoS) Attacks [11]

Smart farming, an essential component of the Internet of Things (IoT), is becoming increasingly popular as a way to address the growing global demand for food. There are numerous ways smart farms can leverage technology and connected devices, from receiving real-time data on crop conditions and soil moisture to using drones for tasks like pesticide spraying. However, the integration of various internet-connected devices introduces vulnerabilities into the innovative farming ecosystem. Intruders can exploit these weaknesses to manipulate or disrupt the flow of data from field sensors remotely, which can have serious consequences, especially during critical times like harvesting, when real-time monitoring is essential. These vulnerabilities underscore the necessity for robust security measures to ensure system reliability and availability.

Phishing Attacks [12]

In today's digital world, phishing poses a significant threat to both individuals as well as organizations. Cybercriminals use phishing emails to extract sensitive information from unsuspecting users. These attacks can compromise personal data, financial details, and expose critical account details.

Man-in-the-Middle (MitM) Attacks

Cybercriminals may intercept and modify communications between two parties without the parties' knowledge in a MitM attack. Attackers could intercept data being relayed from sensors to central systems in the context of smart farming and change the data to interfere with operations or mislead decision-makers.

Spoofing Attacks

Cybercriminals utilize spoofing attacks to trick users or systems by sending fake data. For example, manipulated [13] GPS signals have the potential to deceive autonomous farming machinery, resulting in malfunctions or deviations from the intended course.

Unauthorized Access

Attackers may be able to access smart farming systems without authorization if there are loopholes in the authentication process. Once inside, they can implant malware, disrupt operations, and steal confidential data.

These attacks illustrate the complexity and dynamic nature of cybersecurity risks in smart farming. To defend against these many hazards and ensure the integrity and dependability of smart farming systems, it is imperative to put in place extensive security measures, such as frequent software upgrades, robust encryption, multi-factor authentication, and constant monitoring.

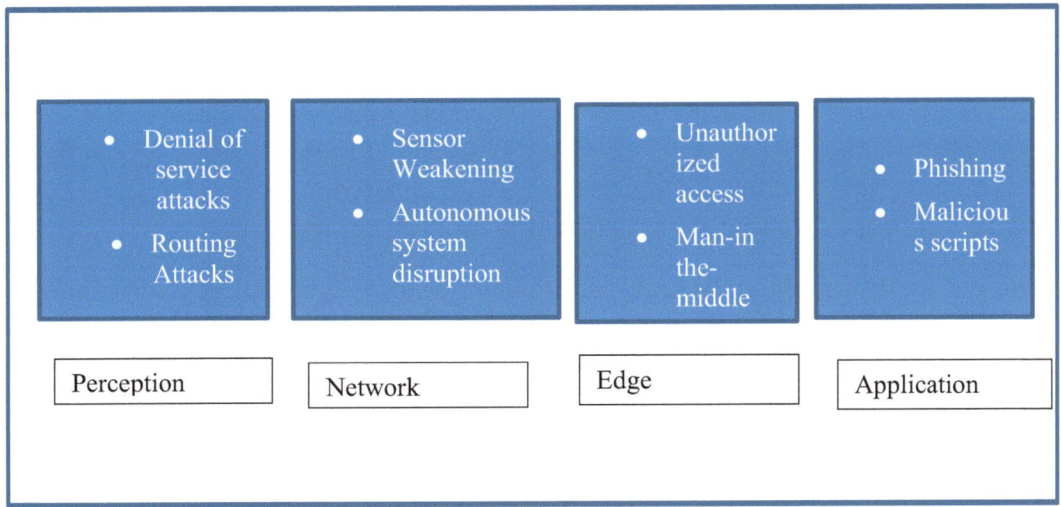

Fig. (2). Depicts some main cybersecurity obstacles facing the agriculture industry based on the four layers of a smart system: i) Perception, ii) Network, iii) Edge, and iv) Application.

ROLE OF AI IN CYBERSECURITY

Due to its versatility, AI is a fantastic tool for addressing global security issues that are always changing with the emerging digital technologies [14]. AI may be used by businesses that handle sensitive data to automate threat detection and keep one step ahead of thieves. AI is utilised in cybersecurity to safeguard user data as well as business assets [15]. AI is particularly well-suited for integration with cybersecurity systems due to several factors, such as continuous learning, managing data, and eliminating complex tasks [16]. With deep learning and machine learning, AI can comprehend network behavior and group recognisable patterns, making it easier to identify potential threats. Moreover, the enormous amounts of data transported and stored in larger enterprises can be scanned automatically by AI for potential dangers [17]. By automating ongoing security procedures, AI can free up knowledgeable cybersecurity specialists to concentrate on developing cutting-edge solutions to the most urgent problems facing the firm.

Integrating AI into cybersecurity systems can lead to better outcomes, including improved IT asset inventory, effectiveness control, and explanation. With AI's IT asset inventory, businesses can receive regularly updated data on users, actions, and performance of hardware and software. This monitoring can help organizations detect weaknesses and adopt improved security procedures. Additionally, AI can automatically evaluate the security performance of enterprise networks to identify areas for improvement. Furthermore, AI can be trained to explain things to key stakeholders in a firm, evaluate systems, and improve their efficiency. This element is essential for winning over both organizational leaders and end-users.

Approaches of AI in Cyber Security

Artificial Intelligence (AI) [18] has become a crucial tool in cybersecurity due to its capability of assisting in the detection and mitigation of real-time potential threats. There are different AI cybersecurity strategies, such as:

Machine Learning (ML): ML algorithms can identify patterns and anomalies in network traffic, user activity, and system logs by training [19] on large datasets. Subsequently, they can detect and prevent cyberattacks.

Natural Language Processing (NLP) [20]: NLP algorithms can comprehend human language and analyze it, which is especially useful in identifying phishing scams and other social engineering tactics.

- Deep Learning [21]: Deep Learning uses neural networks for learning and prediction. Large datasets such as network traffic records can be employed to spot patterns and abnormalities, which is useful for identifying Advanced Persistent Threats (APTs).
- Expert Systems: Expert Systems mimic the decision-making capabilities of a human expert by combining rule-based systems and machine learning approaches. They can detect and respond to security incidents in real-time.
- Behavioral Analysis [22]: Algorithms for behavioral analysis can monitor user activity and identify irregularities that may indicate a security breach. They can also monitor the actions of malicious software.
- Predictive Analytics: Predictive analytics is a process of utilising statistical models and machine learning methods to analyze past data in order to anticipate future events. This technology has the capability to predict the probability of a security breach or identify system vulnerabilities before they are exploited.
- AI can help enterprises detect security incidents and take necessary action quickly and efficiently compared to traditional techniques. However, it should be noted that AI is not a complete solution and should be used in conjunction with other security measures for comprehensive security.

Cybersecurity Challenges in AI

As digital technologies become more prevalent in agriculture, the sector is encountering an increasing number of cybersecurity issues. The incorporation of advanced agricultural technologies like IoT devices, drones, data analytics platforms, and autonomous machinery has transformed conventional farming methods. Yet, this shift to digitalization has also introduced new vulnerabilities that compromise the safety and reliability of farming activities. Here are a few of the main cybersecurity obstacles facing the agriculture industry:

Vulnerabilities of Cyber-Physical Systems

Modern agriculture is more and more dependent on cyber-physical systems that combine digital controls with physical farming procedures. Some instances are automated water supply, temperature-regulated rooms, and tractors guided by GPS. Attacks on these systems can cause instant physical consequences like harm to crops, machinery issues, or loss of stored items, which makes them attractive to attackers.

Risks in the Supply Chain and Ecosystem

The farming industry functions within a complicated, interrelated environment. Every component of the supply chain, from the providers of seeds to the distributors, plays a vital role. An attack on a single part, like a supplier's database or a logistics provider's platform, can cause widespread issues in the agricultural system, impacting production, distribution, and food supply.

Ensuring the Accuracy of Data and Handling Data Manipulation

Modern agriculture depends greatly on decision-making based on data. Information obtained from sensors, drones, and weather stations guides important choices such as when to plant, water, and manage pests. Cyber attackers might focus on this information, changing or controlling it to deceive farmers into making harmful choices, leading to lower crop production, wasted materials, and monetary loss.

Impacts on the Economy

The financial impact of a cyberattack can have a devastating effect on agricultural businesses, especially small and medium-sized farms. Cyberattacks can result in both immediate expenses, such as ransom fees and disrupted operations, and secondary expenses like damage to customer confidence, higher insurance costs, and recovery outlays. For many farms that are struggling to make ends meet, these financial pressures can be extremely damaging.

Compliance with Regulations and Legal Hurdles

With the digitization of the agricultural sector, regulators are also closely monitoring it. Meeting new cybersecurity standards and regulations can be challenging, especially for smaller farms with limited resources to put required security measures in place. Failure to comply may lead to legal consequences, fines, and harm to a farm's image.

Mistakes Made by Individuals and Risks Posed by Insiders

Human errors continue to pose a major cybersecurity challenge within the agricultural industry. Workers can unknowingly put security at risk by opening phishing emails, having weak passwords, or not adhering to security protocols. Moreover, internal risks, whether stemming from intentional wrongdoing or unintentional mistakes, can result in major security breaches.

The Rise of Cyber-Risks

The farming industry is susceptible to the constantly changing landscape of cyber dangers. The adoption of new technologies such as AI, blockchain, and cloud computing introduces fresh vulnerabilities. Cybercriminals continually adjust their strategies, exploiting vulnerabilities in emerging technologies while security measures remain inadequate.

Industry Focused Solutions

Numerous cybersecurity solutions currently available do not meet the unique requirements of the agricultural industry. Customised cybersecurity strategies are necessary due to the distinct difficulties presented by remote operations, legacy systems, and the variety of equipment utilised in agriculture. Agricultural businesses may face challenges in safeguarding against cyber threats without solutions tailored to their industry.

Cybersecurity Skill Gap

There is a significant shortage of cybersecurity professionals with expertise in agricultural technologies. Many farm operators lack the knowledge and resources to implement effective cybersecurity measures. This skill gap leaves agricultural businesses particularly vulnerable, as they may not be equipped to defend against increasingly sophisticated cyberattacks.

AI-DRIVEN SOLUTIONS FOR CYBER SECURITY IN AGRICULTURE

The incorporation of Artificial Intelligence (AI) in farming methods has led to major progress, yet it has also introduced fresh cybersecurity issues [23]. With the increasing prevalence of digital tools and smart farming technologies, the agricultural industry needs to adjust to the changing cyber threat environment. AI-powered solutions offer exciting possibilities for boosting cybersecurity in agriculture by offering sophisticated protection measures, immediate threat detection, and automatic responses to potential security breaches. Here are a few significant AI-powered solutions that can enhance cybersecurity in the agricultural sector:

Analyzing Data to Anticipate and Prevent Potential Risks

AI has the capability to examine large quantities of data produced by agricultural systems, detecting patterns and irregularities that could signify possible cybersecurity risks. Through the use of predictive analytics and artificial intelligence, it is possible to anticipate potential attacks in advance, enabling preemptive actions to mitigate risks. For instance, AI algorithms have the capability to observe network traffic immediately, identifying abnormal activities that could indicate a potential cyberattack, such as a Distributed Denial of Service (DDoS) attack or unauthorized entry attempts.

Automated Incident Response

In the event of a cybersecurity breach, rapid response is crucial to minimize damage. AI-driven systems can automate incident response by detecting and reacting to threats in real-time without human intervention. For instance, AI can isolate infected devices, shut down compromised systems, or block malicious IP addresses immediately upon detection, preventing the spread of malware or unauthorized access. This automation ensures that threats are contained quickly, reducing the potential impact on agricultural operations.

Improved Methods of Verifying Identity and Restricting Entry

AI has the potential to enhance authentication procedures by introducing more advanced techniques like biometric verification, behavioral analysis, and Multi-factor Authentication (MFA). These methods, powered by AI, guarantee that sensitive systems and data can only be accessed by authorized personnel. For instance, AI can evaluate typing styles, voice identification, and even user actions in order to verify users, increasing the challenge for hackers to obtain unauthorized entry.

Detecting Anomalies in Internet of Things (IoT) Networks

The increase of IoT devices in farming, like sensors, drones, and autonomous machinery, has brought about new weaknesses. Artificial intelligence has the ability to observe IoT networks for irregularities that could signal a security breach, like uncommon communication behaviors among devices or unanticipated data exchanges. Through constant analysis of device activity, AI has the ability to identify and respond to possible risks like manipulation of sensor information or unauthorized entry into IoT devices.

Using Machine Learning to Identify Malicious Software

Conventional antivirus programs frequently find it challenging to match the constantly changing form of malicious software. AI-powered machine learning models are capable of analysing large amounts of data to discover novel malware variations that might not be detected using traditional approaches. AI can better identify and stop new malware threats like ransomware and spyware by constantly learning from past attacks and regularly updating its database, thereby ensuring a strong defense against malicious software.

AI to Ensure the Accuracy of Data

Data accuracy is crucial in farming, as decisions often rely on current information gathered from various sources. AI can help ensure the integrity of data by monitoring data streams for signs of alteration or damage. For instance, artificial intelligence algorithms can authenticate data gathered from sensors and drones to confirm the accuracy and reliability of the information used in decision-making. This aids in preventing cybercriminals from altering data in order to disrupt farming activities.

Training in Cybersecurity Powered by Artificial Intelligence

Human errors are a significant factor in cybersecurity breaches. AI has the capability to improve cybersecurity awareness and training through offering customized learning experiences designed for specific users. AI-powered training programs are able to replicate actual cyberattack situations, assisting farm operators and staff in identifying and handling possible dangers. AI ensures that employees are constantly updated on the latest cybersecurity risks by adapting training materials to address new threats.

Utilising Blockchain and AI to Guarantee Secure Transactions

When blockchain technology is integrated with AI, it offers a secure and transparent way to handle agricultural transactions, supply chains, and data exchanges. AI has the ability to examine blockchain transactions in order to identify deceitful behaviors, thus guaranteeing that only valid transactions are logged. The use of these technologies can enhance cybersecurity in the agricultural sector by safeguarding businesses against fraud, unauthorized access, and data tampering.

Adaptive and Flexible Security Frameworks

AI has the capability to aid in creating security systems that can adapt to emerging threats. These systems utilise artificial intelligence to regularly evaluate the security status of farming systems, modifying security procedures and protections according to up-to-date threat information. Utilising an adaptive strategy allows agricultural companies to outsmart cybercriminals, guaranteeing that their cybersecurity measures stay strong amid evolving threats.

CURRENT STATE OF SECURITY IN SMART AGRICULTURE

Traditional internet-connected devices have many security features, such as firewalls, authentication, and access control schemes. As smart agriculture is an emerging field, resources are sometimes inadequate, or there is a lack of personnel to manage them effectively. Therefore, there is a need to utilise techniques such as cryptography [24] and anomaly detection systems to detect vulnerabilities at an early stage [25]. The use of security resources, as shown in Table **1**, can help improve security in smart agriculture.

Table 1. Resources to improve security in smart agriculture.

Security Resource	Possible threats covered
Intrusion detection system	DoS autonomous system hijacking, SQL injection, backdoors, worms, routing attacks, and other cyberattacks
Cryptography	Man-in-the-middle attack, Data capture
Anomaly detection system	Random sensor incidents, autonomous system disruption, and other cyberattacks
Antivirus	Phishing, Virus
Firewall	Unauthorized access

CONCLUDING REMARKS

As agriculture advances in the digital era, it is undergoing a transformation that has the potential to revolutionize the way food is produced, handled, and distributed. The use of modern technologies like the Internet of Things (IoT), drones, autonomous machinery, and advanced data analytics has allowed for precision agriculture, resulting in enhanced productivity, sustainability, and efficiency. Nonetheless, this shift to digitalization has introduced a new array of challenges, particularly in the field of cybersecurity. The modern agricultural industry's interconnectedness has made it vulnerable to various cyber threats like phishing attacks, ransomware, data breaches, and industrial espionage. These dangers pose risks not just to individual farms but also endanger global food security and the wider agricultural supply chain. As cybercriminals continually advance their techniques, the agricultural industry must remain vigilant and take proactive steps to counter these vulnerabilities.

AI is essential for improving cybersecurity in agriculture. The agricultural industry can enhance its cybersecurity by utilising AI tools like predictive analytics, automated incident response, and anomaly detection. AI's capacity to examine extensive data, identify growing threats, and react instantly is crucial for safeguarding the trustworthiness and stability of digital agricultural systems. Furthermore, AI-driven training programs and flexible security frameworks ensure that both technology and personnel are prepared to navigate the ever-evolving cyber threat environment. The path to achieving a completely digitized agricultural industry is challenging but offers many opportunities for creativity and growth. The industry's success in seizing these opportunities depends on its capacity to protect its digital infrastructure from cyberattacks. The agricultural industry can protect its technological progress and ensure durability by implementing a thorough cybersecurity plan featuring AI technology, strong network security, and ongoing training.

Ultimately, the fate of agriculture is closely connected to its ability to adapt to the complexities of the digital realm. The incorporation of digital technologies has incredible potential to improve agricultural productivity and sustainability. Nonetheless, this potential can be achieved only if the industry stays alert to cyber risks. By working together, thinking creatively, and staying dedicated to safeguarding against cyber threats, the agricultural industry can prosper in a world that is becoming increasingly interconnected, ensuring food security and economic stability for future generations.

REFERENCES

[1]   K. Malhotra and M. Firdaus, "Application of artificial intelligence in IoT security for crop yield prediction," ResearchBerg Review of Science and Technology, vol. 2, no. 1, pp. 136–157, Oct. 2022. Available from: https://researchberg.com/index.php/rrst/article/view/150

[2]   Z. Angyalos, S. Botos, and R. Szilágyi, "The importance of cybersecurity in modern agriculture," AGRÁRINFORMATIKA: Journal of Agricultural Informatics, vol. 12, no. 2, pp. 1–8, 2021 Available from: https://real.mtak.hu/197145/

[3]   N.G. Camacho, "The role of AI in cybersecurity: Addressing threats in the digital age", *Journal of Artificial Intelligence General science (JAIGS) ISSN:3006-4023,* vol. 3, no. 1, pp. 143-154, 2024. [http://dx.doi.org/10.60087/jaigs.v3i1.75]

[4]   M. Sharma and C. Patil, "Recent trends and advancements in agricultural research: An overview," Journal of Pharmacognosy and Phytochemistry, vol. 7, no. 2, pp. 1906–1910, 2018 Available from: https://www.phytojournal.com/archives?year=2018&vol=7&issue=2&ArticleId=3745

[5]   C. Pandey, P. K. Sethy, S. K. Behera, J. Vishwakarma, and V. Tande, "Smart agriculture: Technological advancements on agriculture—A systematical review," ScienceDirect, Jan. 2022. Available from: https://www.sciencedirect.com/science/article/abs/pii/B9780323852142000021

[http://dx.doi.org/10.1016/B978-0-323-85214-2.00002-1]

[6]　A.L. Duguma, and X. Bai, "Contribution of Internet of Things (IoT) in improving agricultural systems", *Int. J. Environ. Sci. Technol.,* no. Sep, 2023.
[http://dx.doi.org/10.1007/s13762-023-05162-7]

[7]　J. Boopalamani, P.S.P. Ayswariya, S.P. Raj, P. Yagnitha, N. Sarrvesh, and A. Jha, "A survey of drones in the agriculture sector", *Appl. Mech. Mater.,* vol. 919, pp. 191-200, 2024.
[http://dx.doi.org/10.4028/p-xCMKl4]

[8]　Y. Bai, B. Zhang, N. Xu, J. Zhou, J. Shi, and Z. Diao, "Vision-based navigation and guidance for agricultural autonomous vehicles and robots: A review", *Comput. Electron. Agric.,* vol. 205, p. 107584, 2023.
[http://dx.doi.org/10.1016/j.compag.2022.107584]

[9]　N. Nyoman Kutha Krisnawijaya, B. Tekinerdogan, C. Catal, and R. Tol, "Data analytics platforms for agricultural systems: A systematic literature review", *Comput. Electron. Agric.,* vol. 195, p. 106813, 2022.
[http://dx.doi.org/10.1016/j.compag.2022.106813]

[10]　M. Thakur, "Cybersecurity threats and countermeasures in the digital age", *Journal of Applied Science and Education (JASE),* vol. 4, no. 1, pp. 1-20, 2024.
[http://dx.doi.org/10.54060/a2zjournals.jase.42]

[11]　A. A. Aliyu *et al.,* "An enhanced intrusion detection system for IoT DDoS attacks," KASU Journal of Mathematical Sciences, vol. 5, no. 1, pp. 25–39, Jul. 2024. Available from: https://mathsaccess.com.ng/index.php/maths/article/view/64

[12]　S. Gupta, S. Jain, M. Agarwal, and N. Nanda, "An encryption approach to improve the security and performance of data by integrating AES with a modified OTP technique", *International Journal of Advanced Intelligence Paradigms,* vol. 27, no. 2, pp. 129-149, 2024.
[http://dx.doi.org/10.1504/IJAIP.2024.137187]

[13]　A.N. Alahmadi, S.U. Rehman, H.S. Alhazmi, D.G. Glynn, H. Shoaib, and P. Solé, "Cybersecurity threats and side-channel attacks for digital agriculture", *Sensors (Basel),* vol. 22, no. 9, p. 3520, 2022.
[http://dx.doi.org/10.3390/s22093520] [PMID: 35591211]

[14]　A. Kamilaris, A. Kartakoullis, and F.X. Prenafeta-Boldú, "A review on the practice of big data analysis in agriculture", *Comput. Electron. Agric.,* vol. 143, pp. 23-37, 2017.
[http://dx.doi.org/10.1016/j.compag.2017.09.037]

[15]　B. Geluvaraj, P.M. Satwik, and T.A.A. Kumar, "The future of cybersecurity: Major role of artificial intelligence, machine learning, and deep learning in cyberspace", *International Conference on Computer Networks and Communication Technologie,* vol. vol. 15, pp. 739-747, 2018.
[http://dx.doi.org/10.1007/978-981-10-8681-6_67]

[16]　A. Ponce, "Artificial intelligence: A game changer for the world of work," SSRN Papers, Jun. 2018. Available from: https://papers.ssrn.com/sol3/papers.cfm?abstract_id=3198581
[http://dx.doi.org/10.2139/ssrn.3198581]

[17]　S.A. Bhat, and N-F. Huang, "Big data and AI revolution in precision agriculture: Survey and challenges", *IEEE Access,* vol. 9, pp. 110209-110222, 2021.
[http://dx.doi.org/10.1109/ACCESS.2021.3102227]

[18]　B.T. Familoni, "Cybersecurity challenges in the age of AI: Theoretical approaches and practical solutions", *Computer Science & IT Research Journal,* vol. 5, no. 3, pp. 703-724, 2024.
[http://dx.doi.org/10.51594/csitrj.v5i3.930]

[19]　J.A. Bland, M.D. Petty, T.S. Whitaker, K.P. Maxwell, and W.A. Cantrell, "Machine learning cyberattack and defense strategies", *Comput. Secur.,* vol. 92, p. 101738, 2020.
[http://dx.doi.org/10.1016/j.cose.2020.101738]

[20]　S. Salloum, T. Gaber, S. Vadera, and K. Shaalan, "A systematic literature review on phishing email

detection using natural language processing techniques", *IEEE Access,* vol. 10, pp. 65703-65727, 2022.
[http://dx.doi.org/10.1109/ACCESS.2022.3183083]

[21] J. Hassannataj Joloudari, M. Haderbadi, A. Mashmool, M. Ghasemigol, S.S. Band, and A. Mosavi, "Early detection of the advanced persistent threat attack using performance analysis of deep learning", *IEEE Access,* vol. 8, pp. 186125-186137, 2020.
[http://dx.doi.org/10.1109/ACCESS.2020.3029202]

[22] R. Rukšėnas, P. Curzon, and A. Blandford, "Modelling and analysing cognitive causes of security breaches", *Innov. Syst. Softw. Eng.,* vol. 4, no. 2, pp. 143-160, 2008.
[http://dx.doi.org/10.1007/s11334-008-0050-7]

[23] H. Chaudhary *et al.*, "A review of various challenges in cybersecurity using artificial intelligence," in 2020 3rd International Conference on Intelligent Sustainable Systems (ICISS), Thoothukudi, India, 2020, pp. 829–836.
[http://dx.doi.org/10.1109/ICISS49785.2020.9316003]

[24] S. Gupta *et al.*, "Ensuring data security in databases using format-preserving encryption," in 2018 8th International Conference on Cloud Computing, Data Science & Engineering (Confluence), 2018.
[http://dx.doi.org/10.1109/CONFLUENCE.2018.8442626]

[25] S. Gupta *et al.*, "The potential of blockchain technology in socially responsible crowdfunding platforms," in 2023 Second International Conference on Informatics (ICI), IEEE, 2023.
[http://dx.doi.org/10.1109/ICI60088.2023.10421619]

SUBJECT INDEX

www.ingramcontent.com/pod-product-compliance
Lightning Source LLC
Chambersburg PA
CBHW050810010626
45792CB00029B/1029